Frances Ellen Watkins Harper

Studies in American Popular History and Culture

JEROME NADELHAFT, *General Editor*

For a full list of title in this series, please visit www.routledge.com

Feminist Revolution in Literacy
Women's Bookstores in the
United States
Junko R. Onosaka

**Great Depression and the
Middle Class**
Experts, Collegiate Youth and
Business Ideology, 1929–1941
Mary C. McComb

Labor and Laborers of the Loom
Mechanization and Handloom
Weavers, 1780–1840
Gail Fowler Mohanty

"The First of Causes to Our Sex"
The Female Moral Reform Movement
in the Antebellum Northeast,
1834-1848
Daniel S. Wright

**US Textile Production in Historical
Perspective**
A Case Study from Massachusetts
Susan M. Ouellette

Women Workers on Strike
Narratives of Southern Women
Unionists
Roxanne Newton

Hollywood and Anticommunism
HUAC and the Evolution of the Red
Menace, 1935–1950
John Joseph Gladchuk

**Negotiating Motherhood in
Nineteenth-Century American
Literature**
Mary McCartin Wearn

**The Gay Liberation Youth Movement
in New York**
"An Army of Lovers Cannot Fail"
Stephan L. Cohen

**Gender and the American
Temperance Movement of the
Nineteenth Century**
Holly Berkley Fletcher

**The Struggle For Free Speech in the
United States, 1872–1915**
Edward Bliss Foote, Edward Bond
Foote, and Anti-Comstock Operations
Janice Ruth Wood

The Marketing of Edgar Allan Poe
Jonathan H. Hartmann

**Language, Gender, and Citizenship
in American Literature, 1789–1919**
Amy Dunham Strand

Antebellum Slave Narratives
Cultural and Political
Expressions of Africa
Jermaine O. Archer

**Fictions of Female Education in the
Nineteenth Century**
Jaime Osterman Alves

**John Brown and the Era of Literary
Confrontation**
Michael Stoneham

**Performing American Identity in
Anti-Mormon Melodrama**
Megan Sanborn Jones

**Black Women in New South
Literature and Culture**
Sherita L. Johnson

Frances Ellen Watkins Harper
African American Reform Rhetoric and
the Rise of a Modern Nation State
Michael Stancliff

Frances Ellen Watkins Harper

African American Reform Rhetoric and the Rise of a Modern Nation State

Michael Stancliff

Routledge
Taylor & Francis Group
New York   London

First published 2011
by Routledge
270 Madison Avenue, New York, NY 10016

Simultaneously published in the UK
by Routledge
2 Park Square, Milton Park, Abingdon, Oxon OX14 4RN

Routledge is an imprint of the Taylor & Francis Group, an informa business

Typeset in Sabon by IBT Global.

Library of Congress Cataloging in Publication Data
Stancliff, Michael.
   Frances Ellen Watkins Harper : African American reform rhetoric and the rise of a modern nation state / by Michael Stancliff.
      p. cm. — (Studies in American popular history and culture)
   Includes bibliographical references and index.
   1. Harper, Frances Ellen Watkins, 1825–1911—Criticism and interpretation.
   2. Harper, Frances Ellen Watkins, 1825–1911—Political and social views.
   3. Harper, Frances Ellen Watkins, 1825–1911—Literary style. 4. Rhetoric—
Political aspects—United States—History—19th century. 5. African American social
reformers—History—19th century. 6. African American feminists—History—
19th century. 7. Feminism—United States—History—19th century. 8. Black
nationalism—United States—History—19th century. I. Title.
   PS1799.H7Z87 2010
   818'.3—dc22
   2009054166

ISBN13: 978-0-415-99763-8(hbk)
ISBN13: 978-0-203-84825-8(ebk)

Contents

Figures

Preface

> If this government has no call for our services, no aim for your chil-
> dren, we have the greater need of them to build up a true manhood
> and womanhood for ourselves. The important lesson we should learn
> and be able to teach, is how to make every gift, whether gold or tal-
> ent, fortune or genius, subserve the cause of crushed humanity and
> carry out the greatest idea of the present age, the glorious idea of
> human brotherhood.
>
> Frances Ellen Watkins Harper ("Our Greatest Want" 160)

> We don't yet understand the distinction between the rhetoric of teach-
> ing and the teaching of rhetoric.
>
> Shirley Wilson Logan (*Liberating Language: Sites of Rhetorical
> Education in Nineteenth-Century Black American* 5)

*Frances Ellen Watkins Harper: African American Reform Rhetoric and
the Rise of a Modern Nation State* reconsiders Frances Harper's work as
primarily pedagogical and works towards an interpretation of the pedagogical constitution of nineteenth-century African American rhetorical culture.
From its beginnings in the immediatist politics of early-century uplift organizations, African American reform rhetoric became the platform for moral
suasion from which the nascent African American community employed
social, economic, and theological theory to build a practice of resistance
against the racial politics of the state. Focusing on the work of one historic
exemplar, this book examines the ways in which didactic language, and in
particular rhetorical instruction, can function as part of the political life
of a people. Throughout, I make the case that African American nationalism in the nineteenth century existed largely by virtue of rhetorical action,
the forming and maintenance of communicative networks that are ultimately difficult to conceptualize apart from the broader practices of social
organization among reform communities. Harper helped forge a powerful
political idiom from the perilous social ground of the post-emancipation
era in the United States, and her writing and oratory, exceptional in their
own right, open an important critical window on the innovations of political thought and rhetorical practice within the broader traditions of African American protest. Melba Joyce Boyd's *Discarded Legacy: Politics and
Poetics in the Life and Work of Frances E. W. Harper, 1825–1911* (1994)
remains the only book-length study devoted to Harper's life and work, and
the subsequent chapters are intended to redress in part the relative lack

of comprehensive critical accounts of Harper's career. Across decades of social and political change, for multiple occasions and audiences, and in nearly every available genre, Harper developed an abolitionist theory of moral suasion as a broader discursive practice of movement building and protesting the antebellum slave state and after Emancipation, amidst the first half-century of a constitutively compromised multiracial democracy of the Unites States.

"Our Greatest Want," published in the *Anglo African Magazine* in 1859, is typical of Harper's pedagogical insistence on collective and mutual responsibilities among the reform class of Northern free people of color. *Frances Ellen Watkins Harper: African American Reform Rhetoric and the Rise of a Modern Nation State* is a historical and theoretical inquiry into the tight relational circuit of obligation mapped in Harper's call for African American audiences to attend dutifully to the "important lesson" that they "should learn and be able to teach." For Harper and others, the material commitment to the common work of teaching and learning rhetorical craft was a necessary condition for the future of uplift solidarity. Examining both the cultural sources of Harper's rhetoric and the teaching means she used, I argue that rhetorical pedagogy—the material practice of teaching movement principles and training audiences for reform work—was a central force driving African American reform politics. I argue further that Harper's rhetorical pedagogy was not only persuasive action but also, as it circulated within the networks of the African American and broader reform press, a discursive site for pledging social affiliation. Sounding the call for "true manhood and womanhood" was no simple idealism; the gendered social practices of character were a primary target in Harper's demonstration of the rhetorical habits necessary for race-national uplift and solidarity. My introduction brings into focus how the functionally didactic orientation of characterological rhetoric in Harper's work provided multiple reform communities with a commonplace book of African American national virtue with which they might identify and thus gain political self-understanding.

Risking the correction of historians and philosophers, this book offers a critical portrait of Harper as a pedagogical innovator who challenged the constraining rhetorical culture of nineteenth-century "racial modernity." Historian James Brewer Stewart uses this term to designate changes in the political meaning of race across the nineteenth century, and specifically the increasingly rigid and dichotomous practice of "racially self-referential approaches to politics and reform" (182). Arguing from distinctly different source material, Cornel West and David Brion Davis both conclude that a white supremacist state, though not an inevitable result of modernism, nevertheless defined the racial common sense of the modern era. "New World" modernity propagated a social order of racial and sexual domination that was both a means and end of the imperialist competition that drove both the African slave trade and the subjugation of indigenous peoples in the

Americas. As West argues, "African slavery sits at the center of the grand epoch of equality, liberty, and fraternity" (51), and when Harper calls for the perseverance of "the glorious idea of human brotherhood," she rejects that conflicted modernity's racialized version of democratic statecraft. Protesting and teaching against racial and gender oppression, Harper could not help but engage the unfolding history of the nation state as a rhetorical constraint as well as a humanitarian crisis.

This study takes its place at methodological common ground among several disciplines, primarily rhetorical theory and history, African American studies, literary history, and critical race theory. A common emphasis on the materiality of textual activity across these areas of inquiry informs my reading of rhetorical pedagogy as a socially constitutive cultural practice. Steven Mailloux claims an important place in the humanities for rhetorical methodologies, which provide a "near perfect instrument for overcoming the now artificial distinction between textual and extratextual interpretive approaches." From this critical vantage point, which is "both inside and outside the text," Mailloux asks rhetorical critics to trace the discursive circulation of arguments, tropes, common places, and references, the "rhetorical paths of thought" through which rhetorical action produces social efficacy across situations of production and reception (30). This practice of "rhetorical hermeneutics" has helped me frame my analysis of Harper. Tracing Harper's pedagogical inventions, this study moves toward a general theory of *preceptive rhetorical action* as the inventive site of reading and writing, reception, and production. The following chapters trace such action across the material network of newspapers, lecture circuits, and voluntary allegiances in which Harper published and spoke, which was constitutive of what Frances Foster Smith has aptly termed the "Afro-Protestant press" ("Gender, Genre" 51).

To study nineteenth-century African American rhetorical pedagogy, and to find Harper's place as an innovator of this craft, familiar categories of rhetorical studies must suffer indistinction: theory and practice; knowledge acquisition and knowledge use; textual production and textual interpretation; expert and novice; deliberation and ceremony. As a work of rhetorical theory, this book and its arguments are a response to the rich invitation to inquiry made by Shirley Wilson Logan's provocation regarding the unfixed boundary between "the rhetoric of teaching and the teaching of rhetoric" (*Liberating Language* 5). Harper's public-sphere teaching practice demands a reconsideration of binaries such as these that so pervasively structure critical accounts of education, literacy, rhetoric, and cultural politics. Logan identifies the African American press as an important site of rhetorical instruction, and in fixing Harper's reputation as a pedagogical theorist, I hope to expand our thinking about abolitionist rhetorical culture as a culture of teaching. Teachers rarely acknowledge the *persuasive* intentions of their work, still less perhaps the indispensable articles of cultural faith that orient whatever lessons they ply agonistically. This silence—or, as the case may be, principled denial of political intentionality—elides the extraprofessional, quotidian quality of teaching as well as the rhetorical and historical dynamism of pedagogy as an essential element of cultural inventiveness. Susan Miller argues that communicative subjects learn socially who they are and how to "trust" in ways of speaking and writing; as a teacher of rhetoric, Harper sought to cultivate that trust as a pledge of affiliation, a social investment in a common ethical script. Thought of in these broad discursive terms, pedagogy is not simply a distinct philosophy of education from which more or less congruent curricula might follow. *Pedagogy,* as the term is defined here, names the textual, discursive situation of preceptive circulation and the production of mutually re-enforcing social identities and rhetorical protocols. For Harper, the teaching of rhetoric and the rhetoric of teaching were indistinct on the pedagogical principle of active solidarity.

Harper's place in African American feminist historiography has been widely claimed by scholars such as Carla Peterson, whose study of African American women's writing and oratory in Northern reform communities provides me with a cultural model of rhetorical constraint. Peterson's theorization of the "liminality" of African American women's writing and speech considers the textual acts of Harper and her contemporaries as discursively inventive and ethically daring, enabling new rhetorical ground by risking censure and misunderstanding. Harper is rightly remembered as a key figure in the early tradition of African American feminism. This book is intended to bring to the critical foreground the place of rhetorical pedagogy in her feminist practice. No moment more dramatically illustrates this integrative capacity than Harper's speech at the National Woman's Rights Convention in 1866, a racial watershed in the history of modern feminist politics in the United States. For Harper, as for so many of her contemporaries, the immediatist egalitarian vision of emancipation provided a framework for articulating a politics of African American womanhood. The situation of liminal gender meaning forms another focal point for this study. Though I generally refrain from referring to Harper's politics as feminist, the relevance of my study for feminist historiography of women's reform should be clear enough. Without advancing any general theory of race–gender intersection, I attend to Harper's tactical inventions of manhood and womanhood as complementary ethical positions and the inevitable intersection of race and gender politics.

Though the following chapters proceed chronologically, I have not pieced together the narrative of Harper's life in the manner of a traditional biography. Each chapter is organized around texts I have chosen as exemplars both of her pedagogical innovation and of an evolving politics of rhetorical instruction from abolitionism to Radical Reconstruction. The major questions of policy, leadership, and affiliation, which dominated the extensive volunteer network within which she spoke and wrote were fundamentally arguments about rhetorical instruction and pedagogical politics. The first two chapters examine Harper's appearance as a prominent writer and orator in the context of abolitionism and Reconstruction, respectively. Chapter 1, "Composing Character: Cultural Sources of African American Rhetorical Pedagogy," positions her as a skilled writer and lecturer within the antislavery movement, re-teaching the rhetorical precepts of Protestant and republican communicative ethics. Through an examination of key early works, I read Harper as an accomplished student of African American abolitionist rhetoric. The final section of Chapter 1 recounts Harper's presence in the *Anglo African Magazine* in 1859, initiating an analysis of her theory of the social significance of African American women's rhetoric.

Chapter 2, "Reconstruction and Black Republican Pedagogy," examines Harper's work as a spokesperson for the so-called Radical Reconstruction initiated by powerful Republicans of the 39th Congress, who spearheaded the first national civil rights politics culminating in the Thirteenth, Fourteenth, and Fifteenth Amendments; the Civil Rights Act of 1875; and other key measures. Emancipation, followed by Reconstruction and its abandonment, marked an epochal phase in racial modernity that Harper negotiated with her reform compatriots. From teaching emancipated African Americans and lecturing to race- and gender-mixed audiences in the South, to her tremendous literary production and experimentation in the Northern press, Harper responded persistently to the legitimacy crisis of the state, taking up the Radical agenda in verse, prose, and at the podium. Chapter 2 looks ahead more than two decades to the collapse of Reconstruction in order to illustrate what I take to be Harper's own pedagogical crisis across the brutal first decades of multiracial democracy in the United States. Harper does not simply question the viability of the state and of a hypocritical Republican Party. She taught the rhetorical means of discursive action, the means of organizing resistant political identity and of shaming the state by publicizing corruption.

As an abolitionist, Harper appealed to African Americans in the North to practice solidarity with those in the South. This principle of race loyalty circulated as a primary preceptive idiom of uplift. For Harper, the training of right race character demanded a response to class differences within the African American reform public. Each of the final three chapters is oriented around one of Harper's novels and its pedagogical intervention in the racial modernity of the emancipation era. Published in the African Methodist Episcopal journal the *Christian Recorder*, a major organ of African American reform, these novels taught rhetoric as an integrative practice at the site of multiple and intersecting divisions of social class, region, generation, and education. I read these fictions as pedagogical dramas of persuasion that model a broad social and linguistic practice of voluntary fidelity. Harper theorized this activism as a craft of "living argument," a phrase she uses to idealize one of her late-century pedagogical heroines and to recommend her as a model of social solidarity and rhetorical skill.

Chapters 3, 4, and 5 all treat Harper's late fictions as a cohesive and ongoing practice of teaching uplift principle and speech to African American audiences divided by gender, class, region, education, and generation. Harper circulated a working theory of persuasion, staging perceptive exchanges among the characters of her novels and short fiction. In a satirical turn, Harper wrote one of her most ambitious teaching novels, *Sowing and Reaping*, an anatomy of market speech within the crisis-ridden U.S. economy and its destructively frenzied growth of the liquor market. Teaching the common places of the burgeoning national voluntary network of women's temperance politics, Harper further elaborated her theory of African American women's rhetorical agency. Chapter 3, "Temperance Pedagogy: Correcting Character in a Drunken Economy," traces Harper's work in African American and (almost) exclusively Anglo-American temperance organizations. Harper's temperance villains are of an ethical piece with her earlier representations of slave masters—utterly debased in character, cruel, unthinking, duplicitous, avaricious, incapable of right sentiment, and, didactically in Harper's fictional arrangements, incapable of persuasive or defensible speech. Drunkenness is a moral and a rhetorical failure in Harper's work, the didactic figuration by which to teach the rhetorical habits of uplift and sobriety.

Chapter 4, "Black Ireland: The Political Economics of African American Rhetorical Pedagogy after Reconstruction," surveys Harper's participation in the growing protest of the segregated labor-market color line. This novel maps the direction of African American nationalism and her most detailed discussion to date of life on the colorline and of African American self-determination amid what African American reformers, especially after the 1883 Supreme Court nullification of the 1875 Civil Rights Act, held to be a *post*–civil rights dispensation. Harper, like compatriots including T. Thomas Fortune and Frederick Douglass, found in the Irish American example a pragmatic way of thinking outside of the racial and regional binaries that structured the retrogressive political discourse of the New South. Didactic representations of Irish Americans in *Trial and Triumph* (1888–1889) provided heuristics for thinking through class and gender divisions and inventing a critical position on the crisis of the modern Western world as a result of its own racial waywardness. Through the pedagogical portrait of protagonist Annette Harcourt, Harper offered her most detailed prose lecture to date on the constraints of African American political and rhetorical education within the masculine realm of reform society.

The language lessons of Harper's later fiction raise questions about the class politics of uplift pedagogy. People of all social classes find a place in these fictional scripts of collective solidarity, but not everyone speaks with equal authority. Chapter 4 also extends an ongoing critical discussion of Harper's cautionary stance regarding the public use of African American vernacular. In the novel, vernacular idioms and "slang" are explained away either with loving distance as a legacy of slave generations or, conversely, as a sign of characterological fault. If "respectable" professional class reformers were bound by the code of uplift to the subjects of their benevolence, including former slaves and their descendants, subjects of reform themselves were charged with specific rhetorical duties as well. Protagonist Harcourt unlearns her idiomatic habits in order to shed her signifying edge within the Afro-Irish contact zones of the novel's carefully class-coded urban setting. This novel's reform heroines are quick to correct idiomatic speech as problematic. If Harper disparaged African American vernacular and privileged the English of the black press and the elite classrooms in which she was trained, these biases suggest the degree to which Harper propounded a progressivist liberal racialism that lends historical coherence to the post-racial politics of respectability. The pedagogical politics of *Trial and Triumph* are typical of Harper's recognizably modern, progressivist pedagogy in which African American vernacular is regarded ambivalently and discouraged on pedagogical principle. Following Deborah Brandt's theoretical paradigm, we might think of Harper as a "sponsor of literacy," inviting an important historical discussion of how African American vernacular is read, practiced, or prescribed.

Chapter 5, "Not as a Mere Dependent: The Historic Mission of African American Women's Rhetoric at the End of the Century," analyzes Harper's now widely anthologized fiction and oratory in the 1890s and offers an account of her rise as a leading figure amid an emerging era of women's reform politics. One among a vibrant community of organizers and advocates, Harper stands out as an innovative and prolific teacher of African American women's rhetoric at the turn of the century. During this post-Reconstruction moment, even as the relations of social dependence were increasingly normalized as a matter of economic caste, social independence became the highest characterological virtue in the national justification of a manifestly corrupt state. In response, Harper and her compatriots articulated a national ethic of interdependence, working to revalue dependent social relations as an inevitable political condition that must be fostered, in keeping with the deep ideological commitment to collectivity that had always underwritten African American immediatism. By upholding core republican and Protestant principles of persuadability, a rhetorical disposition of characterological change, Harper bridges the gap between rhetorical and social theory. She and other luminaries of the Black Women's Club Movement, including Ida B. Wells and Anna Julia Cooper, redefined history itself as a system of social dependence, harkening back to the immediatist character of the abolitionist era. The concluding chapter finds common precepts of interdependence in Harper's key late-century texts, including her final novel, published in 1892, *Iola Leroy, or, Shadows Uplifted*, "Woman's Political Future"; the address she delivered as a member of the World's Representative Congress of Women at the 1893 Columbian Exposition; and her 1891 address to the National Council Of Women of the United States, "Duty to Dependant Races."

To be sure, this study of rhetorical pedagogy is unavoidably implicated in the very practice it takes as its subject of analysis. In representing Harper as a modernist dissenter teaching within the racial state of the nineteenth century, I have held up her rhetorical practice as an immediate precursor to our own contentious era of civil rights. In the classroom, Harper is often received as relevant to discussions of contemporary racial politics. Students reading her poetry, fiction, journalism, and oratory find much that is familiar in her rhetoric, and often, in spite of or at times because of her carefully measured tones, students respond viscerally. For some, Harper's carefully cultivated stance of moral clarity resonates strongly, while others receive Harper's prescriptive assertions about lifestyle and duty as presumptuous and narrow-minded. While some students applaud Harper's audacity in denouncing tyranny and corruption, others, remarkably, denounce her race-national appeals as an unfortunate disruption of the racial peace. Conversely, Harper disappoints some contemporary readers as an integrationist undercutting the radicalism of black-nationalist politics. Many applaud her insistence on the power of protest, while others distrust her sentimental vision of social reform. The political legacy of abolitionism, Reconstruction, and the ensuing course of racial modernity remain unsettled no less than Harper's reception. While she no doubt would have had much to say and write about these receptive attitudes, Frances Harper might have been pleased that her work still provokes arguments about the politics of character.

Acknowledgments

I would like to acknowledge the groundbreaking work of Frances Harper scholars preceding me and making this book possible. In particular, I am indebted to the recovery and interpretive work of Frances Smith Foster, Carla Peterson, Shirley Wilson Logan, Melba Joyce Boyd, and Hazel Carby, whose work opened up pathways without which this volume would literally have been unthinkable. Many incredible students in African American literature classes over the years also deserve special acknowledgment. Their insights and pushback against my insistent readings helped me immensely, and their interest and enthusiasm convinced me again of Harper's continued relevance.

For continuous intellectual encouragement and friendship, I thank Eric Wertheimer. Joel Kuszai and I discussed rhetoric and teaching repeatedly over the course of this writing, conversations that helped me think through Harper's pedagogy. For this and much else, he has my thanks. Jennifer Dorsey listened as a friend and historian and provided hilarious distractions, for which I am grateful. Carrie Tirado Bramen and Neil Schmitz guided me early in the process of this writing, and their scholarship and teaching inspired me along the way. Sharon Crowley added her mentorship later in the process, helping me navigate complexities of rhetorical and cultural theory. Thanks also go to Diane Gruber, Patrick Bixby, and Theresa Williams, whose readings of chapters improved them enormously, and special thanks go to Diane for help and support over the long course of this composition. I am grateful to Dennis Isbell and the entire staff at Arizona State University's Fletcher Library for their generous assistance. Additional thanks for advice and encouragement go to Heidi Bostic, Kevin Quashee, Anthony Blake, Stephen Germic, Duku Akua Anokye, Kristie Elmore and Nanette Schuster. For editorial guidance and enthusiasm, I thank Benjamin Holtzman and Laura Stearns of Routledge. Images are reprinted with permission from the New York Public Library. Accessible Archives made key primary documents digitally available. Special thanks go to Jennie Crotero, who rewired so many of my sentences to good effect.

Sharon Kirsch knew all about this book before it was written. She read and commented on every piece of the manuscript and strengthened it each time. Willa Jane Kirsch-Stancliff, more than anyone, insisted that I focus on the joy as opposed to the pain of writing, and Samuel Bodhi Kirsch-Stancliff exuberantly distracted me in a most welcome fashion. The depth of my gratitude and love for Sharon, Willa, and Samuel cannot be fully expressed here.

Finally, this book is dedicated to the memory of Frances Ellen Watkins Harper.

Introduction
Frances Harper and Nineteenth-Century African American Rhetorical Pedagogy

Frances Ellen Watkins Harper taught rhetoric in the African American press throughout the second half of the nineteenth century, helping to train the next generation of activists for the reform work of uplift. Although the African American and broader abolitionist press served as the forum for her speeches and texts, her lessons assumed applications far beyond the podium or printed press where she excelled. Harper taught rhetoric as a holistic practice of everyday duty and devotion, offering communicative resources for the invention of a generative African American publicity and a women's rights practice that by the end of her career were so expansive in their social vision that contemporary human rights workers might claim their legacy. For Harper, African American rhetorical skill, intellect, and imagination were vital resources for social uplift and reform, not simply for protest, but also for building a constitutive self-understanding, a progressive culture of collective respect and humane recognition across lines of gender, race, and economic class.

Harper only rarely drew explicitly on autobiographical sources to craft the commonplace appeals and narratives prescribed in her distinctive rhetorical pedagogy. In 1851, she left the adoptive home of her aunt and aunt's husband, the prominent educator and reformer William Watkins Sr., with whom she had lived in Baltimore, Maryland, after being orphaned at the age of three. For free people of color like Frances Ellen Watkins (she would not gain her married name until her marriage with Fenton Harper in 1860), the Fugitive Slave Law of 1850 had made life all the more precarious, granting slave catchers the profit motive for the abduction and trafficking of free people into bondage. The historical moment of the Fugitive Slave Law witnessed not only the demoralizing power of the slavocracy in the arena of federal law, but also the galvanizing circumstance of political recommitment among abolitionists. A resolution passed at a mass meeting in Springfield, Massachusetts, on September 17, 1850, represents this recommitment as a matter of race-national survival. Conventioneers publicly repudiated "any law that has for its object the oppression of any human being" and formed a Vigilance Association to aid "the panting slave" and resist slave catchers with force if necessary (qtd. in Aptheker 305). In editorial after editorial, the African American press denounced the law as *prima facie* evidence of the corrupt intentions of state power.[1]

By 1853, Harper had become one of many Americans whose antislavery convictions likewise forbade complacency in the wake of the Fugitive Slave Law, which Harper labeled "that abomination of the nineteenth century," according to friend, correspondent, and primary biographer, the abolitionist William Still (757). The tipping point in Harper's life of activism appears to have come when the Maryland legislature revised its slave codes to forbid free people of color from entering the state. Then living and working as a teacher in York, Pennsylvania, Harper indeed became "an exile by law" (758). Learning of the death of a free man of color sold to Georgia under the Maryland statute, Harper wrote to a friend, "Upon that grave I pledge myself to the Anti-Slavery cause." Soon thereafter, she moved to Philadelphia, a center of antislavery activity, living temporarily at a station of the Underground Railroad, where she likely met Still, who was a key operative of the Philadelphia Railroad. While there, Harper wrote protest poems; visited the Philadelphia Anti-Slavery Office, reading, according to Still, "with great avidity"; and sought publication for the book that would ultimately be published in 1854 by J. B. Yerrinton and Sons in Boston as the first edition of *Poems on Miscellaneous Subjects*.[2] From Philadelphia, Harper visited Boston and then went on to New Bedford, Massachusetts, where she gave her first public lecture under the title "The Education and the Elevation of the Colored Race." In a letter to Still dated August of 1854, she reported matter-of-factly, "Well, I am out lecturing," noting a full week of daily lectures and the "success" of these engagements. "My voice," she wrote, "is not wanting in strength, as I am aware of, to reach pretty well over the house" (Still 758). From this moment until beyond the turn of the century, Frances Ellen Watkins Harper would extend the reach of her strong voice at podiums around the country and as an increasingly prestigious contributor to the African American press.

Harper's letters to William Still in these years evince the craft of a rhetor already possessed of experience and training. Having lived within the rarefied reform milieu of the Watkins' Baltimore home, we must assume that Harper's period of political and rhetorical tutelage had been a long time in process. Joining the antislavery lecture circuit, Harper was both student and practitioner of a rhetorical pedagogy already well established in schools like William Watkins's Baltimore Academy for Negro Youth, as well as in the burgeoning print culture of the African American press.[3] Her ardent reports to Still reflect her growing knowledge of the social and political networks in which individual protest voices were amplified and became part of a collective action of political publicity. As Still was careful to point out, Harper was "not content to make speeches and receive plaudits," but undertook rhetorical action as part of a broader reform practice, which included direct financial support for fugitives and their families, something she provided throughout this period. Beyond "money or words," inquiring

GRACE ANNE LEWIS.
See p. 748.

MRS. FRANCIS E. W. HARPER.
See p. 752.

JOHN NEEDLES.

EARNEST IN THE CAUSE.

Figure I.1 This page from William Still's 1872 history, *The Underground Railroad*, gathers portraits of Harper and fellow abolitionists Grace Anne Lewis and John Needles. Picture Collection. The New York Public Library, Astor Lenox and Tilden Foundations.

about a failed rescue attempt in Cincinnati, Harper offered her services in whatever "rough work" might be necessary in future endeavors. Her time in York, Philadelphia, and Boston suggest great confidence in the collaboration mobilized in the face of the ongoing slavery crisis and the complex networks of persuasion in which she labored. Of the antislavery "Maine ladies" she found so praiseworthy while on the Maine Anti-Slavery Society lecture circuit, Harper wrote, "They are putting men of Anti-Slavery principles in office . . . to cleanse the corrupt fountains of our government by sending men to Congress who will plead for our down-trodden and oppressed brethren, our crushed and helpless sisters" (Still 759). In this collaborative vision—abolitionists contending in politics, championing politicians who would further advocate for the enslaved at a governmental level—we can discern her belief in the power of reform as a social chain of persuasion capable of transforming the state.

A letter from Tiffin, Ohio, dated March 31, 1856, indicates that Harper's sense of her own work as a moral and spiritual duty was complicated by a determination to assert freedoms of her own. Seemingly measuring her

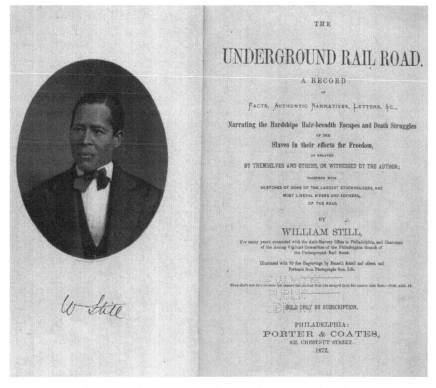

Figure I.2   Title page and portrait of William Still, Harper's friend, correspondent, and the author of *The Underground Railroad*. Manuscripts, Archives and Rare Books Division, Schomburg Center for Research in Black Culture, The New York Public Library, Astor, Lenox and Tilden Foundation.

own transgressive entry into the masculine realm of political speech against that of the Maine abolitionists she admired, she wrote, "I have a right to do my share of the work" in the "common cause" of antislavery reform work that demanded the assertion of both "manhood and womanhood" (Still 761). Harper's practice of public instruction made new claims for mothers, daughters, and wives as rights-bearing subjects, and in so doing, helped to build the commonplace language of nineteenth-century African American women's reform.

By the end of the century, Harper would become one of the founders of a national African American women's politics and a spokesperson for the emergence of a "woman's era," which she, like her compatriots, heralded as the historical resolution of an ostensibly waning age of masculine barbarism. Harper most famously made such claims as one of the few African American women allowed to speak at the World's Congress of Representative Women at the 1893 Columbian Exposition in Chicago. With the woman's era still a matter of theory rather than practice, abundant evidence of continued white racial terrorism existed, and Harper was distinctive among her contemporaries in her ability to simultaneously negotiate and criticize the color line. Ida B. Wells, Frederick Douglass, Irvine Garland Penn, and Ferdinand L. Barnett published a pamphlet titled *The Reason Why the Colored American Is Not in the World's Exposition*, a critical exposé denouncing lynch law, the convict lease system, and the exclusion of African Americans from planning and participating in the Columbian Exposition.

Harper envisioned a turn-of-the-century United States deeply flawed and in need of women's reform, a historical mission to be realized through the social processes of moral suasion. Her suasionist's view of the state hinges on a characterological frame of individual and communal rhetorical agency trained and exercised in history and culture. Harper disparages "legislators . . . born to an inheritance of privilege," the subjects of "ages of education, dominion, civilization, and Christianity" ("Woman's Political Future" 434–435). Inevitably, the cultural legacy of these privileged but corrupt politicians required the intervention of women's rhetorical action:

> To-day women hold in their hands influence and opportunity, and with these they have already opened doors which have been closed to others. By opening doors of labor woman has become a rival claimant for at least some of the wealth monopolized by her stronger brother. In the home she is the priestess, in society the queen, in literature she is a power, in legislative halls law-makers have responded to her appeals, and for her sake have humanized and liberalized their laws. The press has felt the impress of her hand. In the pews of the church she constitutes a majority; the pulpit has welcomed her, and in the school she has the blessed privilege of teaching children and youth. To her is apparently coming the added responsibility of political power; and what she now possesses should only be the means of preparing her to

use the coming power for the glory of God and the good of mankind; for power without righteousness is one of the most dangerous forces in the world. (435)

The social ascendance of women's influence envisioned in Harper's speech maps the culture-making power of speech and writing. Harper offers a rich view here of African American women's rhetorical culture in the pulpits and presses, in literature and law, and perhaps most important, as part of the vast system of influence among black churches. If Harper had a nearly millennial confidence in the political potential of women, it must be noted that she developed her women's reform agenda in tandem with her long-held commitment to African American reform communities. Harper's landmark address, "Woman's Political Future," is of a political piece with the work of her companions who disputed the legitimacy of the Exposition from without. Harper denounced the government's legal failure to protect African Americans from lynch law and refused the nationalist pedagogy of the Exposition.[4] Like Wells, Harper protested lynch laws in the South as a national failure of state. Harper's speech cannily elides explicit racial terms, but she closes demanding "justice, simple justice, as the right of every race" (437). As Nell Irvin Painter said of Harper, she "[r]efused to separate her sex from her race" (224).

No less than her white reform contemporaries, Harper practiced a textual reform politics of "republican motherhood," a pedagogical stance of national character formation. Sarah Robbins writes, "In the first days of republican motherhood, proponents argued for reforming American female education." Robbins notes that "enhanced education for women" took on legitimacy as a function of state loyalty (27). Through the habits and sentiments that constitute her career-long composition of social virtues, Harper sought to instill a new brand of race-national allegiance that would frame the current struggle as a passing phase in a historical mission of African American national progress. She inhabited the nationalist ground that feminist historians such as Nancy Cott identify as a guiding principle in the early republic, and thus a point of commonality through which social reform messages could be transmitted: "The project of characterological training provided an important point of access for the woman-led reform movements and for the re-teaching of public–private relations" (Cott 104–105). Early reform women constructed the boundaries of national character differently than Benthamite Benjamin Rush and subsequent generations of social architects, who were proponents of the citizen-training function of motherhood only inasmuch as it contributed to the maintenance of patriarchal hegemony.[5] While patriarchal precepts of republican motherhood relegated women's teaching work to the private sphere, African American women reformers found women's pedagogical dominion of home life a powerful conceptual framework in for inventing countervailing logics of women's influence in the public sphere.

The domestic precepts of African American republican motherhood, at least as articulated by Harper, added an important ethical register to the cultural rhetoric of black nationalism. To be sure, Harper's economic thought was inseparable from her rhetorical pedagogy as well; she theorized subjects of persuasion as the characterological impetus behind every economic decision. As Patrick Rael argues, African American protest language relied on market logic. Dominant notions of a "respectability" of character assumed economic virtues such as honesty, diligence, and generosity ("Market Values" 28–29). The rhetorical force of these virtues practiced and prescribed were meant to check the masculine mastery characterized by "the greed of gold and the lust of power" ("Woman's Political Future" 433). Such unchecked desire was for Harper an ethical disorder, the core moral ignorance to be addressed, and the proper target of abolitionist moral suasion. Her often-recorded confidence in persuasion as a rarefied democratic force to guide the state, and her quintessentially republican faith in the power of a virtuous citizenry to check the corrupt excesses of national institutions, extended to economic forms of action. Harper's understanding of state corruption, across her career, was oriented by a critique of economic violence. As a teacher of economic protest, Harper always focused on the symbolic force of economic systems, and as I argue throughout the following chapters, economic and rhetorical action always orient around the same precepts in Harper's pedagogy. By 1854, Harper claimed herself to be an adherent to the boycott politics of "Free Produce" abolitionism, a direction taken, perhaps in part, as a result of reading Solomon Northrop's autobiographical narrative, *Twelve Years a Slave*, which offers a harrowing depiction of the cotton economy from the inside.[6] In a letter to Still, she offers the apostrophic observation, "Oh, could slavery exist long if it did not sit on a commercial throne?" (Still 759).

The early poem "Free Labor" configures the scene of commodity consumption as a liminal site of intersubjective connection and a field of ethical choice, one with human loyalty in the balance:

> I wear an easy garment,
>   O'er it no toiling slave
> Wept tears of hopeless anguish,
>   In his passage to the grave.
>
> And from its ample folds
>   Shall rise no cry to God,
> Upon its warp and woof shall be
>   No stain of tears and blood.

> Oh, lightly shall it press my form,
>   Unladen with a sigh,
> I shall not 'mid its rustling hear,
>   Some sad despairing cry. (*Complete Poems* 25)

Any boycott politics demands the education of consumers, and the lesson is one that addresses the importance of social fidelity as a kind of listening. In these stanzas, Harper's practice of persuasion and advocacy challenges readers with their own potential culpability within the slave system. Figuring the brutality of that system as slave voices woven into the fabric of its products, Harper constructs an ideal consumer/subject who discovers her position within the social totality the poem articulates as a frame for critical self-reflection. Readers of this poem, perhaps clad in Southern cotton, are confronted with the anguished plaints of slaves, and through the political and geographical network charted by the poem, discover their own relationship to the laborers whose cries haunt the commodity and consumer conscience.

Beyond its dissection of economic and ethical choices, Harper's fiction as a whole can be considered a rhetoric in the classical sense insofar as it provides heuristics for communicative action. In her study of the activism of African American women in the nineteenth-century urban North, Carla Peterson provides a model analysis of the way public institutions of literature, media, and government "connect . . . people by articulating a sameness of purpose and providing a common means of executing designs" (*Doers* 11). Peterson's phrase "executing designs" aptly suggests the functional manner in which a group can share a inventive social script. Minnie and Louis, the protagonists of Harper's first novel *Minnie's Sacrifice*, are exemplary or "ideal" not only in their uncompromising race loyalty and dedication to reform, but also in their rhetorical practice as speakers of the precepts of Reconstruction uplift. Like all of Harper's fiction and much didactic literature, *Minnie's Sacrifice* is dialogue heavy, and one might fairly say that you get a good "talking to" when reading a Harper novel. These many dialogues make up the drama of persuasion through which Harper so often taught, and her didactic conversational topoi serve as an index of the broader political-economic forces that underwrite the exchange; people say what they must, in a sense, given their place within an economic totality.[7]

In Harper's rhetorical pedagogy, the subject of persuasion exists amid these intersubjective circuits, unknowingly or actively closed off from the collective sense of responsibility and mutual dependence, a precept at the core of Harper's ethics. Throughout her career, Harper taught this idiom as a lecturer, poet, novelist, and journalist, not simply as a series of talking points or set arguments but as a lived ethics of connection, a structure of identification within an intersubjective social network. Contemporary theories of subject formation, personhood, hybridity, and ideological interpolation all provide the framework for studying political identity as a group phenomenon, and many of these theories inform my reading methodology. However, to analyze the politics of subject formation with historical sensitivity, we need to begin with the most pervasive conceptual model of personhood in the nineteenth century, that is, *character*. Harper, like many of her compatriots, found a rhetorical dynamism in the discursive structures of character, one that emerged with the politics of African American abolitionism. African American protest, and more specifically African American women's rights protest, uncoupled national fealty from state allegiance, the powerful cultural imperatives of *national* character. As a matter of rhetorical pedagogy premised on a model of persuadable subjectivity, calling on a collective political will—a black-national gesture—served to materially organize the African American character, which in turn became the engine of social reform and the germinating subjective ground of community. This craft was at its core the invention of a commonplace teaching idiom meant to be emulated as practical political wisdom on the color and gender lines encountered daily by her primary audience, the readership of the African American press.

Character talk is a shorthand term I use to designate the pervasive conceptual reliance on cultural forms of characterological virtue in nearly all manner of social address, the communicative manner of ethical subjects negotiating general principles of ethical personhood. Harper's adherence to the inventive possibilities of self in society was quite conventional, but the new disciplinary politics of character articulated in her work marked a sea change in the history of character itself.[8] My choice of the word "talk" is meant to suggest the pervasive and ordinary quality of characterological rhetoric and its context within the oratorical culture of reform communities in the nineteenth century, what author and cultural observer Edward G. Parker referred to as the "golden age of American oratory." As Peter Gibian notes, conversation was a bedrock element of political culture in the nineteenth century. According to Gibian, reformers viewed conversation as "a model for the larger culture" and as "a privileged vehicle for their efforts at personal and political emancipation." The "problems of American diversity and American dividedness and the possibilities of American pluralism," Gibian argues, were often figured as "problems and possibilities of American conversation" (8). Particularly in her fiction, Harper found rich possibilities for social change in her practice of character talk as an art of conversation, modeling a general theory of rhetoric that formulates human relations as an ever-expanding circuit of addressor–addressee. Harper's formidable presence within this elite culture should not obscure the quotidian impulse of her teaching; she crafted rhetorical scenarios at sites of contested power in homes, work sites, the marketplace—the loci of myriad daily encounters along color and gender lines where that power was transacted. Harper pointedly taught the quotidian art of conversation as a vital political resource.

Voluntary organizations, publishing, and journalism formed the primary discursive ground of African American nationalism as a rhetorical and pedagogical project of character formation. Through these channels, Harper addressed audiences not as stable, independent subjects but as dynamic and intersubjective members of a race-national community, a practice contemporary rhetoricians have theorized as constitutive rhetoric.[9] Despite the high theoretical underpinnings of this critical discourse, we should not ignore the place of teaching and popular literature in the cultural work of constitutive rhetoric. Dexter B. Gordon theorizes the constitutive rhetoric of black nationalism not as a "philosophical ideal" but a working theory of "discourse in action" that is "constantly responsive to the exigencies of the contingent situations in which it operates," a rhetoric meant to generate race-national collectivity in the face of profound disenfranchisement and alienation (5–6). "Nation language" is Eddie S. Glaude's term for this constitutive lexicon of African American uplift and race pride. According to Glaude, the "cultural idea of the nation" developed amid the National Negro Convention Movement's "focus on moral reform and social uplift," a discursive practice that "confronted directly the practices of white supremacy of the American nation state" (18). Harper was trained in this context, and her constitutive rhetorical practice is consistent with that of the convention reformers who preceded her.

The continuity of tradition relies on inventive rearticulation. This is the craft Harper taught. Susan Miller makes a strong argument for analyzing rhetoric outside of dominant assumptions about tradition, lineage, and formal training, emphasizing instead that the "multiple forms" of rhetorical practice "constitute a plurality of instructive, variously situated lessons in language and in aesthetic, formal, and ordinary discourses that create contexts for choice." This paradigmatic shift, for Miller, demands that rhetoricians write their histories not according to "canons formed around concepts" but, instead, according to "situated uses" (1–3). This book takes up Miller's challenge. Taken as a whole, Harper's lifework should be seen as a cohesive book of working theory written with the civic function of rhetorical force in mind and generative of "contexts for choice," to use Miller's apt formulation.[10] Miller limns the interwoven, affective, cultural structure of these situated lessons, which transmit knowledge while concurrently eliciting trust in specific versions of rhetorical efficacy, ways of speaking we believe wield power. Harper's craft was forged from within that "web of situated lessons." She reinvented resonant commonplace knowledge as a grammar of preceptive statements that grounded the teaching idiom she intended readers to "take into their lives," as Frances Smith Foster describes the rhetorico-political use value of Harper's didactic address ("Gender, Genre" 54).

In Harper's public teaching texts, we find a striking continuity across years of political upheaval and crisis. After the Civil War and the abolition of chattel slavery, the pressing and hopeful demands of Radical Reconstruction created a new political urgency for Harper, who by this time had earned a strong reputation as a gifted and devoted writer and speaker. In the concluding installment of *Minnie's Sacrifice*, serialized in the *Christian Recorder* in 1869, Harper breaks fictional frame and addresses her audience directly. Herein, Harper offered her readership an interpretive framework for reading her novel. As I tell students only half-jokingly, we are fortunate as critics that Harper so often tells us exactly *how* to read her work. Minnie and Louis, the novel's sentimental heroine and hero, are, as Harper acknowledges, "ideal beings" meant to instruct, literally to model, race-national character as a practice of language.[11] The language of character, that core conceptual structure of personhood in the nineteenth century, grounded Harper's pedagogical address to audiences across the century. Over the course of the novel, both Minnie and Louis model an ethics of personhood that engaged directly with the political discourse of the moment. Both Minnie and Louis "sacrificed" the white privilege of racial "passing" and devoted their lives to the so-called Radical Reconstruction of the 39th Congress, which at the time seemed the most likely means of continued liberation for the newly emancipated Southern population. Harper was dedicated as a neo-abolitionist reform speaker traveling in the South during these years, addressing African and Anglo-American audiences, meeting with groups of African American women in their homes, and promoting Radical Republican politics and education.[12] From Athens, Georgia, in February of 1870, she wrote, "Here there is ignorance to be instructed, a race that needs to be helped up to higher planes of thought and action" (Still 770). For Harper, this was no less true when addressing a white reform audience or African American reform elite.

Harper's primary discursive site for teaching such ethically needful audiences was what Frances Smith Foster calls the "Afro-Protestant press" ("Gender, Genre" 52). Peterson argues that Harper's magazine fiction was a hybrid form combining conventionally didactic "tutelary activity" with journalism from an African American perspective ("Literary Reconstruction" 40–43). Over the course of her career, Harper published her work in the most influential abolitionist and African American newspapers, among them the *Weekly Anglo African Magazine*, the *African Methodist Episcopal Church Review*, *The Liberator*, the *National Anti-Slavery Standard*, and extensively, for over fifty years, *The Christian Recorder*, which circulated more of Harper's work than any other periodical. Harper tailored her call for rhetorical action to the African American reformers who like her had enjoyed the benefits of education and some economic stability. Her address to *Christian Recorder* readers in 1869 targeted an ignorance she found far less tolerable than the rhetorical and social underdevelopment of the recently emancipated slave class. In the conclusion of *Minnie's Sacrifice*, Harper reminds her readers of the black-national precept of solidarity, charging them with a duty-bound advocacy of which Minnie and Louis are fictional exemplars. Hers was no simple project of indoctrination, but the training of a collective literacy of uplift:

> We have wealth among us, but how much of it is ever spent in build-ing up the future of the race? In encouraging talent, and developing genius? We have intelligence, but how much do we add to the reservoir of the world's thought? We have genius among us, but how much can it rely upon the colored race for support?
>
> Take even the *Christian Recorder*; where are the graduates from colleges and high school whose pens and brains lend beauty, strength, grace and culture to its pages? (91)[13]

Harper presses here a specific strain of uplift rhetoric, one I trace in the chapters that follow, lamenting a regrettable lack of compositional energy in the African American community implicated in broader material and political dysfunction. As Shirley Wilson Logan argues, an important part of rhetorical pedagogy is the "invocation" of rhetoric. Harper's invoca-tion here could not be any more site specific (*Liberating Language* 98). With the caveat that she wished not to be "officious or intrusive," Harper insists on the moral duty accompanying literacy, claiming that the readers' "disused faculties" will "avenge themselves by rusting" (91). This wasting of vital community resources is for Harper a kind of communicative immo-rality, a viciously involuted practice of literacy antithetical to the rhetorical pedagogy she had developed in the first decade and a half of reform work. This pedagogy of social connection claimed the "gifts we possess," be they "genius, culture, wealth or social position," as a resource for serving the interests of the race. Harper's prescribed practice of "loving diffusion" required of her audience a renunciation of "narrow and selfish isolation." These assertions instruct readers about the preceptive characterizations of Minnie and Louis, which chart a Reconstructionist's path into the South-ern field of relief and educational work. Harper concludes the call to action in the novel's final installment, asserting a dialectical complicity of self and society by which individual actions embodied the immorality of institu-tions as "one type of the barbarous and anti-social state" (92).

The subtending spatial metaphors of "diffusion" and "isolation" sig-nal the conceptual core of Harper's rhetorical politics and her didactic intention toward her learning subjects, in this case, a potential African American national community as yet separated by class, gender, educa-tion, and region, the very fractures that African American reformers had sought to heal since the Negro Convention Movement of the early century. Like the readers Harper addressed in the poem "Free Labor," the *Chris-tian Recorder* readers of *Minnie's Sacrifice* are addressed as ethical subjects enmeshed in systems of literacy and economics that ultimately cannot be separated. Harper's barely constrained disparagement works an ancient persuasive channel, of course—a characterological charge of greed and excessive self-interest that was perhaps the most serious charge an African American reformer could bring against her or his own community. David Walker was among the first early black nationalists sounding this critical note forty years earlier in his *Appeal to the Coloured Citizens of the World*, when he anticipated a hostile reception to his text by members of his own community, African Americans who were "ignorantly in league with slave holders or tyrants, who acquire their daily bread by the blood and sweat of their more ignorant brethren" (4). The dormant pens and sequestered intellectual and monetary resources of the *Christian Recorder* readership are thus another "type" of racial and economic immorality underwriting the "barbarous and anti-social state" that nineteenth-century African American reformers worked to transform. Like that of Walker, Harper's call to conscience is socially constitutive in its rhetorical function insofar as it solicits, and gauges, race loyalty as a point of ethical identification.

AFRICAN AMERICAN RHETORICAL PEDAGOGY AND THE EDUCATION OF CHARACTER

Any approach to a general account of Harper's work requires coming to terms not simply with her *ethos*, but with her *ethical theory*, the system of recurring characterological precepts she taught as a matter of lived principle and committed linguistic practice. Before the secularization and professionalization of teaching, the inevitability that literacy acquisition constituted a moral training ground was for better and for worse generally expected by educators, particularly those who worked in the name of reform. Hugh Blair's *Lectures on Rhetoric and Belle Lettres*, one of the most influential nineteenth-century works of rhetorical pedagogy, lists the "development of character or moral improvement" as the first means of "improving eloquence." (qtd. in Logan, *Liberating Language* 97). Given that "eloquence" was predicated on access to education within the racial state, Blair's is a cruelly ironic precept to say the least.[14] Nevertheless, Harper's rhetoric garnered praise, and her oratory in particular was thought to be exemplary. This much can be deduced from contemporaneous assessments of her speeches, the influence she wielded, and her appearance at landmark events.[15] As Harper argued throughout her career, eloquence was only as valuable as it was instructive and only properly instructive if it proved corrective of character. Patrick Rael argues that without other recourse, African American reformers entered as contestants the characterological language game of "elevation," "improvement," or "development" (*Black Identity* 130–132). For Rael, despite its characterological paradoxes and corruptions, the market revolution also created the fundamental possibility for African American character to emerge as the guiding preceptive structure for social protest. The generation of writers and speakers preceding Harper had derived their appeals for racial justice while carefully preserving a network of commonly accepted ideas concerning an impersonal and rational marketplace, meritocracy, and a vision of market culture as the proper ground of moral as well as economic self-determination (Rael, "Market Values" 22–25). By revealing the characterological underpinnings of slavery and racial prejudice and reclaiming the realm of character formation from the marketplace, Harper formulated a language of protest that would ultimately emerge at the center of the free labor antislavery platform.

As a model for social self-understanding, the interpolative resonance of characterological rhetoric is more distant for twenty-first century thinkers than it was for Harper and her contemporaries. The absence of the word "character" from Raymond Williams's canonical *Keywords: A Vocabulary of Culture and Society* is surprising given the author's astute selection of epochal English words. *Keywords* dramatizes, at the lexical level, Williams's tripartite model of cultural-historical dynamism: the practice of language evolving in "dominant," "emergent," and "residual" phases. Tracing shifts in the definition and usage of powerful words such as "tradition," "generation," "art," and "family," Williams illustrates the resilient epistemic authority of language over time. Taken as a whole, the rich etymologies and usage notes of the *Keywords* entries locate language within a web of cultural dynamism and assume that any account of language will perforce be an account of the discursive practices in which language emerges, circulates, and changes. Where, then, is character, in the Anglo-European master index of language?[16]

As a locus of moral identity and as a powerful heuristic for civil belonging, perhaps character eluded Williams's lexical schematics because of its simultaneously pervasive and diverse cultural articulation, its rhetorical diffuseness. To be clear, I am not suggesting that character could be invoked with anything like univocality. Rael notes that such everyday moral distinctions "took place over hierarchies of character traits on which humans and societies might rise and fall." The morally inflected vocabulary of "elevation" and "progress" was a ubiquitous feature on the antebellum "conceptual landscape," one that most Americans "took so much for granted . . . they would have been hard pressed to elucidate [it]" (*Black Identity* 125–127). Despite the common-sense quality of character and its inevitable omnipresence as the rhetorical framework for ethical identification, many writers and orators viewed themselves as technicians of character, inventing and circulating political identity as a claim to diverse sources of social authority. Rael notes the common-sense certainty with which people invoked character as a moral measurement without defining the term assured a diversity of usage where consensus was merely assumed (131). From a rhetorical perspective, this inevitability of variation within a broad common understanding allows for powerful inventive possibilities. Character, understood to be the practice of self-discipline or the ethical principles of social personhood, must be considered as a broadly discursive practice of identity. Questions of character are still operative in political debate; think, for instance, of the way it animates the contest of political elections. This old way of thinking about moral identity might emerge, or re-emrge, in moments when the distinctions between the political and the personal, between the public and the private spheres, invite scrutiny.

Warren Susman's assessment of the nineteenth-century United States as a "culture of character" does not overreach in claiming that notions of character were "fundamental in sustaining and even in shaping the significant forms of the culture."[17] Modern architects of character stipulated self-control as a matter of civic virtue—no person's moral status could be adjudicated in isolation from the larger community. Scholars and students of the nineteenth-century United States should be able to attest to the archival pervasiveness of the language of character in governmental documents, treatises on the sciences and arts, personal journals and letters, all the records that are left to us. The power and dynamism of character as a cultural formation arise, as Susman notes, from a presiding ambiguity, its functionality as a mode of "both mastery and development of the self" (273). All the European sources of characterological thought posit this general notion of mutable identity as a social happening—free will, self-government, the covenant of work and mutual obligation, enlightened self-interest, as well as ancient thinking about the cultivation of virtuous habit, all endlessly negotiated through constant and myriad encounters between the self and society. Protestant non-conformists and dissenters would bring these ideas and practices to North America, where they grounded early national thought. Evangelists of the Great Awakening saw themselves as the vanguard of a continuing process of social perfectionism in which antinomian character embodied, as it had for Martin Luther, anti-institutional virtue.

Antinomian conceptions of the self would ground the ethical perspective of the abolitionist movement, of African American reform thought, and more specifically, of the lineage of African American feminist moral teachers to which Harper belongs. Thought of in this way, we might understand the "slave poet" Phyllis Wheatley as a foremother of this pedagogical tradition, her rhetorical practice a radical continuation of the Reformation, cautioning and admonishing white male Christendom about the excesses of an unbalanced character. Wheatley's poem "To the University of Cambridge in New England" delivers no quiet pieties, but bold declarations of principle and theological pedagogy meant to put the Cambridge elite on guard against sinful influence, their "greatest foe." Moving from the premise that "the whole human race" exists in a "fall'n" state, Wheatley exhorts the Cambridge "pupils" to "improve your privileges while they stay" and "each hour to redeem, that bears good or bad report of you to heav'n." Christian theology provides a framework for didactic address here, so that anyone among the "fall'n," that is, all of humanity, might address her fellows in this way. Wheatley, however, carefully marks the racial distance between addressor and addressee even while her appeal to Christian virtue attempts to close that distance. She reminds the Cambridge students, those "sons of science," of their relative social position and its duties; that to them "'tis giv'n to scan the heights / Above, to traverse the ethereal space, / And mark the systems of revolving worlds." Wheatley thanks gracious "Father of mercy" for bringing her to North America from her "native shore / The land of errors, and *Egyptian* gloom;" whether we read this thanks for enslavement as sincere or tactical, Wheatley reminds readers that the neoclassical verse before them was written by "an Ethiop" (*Collected Works* 13–14). While never matching Wheatley's evangelical zeal, Harper likewise invoked Christian sentiment to frame her rhetorical pedagogy and articulate the precepts of an ethically composed self.

Ultimately we cannot cogently read the history of character talk in the United States without acknowledging its gaps and absences. For the English gentry and their colonial American counterparts, the concept of character was nothing less than the mark of white patriarchal privilege. Character as a pedagogical function assumed a social field of white contractual and affective fealty. Without question, as a byword of cultural currency and public access, character was the province of white men. I take the cultural exclusivity of character as axiomatic, and this study attends to the function of characterological rhetoric as a legitimating code in the systematic atrocities of racial statecraft.[18] Institutional arbiters of character in churches, schools, and government carefully wrote African-descended people out of the character-based social contract in both law and custom. Thomas Jefferson's assessment of ostensible African instinct, as opposed to character, suggests the ingrained and oppressive hierarchies of race and gender strictures in the American Enlightenment. Jefferson's most potent character assassination, his *Notes on the State of Virginia*, was a landmark moment in the philosophical justification for African slavery. Generations of white supremacist ideologues would return to Jefferson's key claim that Africans were incapable of reason and thus of self-government. Jefferson paints the picture of essentially animalistic African nature.

We should note that women's character never even emerges as a category, the possibility of character in African American women being for Jefferson, we must deduce, not even worthy of dismissal. African American women serve only as a rhetorical device to further de-humanize African American men. Jefferson asserts that "[t]hey are more ardent after their female: but love seems with them to be more an eager desire, than a tender delicate mixture of sentiment and sensation." Jefferson does acknowledge that as slaves "confined to tillage," a lack of opportunity for improvement might be forwarded as a cause for characterological incapacity, suggesting that Africans' ostensibly imitative and thus deficient cultural productions may be evidence of some "germ in their mind that only wants cultivation." As a refutation, Jefferson argues that even those slaves who "have been liberally educated" lack still the capacity for written expression.[19] Jefferson assessement of Phyllis Wheatley's poems as "below the dignity of criticism" and of African American epistolary artist Ignatius Sancho as "wild and extravagant, fugitive" from "restraint of reason and taste," are examples of Jefferson's pedagogical assault on the incapacity of African character (139). To say the least, Jefferson's disparagement in its entirety is rife with circular justifications of North American slavery.[20]

While historians of character like Susman and Rael demonstrate the utilitarian functionality of character in the racial caste system of the state, the more critical pedagogy enabled by the conceptual model of character has been left largely unexplored. The racial theory emerging from the black national public sphere reinvented character as a powerful set of egalitarian precepts. "The Colored People in America," the prose introduction to the 1857 version of *Poems on Miscellaneous Subjects*, exemplifies Harper's rescue of characterological rhetoric, mapping how popular conceptions of character were employed to rationalize human degradation, positioning her own pedagogical use of character through her insistence on well-disciplined living. The shibboleth of debased African character becomes for Harper the framework for political-economic critique. Directly addressing white supremacist opinion, she suggests the legacy of enslavement's "degradation" as a refutation to any intrinsic argument about race character:

> [L]et them, when nominally free, feel that they have only exchanged the iron yoke of oppression for the galling fetters of a vitiated public opinion;—let prejudice assign them the lowest places and the humblest positions, and make them "hewers of wood and drawers of water,"— let their income be so small that they must from necessity bequeath to their children an inheritance of poverty and a limited education,—and tell me, reviler of our race! Censurer of our people! If there is a nation in whose veins runs the purest Caucasian blood, upon whom the same causes would not produce the same effect; whose social condition, intellectual and moral character, would present a more favorable aspect than ours? (qtd. in *BCD* 99–100)[21]

The catalogue compiled here and the rhythmic force of Harper's periodic phrasing refutes the precept of essential African degradation. The "purest Caucasian blood" would not, for Harper, transcend the cause and effect of material oppression and characterological quality. Harper's indictment of a "vitiated public opinion" casts the rhetorical culture in which African Americans labored as itself a production of racial-state oppression.

In Harper's address, this defense of African American character is often joined with sympathy or rebuke for her readership's damaging internalization of that "vitiated public opinion." Among the elite African American readership making up her primary audience, Harper asserted the presence of "a disposition to censure and upbraid each other," a disposition Harper attributes to "a want of common sympathy" engendered by

> misery, nurtured in degradation, and cradled in oppression, with the scorn of the white man upon his soul, his fetters upon their limbs, his scourge upon their flesh, what can be expected from their offspring, but a mournful reaction of that cursed system which spreads its baneful influence over body and soul; which dwarfs the intellect, stunts its development, debases the spirit, and degrades the soul?

Here, for Harper, is the fundamental characterological ill of the African American nation, the perverse training of an oppressive system carried out over generations, deforming race pride, racial solidarity, and the inherent human potential of the enslaved and their descendents. Racial self-hatred is shown to be the reproduction of white supremacist ideology, and it is this "system" that "stunts" moral character, "the intellect . . . the spirit . . . the soul" (99).

Harper was consistent with her teachers in her view of education, largely rhetorical in emphasis, as a powerful stay against this oppressive cultural pedagogy. Under his own name and as "The Colored Baltimorean," Harper's uncle, William Watkins Sr., published consistently in *The Liberator* and *The Universal Genius of Emancipation* and ran the highly esteemed Watkins Academy for Negro Youth in Baltimore. In an 1886 *African American Episcopal Church Review* retrospective of Watkins's career, James H. A. Johnston noted the exacting instruction he employed in both the classroom and the African American press, especially the emphasis on oratory and composition at the Watkins Academy. Its curriculum consisted of history, geography, mathematics, English, natural philosophy, Greek, Latin, and rhetoric. "[Watkins's] forté as a teacher," Johnston wrote, "was an amazing command of English . . . Every example of etymology, syntax and prosody had to be given as correctly as a sound upon a keyboard . . . every rule had to be repeated and accurately applied . . . every peculiarity of declension, mood and tense readily borne in mind." Harper studied at her uncle's school and even assisted with the instruction. Johnston also noted, "Frances Ellen . . . excelled" in the near-daily compositions that Watkins required (qtd. in Gardner 623). Harper's uncle was also a cofounder of the American Moral Reform Society, which was an outgrowth of the 4th and 5th Conventions of the Free People of Color in 1836. Watkins was central in developing the organization platform which held as its main tenets "Education, Temperance, Economy, and Universal Liberty" (624). He embraced the character-forming responsibilities of education, though his sense of the cultural scope of pedagogy was far from limited to official works of rhetorical or educational theory or even to scholastic institutions. In his 1836 address to the Moral Reform Society, Watkins began with the premise that "all civilized nations have always regarded, as of paramount importance, the education of the rising generation." The subject of education is "continually receiving impressions" and "perpetually forming habits." The education that attends only to intellectual cultivation is morally bankrupt for Watkins. He stipulates that a "good education" will be "one as will soundly instruct this compound being." Harper's rhetorical pedagogy assumed a similarly dynamic and socially located learning subject. A "good" as opposed to "pernicious" education will enable the student "at all times, in all places and under all circumstances" to maintain a virtuous character (157). Her didactic novels, modeling moral suasion as a dispersed, public-sphere practice, attend especially well to the temporality of rhetorical subjectivity.

Harper's family history coincides with the increasing prominence of African American leadership within the national abolitionist movement. Accompanying this shift in leadership was a political reorientation of abolitionist rhetorical theory toward immediatism.[22] Immediatists required a relinquishing of allegiances to and a rejection of compromise with what they argued was a fundamentally corrupt ruling class. As a constitutive pedagogical rhetoric, immediatism and its signature rhetorical practice of moral suasion extended to readers and auditors a pledge of action, a call to allegiances more profound than those of the state. John Goodman notes that African American abolitionists were the first immediatists. As a political platform, immediatism responded to the African colonization movement, which abolitionists refuted as a project of white supremacist logic and the economic expediency of Northern compromise with the slave power (106–107). Colonization, then, was not a means to African American independence, but a stall tactic and capitulation to the dangerous ideology of essential hierarchical difference based on race (41–57). The anti-colonization argument of William Watkins Sr. and other African American reformers was a great influence on William Lloyd Garrison's *Thoughts on African Colonization*, by all accounts a crucial document in the progression of the immediatist cause. Goodman refers to this as Garrison's "conversion" to immediatism.

RHETORICAL PEDAGOGY AND THE POLITICAL ECONOMY OF THE RACIAL STATE

The nation state was the premier political achievement of racial modernity in the Western Hemisphere, and the Atlantic slave trade served as the engine driving the state-building processes of colonial imperialism. David Brion Davis notes the scholarly consensus that the slave system in the Americas, plantation slavery in particular, was "far from archaic" but in fact "anticipated much of the efficiency, organization, and global interconnectedness of industrial capitalism" (77). Modern racial states in the nineteenth century, the United States among them, propagated racial control of non-white peoples through political-economic violence perversely legitimized as the inevitable and benevolent outcome of Enlightenment statecraft. Though ancient in its ideological sources, as Davis demonstrates, anti-black thought pervaded the slave economies of the early modern era in the Atlantic world. White supremacist precepts binding with the power of law governed what scholars have understood as "the racial state" of the nineteenth-century United States. As David Theo Goldberg argues, nation states organized according to capitalist economies have most often been characterized by two concomitant forms of racial hegemony, what he calls "naturalist" and "historicist" racism (74–82). Naturalist racism, according to Goldberg, is based in biologistic and theological premises, while historicist racism depends on narratives of racial development over time, retaining white supremacism as the inevitable telos of historical progress. Across the era of Emancipation and Reconstruction, these interacting cultural formations of racial domination provided the rationale for political retreat from racial justice within the context of an ostensibly ascendant democracy.

However, in the end, nineteenth-century slave emancipations amounted, at best, to a partial reform of race relations in the Western Hemisphere. The first national era of civil rights emerged a decade after Harper began her career. The transformational events of Emancipation, the Civil War, and Reconstruction marked the epochal end of what Michael Omi and Howard Winant fairly characterize as a pre-Emancipation "racial dictatorship."[23] In the United States, nonetheless, Union victory in the Civil War accelerated the nation-state modernization that ultimately nullified much of the promise of Emancipation. Presiding over this era of reform and reaction was the administration that had prosecuted war on the seceding Southern states, the Republican Party of Abraham Lincoln and then of Andrew Johnson. Initially a staunch advocate of Radical Republican politics, including the extension of suffrage to African American men, Harper made no secret of her frustration over the forestalled Emancipation in her address to the predominantly white audience of the 1866 Woman's Rights Convention in New York. Harper delivered her lesson by turns with bracing calls to justice and strong disparagements of Andrew Johnson's aggressive executive assault on Radical Reconstruction initiatives.[24] Harper's character assassination of Johnson posits his political misbehavior as the product of a corrupt and failed pedagogy, a moral and intellectual deficiency that renders him dangerously ignorant. This address presciently anticipates an epochal shift in the history of "racial formation," what Omi and Winant identify as "the socio-historical process by which racial categories are created, inhabited, transformed, and destroyed" (55–56). Johnson is unable to "catch the watchword of the hour," which for Harper heralds the "grand glorious revolution" of Reconstruction, and this historic failure of interpretive wherewithal becomes the preceptive exemplar structuring Harper's characterological argument (*BCD* 218).

David Theo Goldberg identifies the discursive means by which racial states utilize race as a category of control, a "set of projects and practices, social conditions and institutions, states of being and affairs, rules and principles, statements and imperatives" (5). This schema is helpful insofar as it allows us to think in more detail about the dissemination of race as a political idea, and more specifically, as a set of didactic if diffuse cultural precepts that legitimize the organization of human relations in service of the dominant political economy. Insofar as they derive ethical authority from widely held belief in their culture-building processes and social functions, political economies are pedagogical. As a material, socially constitutive rhetorical practice, Harper's reform work articulated a preceptive language that engaged the dominant racial lessons of the antebellum racial state. Harper and her abolitionist compatriots often berated the pedagogy of the slave system, detailing the lessons of slavery's "school" for both slave and enslaver. The great counter-example for Harper was the ostensibly dawning and much heralded age of a virtuous "free labor" society, a civic system of open opportunity, in which accumulative desire, "avarice" as Harper so often called it, would be understood as contrary to the public good both theologically and as a matter of economic utility.[25] Despite the "progress" of nineteenth-century social reform and much ceremony regarding free-labor principle, the United States remained an oppressive racial state moving back toward racial dictatorship.

Harper's rhetorical pedagogy, exemplary of much black-nationalist thought, imagined a different emerging modernity in which the uplift principle of solidarity gave a "subaltern class" of African Americans new economic power. Peterson argues that "African Americans needed to resist, and to adapt themselves, not only to the forces of white racism but also to a growing capitalist economy in which the wealth was increasingly concentrated in the hands of a small number of manufacturers who controlled the wage labor." "At the very bottom of this workforce," Peterson notes, "black men and women strove to transform their marginal status into a source of strength, to achieve social and economic autonomy by circumventing capitalist structures and holding on to pre-capitalist forms of behavior" (*Doers* 9). It was not capitalism *per se* that Harper resisted. She continually recorded her hopes for a reformed and humane culture of labor and commerce, often equating economic opportunity with racial uplift in her labor and land-reform advocacy. However, Peterson notes that the free-labor ethic was championed by Harper and much of the rest of the country just as the era of independent small producers was coming to an end. Though it lost its material base, the residual power of the republican ideology provided Harper and her contemporaries with a cogent critique of the disruptive civic forces of American capitalism, which had built a world of social caste and stolen labor. By the time of Reconstruction, artisanal social relations may indeed have been considered "pre-capitalist," as Peterson notes, but in the abolitionist imagination, they were nonetheless a guiding figure of a projected emerging age.

White nationalism underwrote the cultural pedagogy of the nineteenth-century racial state, a preceptive script that exists to this day, but as Davis's discussion makes clear, the sovereignty of white nationalism was contested from the beginning of Western modernity. While a strict Marxian understanding holds the state to be the protectorate of capital, "nation" is meant to designate a constellation of ideological exclusions by which the social relations and sovereignty of the state are legitimated. The resulting institutional scripts, of the public good, of market orthodoxy, or of military patriotism, serve a training function for the promotion of state allegiance.[26] Sticking to the script of this allegiance, so to speak—circulating and bonding over its commonplace statements—produces the discursive space of nationalism, either in moments of deliberation, that is, policy matters, or as ceremony, that is, children pledging allegiance or legislators invoking national duty as a warrant for action. The following chapters attest to Harper as a tactically ambivalent participant in nationalist discourse. So often in her work, the call to character, to self-discipline, forbearance, and duty, appeals to the authority of natural-rights social theory, a cultural pedagogy she could neither reject nor claim in full, insofar as the theory had always served to further white nationalism.

Charles Mills's formulation of the "racial contract" brings critical attention to the fundamentally exclusionary cultural lineage of natural-rights theory as a continually self-producing practice of racial hegemony. Mills offers an important critique of the essential racism of democratic political culture in the West, demanding an account of the "the racial contract," his term for the linguistic script of loyalty for white privilege and racial hierarchy. According to Mills, when we make rights-based appeals to the core principles of equality, we partake of a political idiom that has historically maintained white citizenship as a powerful norm. The codification of the racial state in the form of the Naturalization Acts of the 1790s, the 1857 Dred Scott decision, and successive fugitive slave laws indicates the *"prescribed"* quality of the epistemological "general rule" of white contractarian, the dissemination of *"white misunderstanding, misrepresentation, evasion, and self-deception on matters related to race,"* what Mills calls the "most pervasive mental phenomena of the past few hundred years" and the "cognitive and moral economy psychically required for conquest, colonization, and enslavement." The persuasive historicity of the racial contract comes in its function as "the differential privileging of the whites as a group with respect to the non-whites as a group, the exploitation of their bodies, land, and resources and the denial of equal socioeconomic opportunities to them" (1–19). Racial-contract language, held by Mills to be the discursive site of white privilege, is constitutive for its white "signatories" even if they make no explicit pledge of faith to a white racial state or to one another (11).

Character talk, understood as an intersubjective social process of hailing one another, cannot be separated from the constitutive common places of contractarian rhetoric. The public discourse of abolitionism also relied on social-contract precepts, testing their egalitarian potential. As will be reviewed in detail in Chapter 1, African American nationalists took up print culture and the lyceum as both emblem and operation of racial solidarity and progress. Michael Warner examines the historical beginnings of this linguistic commonality in his study of early national rhetorical culture in the eighteenth-century United States, demonstrating the symbiotic development of mass media and the republican public-sphere ethic. Warner explains the formation of an early New England bourgeoisie as continuous with this emergence of technology and technological self-consciousness, arguing that "an emerging political language—republicanism—and a new set of ground rules for discourse—the public sphere—jointly made each other intelligible." As a space of ostensibly democratic debate, public-sphere discourse becomes a political ideal, an imaginative space where individuals define and participate in their own citizenship, articulating political identities and "becoming part of an arena of the national people that cannot be realized except through such mediating imaginings" (viii).[27] In Susan Miller's formulation, such "imaginings" are rhetorically constitutive insofar as they function as a site of trust in a historically specific communicative practice, a constitutive article of faith in an efficacious political language (2).

In the opening sentences of her 1859 essay "Our Greatest Want," published in the *Weekly Anglo African Magazine*, Harper identifies the constitutive power of linguistic trust in the form of "public opinion." The rhetorical pedagogy articulated in the essay sounds the precepts of contractarian ideology. For her elite audience, Harper sketches the discursive frame for a practice of reform publicity:

> Leading ideas impress themselves upon communities and countries. A thought is evolved and thrown out among the masses, they receive it and it becomes interwoven with their mental and moral life—if the thought be good the receivers are benefited, and helped onward to the truer life; if it is not, the reception of the idea is a detriment. A few earnest thinkers and workers infuse into the mind of Great Britain, a sentiment of human brotherhood. The hue and cry of opposition is raised against it. Avarice and cupidity oppose it, but the great heart of the people throbs for it. A healthy public opinion dashes and surges against the British throne, the idea gains ground and progresses till hundreds of thousands of men, women and children arise, redeemed from bondage, and freed from chains, and the nation gains moral power by the act. (160)

These confident assertions regarding the power of language present rhetoric, in the agency of public opinion, as the movement of history itself. The state would be reformed by the discursive training of the citizenry into interpretive interaction with the world, a process Harper figures as a weaving of "mental and moral life." The "moral power" of the "nation" depends on this reform, and pedagogically, on the nurture of a "healthy public opinion."

Despite the sweeping historical scope of this rhetorically ideal narrative, at the core of Harper's pedagogy lies a belief in the workaday importance of rhetoric as the substance of common talk, of conversational readiness. The ethic of rhetorical invention forwarded in Harper's late poem "Songs for the People" models this practice of socially committed language:

> Let me make the songs for the people,
>   Songs for the old and young;
> Songs to stir like a battle-cry
>   Wherever they are sung.
>
> Not for the clashing of sabers,
>   For carnage nor the strife;
> But songs to thrill the hearts of men
>   With more abundant life.

Attention to the expansive temporal reference of the first stanzas reveals the poem's pedagogical functionality, as Harper marks the ethical use value of her poem across contexts, beyond the scene of her own composition. The stirring quality of the prescribed "songs"—aggressive but pointedly not martial as the poem goes on to stipulate—is meant to circulate, to have effect "[w]herever they are sung." Songs meant to "thrill the hearts of men" have emotional impact and exponential effect, inspiring as they should "more abundant life." By the time this poem was published, Harper's political criteria for life's "abundance" was a matter of prolific public record.

Harper's poetry, like her fiction, journalism, and oratory, enacts theory even as it persuades and teaches. The analysis in the following chapters seeks to make clear that tripartite discursive action. Patricia Hill Collins argues that for Harper and fellow nineteenth-century African American "clubwomen" such as Anna J. Cooper, Ida B. Wells, and Mary Church Terrell, theory and practice were inseparable (33). These intellectuals, without the leisure of "purely theoretical work," theorized and set into motion their own persuasive practices. They recognized rhetorical pedagogy as the functional link between theory and practice. Whatever persuasive gambits are at play, Harper's rhetorical pedagogy hails audiences *as* communicative subjects. Audiences are moved, then, not only toward some political end— though Harper was most often quite pointed in her policy prescriptions— but are invited into the community of a timely idiom and bid to accept a communicative methodology as a matter of pressing political necessity.

1 Composing Character
Cultural Sources of African American Rhetorical Pedagogy

ADDRESSING ANGLO-AFRICANS, CIRCA 1859

Before the Civil War and Emancipation, the African American press emerged as a powerful pedagogical institution, though instruction was only one of its rhetorical functions. Frances Harper was among the abolitionist luminaries who published in Thomas and Robert Hamilton's prestigious *Anglo African Magazine* in its three-year run from 1859 to 1861.[1] We can begin to assess her prominence within a galvanizing national African American reform society simply by surveying the in-print company Harper kept. Her fellow contributors in the magazine's inaugural year of 1859 included Martin Delany, Sarah H. Douglass, J. W. C. Pennington, J. Holland Townsend, J. Theodore Holly, James McCune Smith, and William J. Wilson. Harper and the other reformers pledged themselves to the duty of cultivating a knowledgeable readership by writing in explicitly didactic genres that addressed a range of topics, primary among them, the abolition of slavery and the importance of education for the social reform of the racial state. Pennington's praise for the race character of a rising people and his confident predictions about the future of the race chorused across the wide range of compositions filling the *Anglo African*. Theodore Holly's series "Thoughts on Hayti" surveyed the heroic attainment and fifty-year maintenance of this "negro nationality" as an international precedent and a definitive refutation of white supremacist arguments that non-whites must be dependant races at best. Amos Gerry Beman perhaps best expressed the didactic ethic of the *Anglo African Magazine* in "The Education of the Colored People," the cover article of the November 1859 issue. Insofar as the modern world would be governed by "force of mind—cultivated mind," as Beman claimed, "instruction is the great want of the colored race" (339). Cultivating the political sensibilities of the readership and calling them to a pledge of collective character, Harper and her abolitionist compatriots made the *Anglo African Magazine* a constitutive site of African American rhetorical pedagogy.[2]

Among the contributors, the training of character became the principal rhetorical intention of such needful instruction. While no final consensus emerged among *Anglo African Magazine* contributors regarding the proper course of uplift and racial self-determination, the intellectual and social event of characterological redemption through education bore historic importance. In the "Apology," opening the magazine's first issue, the editors promise to "uphold and encourage the now depressed hopes of thinking black men, in the United States," appealing to the convention movement activists, editors, preachers, and speakers who, despite their best efforts, "see, as the apparent result of their work . . . only Fugitive Slave laws and Compromise bills, and the denial of citizenship on the part of the Federal and state Governments" (3). This litany of crimes in the racial state on the brink of epochal transformation will be familiar enough to readers of African American reform and protest writing. The clarion call for education pervaded the social mission of the African American reform community, but very few in the African American press exhibited a dedication to rhetorical education comparable to Harper's. Harper borrowed from rich cultural sources such as theology and republicanism to build the language of her constitutive rhetoric. This chapter examines the innovations of Harper's rhetorical pedagogy, focusing primarily on her essays and fiction published in the *Anglo African Magazine* and other periodicals in and around the incredibly productive year of 1859, the zenith of the abolitionist movement.

Among the many pieces Harper wrote for the *Anglo African* in its inaugural year of 1859, her essay "Our Greatest Want," which rounded out the May issue, perhaps most powerfully integrates sacred and secular sources of social virtue as resources for the composition of a protest ethos. In what had become by this date a characteristic rhetorical stance, Harper takes readers to the text of Exodus, which Eddie S. Glaude Jr. has argued is a great storehouse of the commonplace arguments, tropes, and figures that infuse what Glaude refers to as "nation language," arguably the rhetorical backbone of African American nationalism in the nineteenth century (14).[3] Harper's invention of a Mosaic character not only depends on a specific biblical interpretation, it models a hermeneutical method of self-reflection, a political literacy that would promote collectively responsible action among otherwise estranged segments of the race. In the following passage, she challenges that readership to compose its own ethical personhood through reference to Moses:

> I like the character of Moses. He is the first disunionist we read of in the Jewish Scriptures. The magnificence of Pharaoh's throne loomed up before his vision, its oriental splendors glittered before his eyes; but he turned from them all and chose rather to suffer with the enslaved, than rejoice with the free. He would have no union with the slave power of Egypt. When we have a race of men whom this blood stained government cannot tempt or flatter, who would sternly refuse every office in the nation's gift, from a president down to a tide-waiter, until she

shook her hands from complicity in the guilt of cradle plundering and man stealing, then for us the foundations of an historic character will have been laid. (160)

Harper's disunionist Moses represents the characterological discipline necessary for race-national survival, a collective future unthinkable without uncompromising loyalty to African American slaves, which Harper exhibited not only through writing, but through action as well. Because of William Still's documentation and the efforts of other contemporaneous commentators, we now know that Harper was an active member of the Underground Railroad, a woman who lent material aid to no less a radical group than John Brown and his compatriots. Harper is careful to present her Moses as a "disunionist," a non-state abolitionist position rejecting party politics and the longstanding mission of "saving the union," to which the political compromises of the Jacksonian period can fairly be attributed.[4] Harper calls for a national ethic of non-participation, a turning away from the barbarity of white America writ large and Northern "complicity," in which even wayward members of her *Anglo African* audience might be culpable. As argued in the Introduction, political and rhetorical theory is inseparable in this immediatist stance. Immediatism, the radical belief in swift and complete abolition, refused the compromises of perpetually deferred political solutions, such as colonization, and insisted that moral suasion would re-educate racial sensibilities and create a revolution of hearts and minds, much as Harper's words above indicate. We can think of "disunion," then, as the political orientation of immediatist rhetoric, the social vision grounding its pedagogy. The *topoi* or constitutive commonplace precepts of disunion serve as the inventional ground of the abolitionist pledge language adopted by Harper and others to voice the political demands of the emerging race-national character.

The pedagogy of race womanhood Harper brought to the African American press was also based on this ethic of rejection. In this pedagogy, teaching rejection of both the racial state and the patriarchal control of African American women were one and the same practice. The appearance of Harper's "The Two Offers," serialized in the September and October, 1859, issues, signals her most distinctive feminist arguments in the form of the critical narrative, or "dramatic essay," Frances Smith Foster apt term for Harper's pedagogical fiction ("Gender, Genre" 57). The final section of this chapter argues that "The Two Offers," carrying forward the rhetorical precepts of her early poems, marks a watershed moment in Harper's elaboration of the women's rights idiom she would deliver to her readership for the remainder of her writing career. As Carla Peterson suggests, fiction rather quickly became Harper's primary means of rhetorical pedagogy, a "tutelary activity" meant to model a sustaining discipline of race-national character ("African American Literary Reconstruction" 46–47). Across genres, Harper taught her audiences among the Northern African

American elite a variety of character talk—common places and common-place rhetorical habits that were part of a broader process of establishing compositional space for African American women. Like much of Harper's subsequent fiction, "The Two Offers" directly addressed the gendered constraints of separate-spheres doctrine, therefore making inseparable claims for both women's rights and rhetorical action.

A pledge to rhetorical action, to participation in the discursive making of race-national collectivity was, for Harper, the "important lesson we should learn and be able to teach." Thus, the preceptive call to both "learn" and "teach"—the co-production of vital political knowledge—served as a constitutive bond among the African American nationalist community represented by the *Anglo African Magazine* readers. Her pedagogy of character formation emphasizes the discipline necessary to "make every gift, whether gold or talent, fortune, or genius," a community resource subserving "the cause of crushed humanity" ("Our Greatest Want" 160). This economic and collective ethical self-assessment to which Harper called her audience is echoed in the works of other *Anglo African Magazine* writers and in the rest of the African American press. For Harper and other disunionists, the reformation of corrupt government would occur from the ground up, through the rhetorical historical force of "public opinion"; and as the rest of this chapter illustrates, this grassroots politics was just as much a matter of rhetorical theory as of organizational principle.

BLACK REPUBLICANISM: NATIONAL VIRTUE
AND VICE IN THE RACIAL STATE

Southern Democrats used the term "Black Republican" as a racialized denunciation of Abraham Lincoln during the election of 1860.[5] In distinction, use of the term "black republicanism" here attempts to capture the idealism proudly dared by African American claimants of the revolutionary heritage, those, like Harper, who would take up the cause of popular democracy and the pedagogy of public-sphere citizenship. Returning to the passage of "Our Greatest Want" casting Moses as an immediatist exemplar, we can discern this framework as the historical logic underwriting the constitutive rhetoric Harper delivered to her *Anglo African Magazine* readers, potential members of her projected black-nationalist community. Identifying them as "a few earnest thinkers and workers," Harper recalls English abolitionists, who "infuse[d] into the mind of Great Britain, a sentiment of human brotherhood. The hue and cry of opposition is raised against it. Avarice and cupidity oppose it, but the great heart of the people throbs for it" ("Our Greatest Want" 160). Harper posits this idealized vision of public-sphere rhetorical politics as a foil against gag laws prohibiting antislavery petitioning, the policing of slave literacies, the stigmatizing of abolitionists, and the profound complacency and self-interested silence of white Northerners and elite African Americans. The rhetorical force of public opinion as a practice of principled iconoclasm is quintessentially republican in the pedagogy it elaborates, evoking grassroots democracy as a discursive project, a popular democratic will rising up in opposition to guard against corrupt and nefarious government. Popular democracy, and the rhetorical means necessary for the de-centralization of power, inspired mixed reactions among social elites. Kenneth Cmiel richly illustrates the political and cultural complexity of "eloquence" in the generation succeeding the revolution. Eloquence, be it high oratorical flourish or, increasingly, the plain style recommended by the increasingly influential texts of Scottish Common Sense philosophy, was previously attributed only to elite, educated gentlemen who through their reason and right feeling would obstensibly rule a republic benevolently (39–40). Harper's rhetorical pedagogy contributed to the de-centering of eloquence, transforming an exclusive mark of political power into a skill that could be taught and learned by any participant in popular democracy.[6]

Harper's reflections on the force of public opinion always cast African Americans as both subject and object of publicity, by turns agents of its political possibilities and made abject in its oppressive grasp. Though only implied, Harper offers readers a structure of rebuke to "learn" and to "teach," a corrective for those enthralled with profit and status. Such corrupt human sensibilities were for Harper the subjective site at which rhetorical pedagogy must do its work. In Harper's rendering, abolition in the Western Hemisphere is the test case of republican morality and the great measure of morally efficacious speech. Her reform argument owed as much to the revolutionary legacy of civic republicanism as to evangelical Protestantism. Harper found in a Protestant god a democratic ideal because the belief in spiritual free will mirrored the freedom of social agency inherent in Harper's ideological construction of the public sphere. The pervasive immediatist ethic of Harper and other moral suasionists projected the millennial script of individual and societal transformation onto the secular drama of public debate. "Free speech" had long been at the core of republican rhetorical culture, serving as the constitutive agency of the United States exceptionalist narrative; for reformers, it became the mechanism through which government might plausibly be dictated "by the people."

The didactic analogy of the pulpit and the press, of conversion and persuasion, grounded the reform argument in much of Harper's writing. "Our Greatest Want" illustrates the co-functionality of Harper's Protestant faith and republican national creed, as does her *National Anti-Slavery Standard* article of 1857. In this figurative soul searching, moral character is represented not as a static entity but as a site of moral interpretation, a politicized literacy of heart and soul:

> Could we trace the record of every human heart, the aspirations of every immortal soul, we would find no man so imbruted and degraded that we could not trace the word liberty either written in living characters

upon the soul or hidden away in some nook or corner of the heart. The law of liberty is the law of God, and is antecedent to all human legislation. It existed in the mind of [the] Deity when He hung the first world upon its orbit and gave it liberty to gather light from the central sun. (*BCD* 100)

The claim that for every person "the word liberty" was "written in living characters upon the soul or hidden away in some nook or corner of the heart" suggests how, within a Protestant dispensation, language could become something vital, literally, a word alive. As well, the representation of the "heart" or "soul" as a receptor of language and an agent of literacy is a recurring symbol of moral character in Harper's reform argument. Her abolitionist writing participates in a discursive drama played out in the "heart" as well as at the national level of public discourse. The scenes of political insight and spiritual transformation are represented as coincident in a hermeneutical moment, the scene of reading and writing; to be sure, such representation took on self-referential importance in the burgeoning abolitionist press. Thus, the press and the pulpit, all media, were viewed as the conduits of persuasion, the channels connecting individual agency to a common historical destiny.[7]

According to Harper, the national character was only as healthy as that of its "public opinion," and public opinion was the moral pulse of character writ large. Radical abolitionist and famed orator Wendell Phillips was another among the republican-minded abolitionists who argued that democratic sovereignty was a broad discursive project mediated by print.[8] "Public Opinion," Phillips's 1852 speech before the Massachusetts Anti-Slavery Society, exemplifies how reformers used the theoretical conjoining of republican and abolitionist rhetoric to harness the power of public opinion. Phillips locates democratic intelligence in the institutions of public discourse, institutions clearly separated from governmental institutions:

The accumulated intellect of the masses is greater than the heaviest brain God ever gave to a single man . . . A newspaper paragraph, a county meeting, a gathering for conversation, a change in the character of a dozen individuals—these are the several fountains of public opinion . . . The penny papers of New York do more to govern this country than the White House at Washington. Mr. Webster says we live under a government of laws . . . He never was so mistaken . . . We live under a government of men—and morning newspapers. (44)

Stronger than the governmental power of "the White House at Washington," the power of public language affects a "change" in the "character" of citizens who are placed in rhetorical relation to one another. This is the social collective, which in Harper's estimation generates its own moral power through public discourse. Phillips's hyperbole also suggests the teleological confluence of Christian and republican ideals: "I hail the almighty power of the tongue. I swear allegiance to the omnipotence of the press. The people never err. '*Vox populi, vox Dei*,'—the voice of the people is the voice of God" (45). Phillips's ethical charge is a striking example of the manner in which immediatists made abolitionist speech the measure of moral character. "Now the duty of each antislavery man is simply this," Phillips claims: "Stand on the pedestal of your own individual independence, summon these institutions about you, and judge them." Freedom of speech, then, is an abolitionist resource and the mark of citizenship, the republican essence of the nation. As Phillips has it, "Republics exist only on the tenure of being constantly agitated" (36–49). This fairly well states the abiding precept of republican rhetorical pedagogy. Phillips stressed repeatedly the primacy of an invigorated moral character in the antislavery project, voicing his distrust for the Constitutional allowance of enslavement and churches that took accommodationist stances on the slavery question. The "press, the pulpit, the wealth, the literature, the prejudices, the political arrangements, the present self-interest of the country . . . [the] elements that control public opinion and mould the masses are against us" (106).

As a rhetorical action, moral suasion joined the moral perfectionism of evangelicalism with natural-rights precepts—the universally inherent rights of the individual. Liberty, in the immediatist jeremiad, is the socio-rhetorical ground on which the individual struggles with earthly desires, always construed in immediatist polemic as anti-democratic impulses. This immediatist conception of character as the site of social change and national integrity relies on a crucial ambiguity, highlighted by Phillips's assertion that "republics" must be "constantly agitated"; character as a lived ethic is as much an act of national disruption as cohesion. By figuring the state as a dissembling force, a text to be reinterpreted and exposed in its hypocrisy, Harper incorporated this seeming contradiction into her pedagogy, promoting a non-state literacy in service of remaking the state. In the public imaginary, definitions of citizenship and national identity became inextricably linked with the acts of language, imbuing the communicative ethic with nationalist identification. Even as their discursive politics challenged the boundaries of the nineteenth-century ideal of a "marketplace of ideas," abolitionist and feminist reformers bolstered the moral authority of their arguments by appealing to the revolutionary code of civics that held public-sphere debate to be the generative site of an organic, if fractious, democracy *of the people*.

Harper's black-nationalist ethic, then, was itself a theory of rhetorical pedagogy in which citizens met one another as subjects of persuadability, agents of mutual influence, at fateful, coalitional crossroads. Democratic social relations, unlike a Calvinist conception of grace, could be brought about through persuasion, through an address to a social collective called to order as a national people as well as the people of a Christian God. Given the number of journals and organizations that sponsored abolitionist lecture

Figure 1.1 Radical abolitionist and renowned orator Wendell Philips. Picture Collection. The New York Public Library, Astor Lenox and Tilden Foundations.

series under church auspices, it is easy to see how nineteenth-century reformers could conceive of journalism as a kind of editorial sermon. Harper's theological claim for the freedom of the individual will, and, more specifically, the will to "speak," imbues her theory of republican character with the cultural authority needed to permeate the realm of civic discourse.

The degree to which Harper's own rhetorical theory resonated with Wendell Phillips's non-state philosophy is evident in an 1859 piece published in the *National Anti-Slavery Standard*. Appearing as "Miss Watkins and the Constitution," the letter is in part a response to Phillips's interrogation of James Madison's papers titled "The Constitution, A Pro-Slavery Document" (*BCD* 47). Therein, Phillips argues that "with deliberate purpose, our fathers bartered honesty for gain, and became partners with tyrants, that they might profit from their tyranny" (qtd. in Stewart 123). Endorsing Phillips's estimation of the foundational violence of institutional democracy in the United States, Harper's disunionist salvo begins with an exclamation of her own sense of discovery in reading:

> I never saw so clearly the nature and intent of the Constitution before. Oh, was it not strangely inconsistent that men fresh, so fresh, from the baptism of Revolution should make such concessions to the foul spirit of Despotism! That, when fresh from gaining their own liberty, they could permit the African slave trade—could let their national flag hang a sign of death on Guinea's coast and Congo's shore! Twenty-one years the slave-ships of the new Republic could gorge the sea monsters with their prey; twenty-one years of mourning and desolation for the children of the tropics, to gratify the avarice and cupidity of men styling themselves free! And then the dark intent of the fugitive clause veiled under words so specious that a stranger unacquainted with our nefarious government would not know that such a thing was meant by it. (*BCD* 47–48)

Here is Harper in the familiar rhetorical stance of *reading with* her audience, and in this instance, the Constitution is represented as the object of conflicting interpretations. The Constitution, like the Fugitive Slave Law of 1850, exhibits an obfuscatory quality and is a textual manifestation of the character of the falsely "styling" patriots of the Republic. Harper highlights the instability of the national symbol—signifying liberty for the patriot-hypocrite and death or enslavement for "the children of the tropics." This archetypal gesture of abolitionist protest—shaming the crimes of a racially oppressive state—is presented as an active political literacy, a way of reading history and political pretension. African Americans, as legislative or juridical figures and as enslaved workers, are instrumentalized in this representation of a national will embodied in the form of the glutinous "sea monsters" escorting the ships of the Middle Passage. Only careful reading on the part of citizens, the practice Harper models in her own writing, exposes the logic of the racial state, the imperialism of "the new Republic" and its root in an avaricious desire for profit.

Near the outbreak of the Civil War, Harper's republican faith in rhetorical solutions to political problems was tested; we can judge as much from her response to the raid on the national armory at Harper's Ferry led by radical abolitionist John Brown. If Harper urged her reform audience to adopt a Mosaic character of sacrifice, this did not preclude more dramatic forms of giving. Writing to John Brown on November 25, 1859, while he awaited execution, Harper offered her sincerest thanks to the soon-to-be-martyred radical. In the letter, Harper estimates the achievement of the failed insurrection in typological terms, as an event of unquestionable signifying power. She assures Brown that "from [Brown's] prison has come a shout of triumph against the giant sin of our country." While many abolitionists compared Brown to John the Baptist, the typological lineage Harper constructs assigns Brown even greater prominence as his impending death is compared to that of the biblical Christ. "The Cross," Harper writes, "becomes a glorious ensign when Calvary's page-browed sufferer yields up his life upon it." Assuring Brown that he had "rocked the bloody Bastille," she qualifies her praise tellingly:

> I would prefer to see Slavery go down peaceably by men breaking off their sins by righteousness and their iniquities by showing justice and mercy to the poor; but we cannot tell what the future brings forth. God writes national judgments upon national sins; and what may be slumbering in the storehouse of divine justice we do not know. (*BCD* 49)

Harper's faith in a peaceful revolution of character wavers interestingly here. Alluding to the uncertain "future," she posits a possible scenario beyond her own non-state ethic, and if we follow the logic of the pun, we can understand Harper's acknowledgment that it could well fall on military agency to mete out God's "national judgment." Brown had attempted to access the national arms at Harper's Ferry, and Harper positions the untapped potential of the armory, a synecdoche for federal military power, as the means of millennial retribution waiting in a heavenly "storehouse of divine justice." Thus as the possibility of war loomed ever larger, Harper, the pacifist, at least metaphorically, seemed willing to consider war as a possible means of social reformation. Even the revolution of moral character—in other words, "men breaking off their sins by righteousness" en masse—might be cut short as providential history unfolds. The great irony, of course, is that it is in praise of insurrection that Harper is able to imagine right moral action on behalf of the government. Harper contemporary Sarah H. Douglass also represented the "hero of Harper's Ferry" as a figure at the borders of typological intelligibility, arguing that the United States "is too fat with the lost sweat and warm blood of slaves driven to toil and death; our civilization yet too selfish and barbarous; our statesmen are yet too narrow, base and mobocratic; our press is yet too venal and truckling . . . to understand and appreciate the great character" of John Brown (387). In the immediatist vision of a reformed nation, Brown's rebellion could be appropriately interpreted as a sign mediating between civic morality and divine will.

In these years before the war, Harper's claims for the power of protest and the ultimate weakness of a state built on anti-republican structures of domination would approach the idealism of Phillips's non-state ethic. Harper crafted a republican allegory of the abolitionist moment within Jacksonian culture in "The Triumph of Freedom—A Dream" (1860). Published in the *Anglo African Magazine* at the apex of antislavery sentiment, the short fiction serves as a brief history of abolitionist rhetoric, a figuration of its providential import and its place in the progress of the republic. The fiction begins as an idyll in which a languorous narrator is enjoying a spring day, but suddenly, the narrator's perspective shifts to that of the typological reader. She looks into the sky, which is "eloquent with the praise of God." The communicative quality of a sanctified universe is further invoked when we are told that the earth the narrator beholds is "poetic with His ideas." She is then "roused to a sudden con[s]ciousness" by a shrieking spirit who takes her on a Dickensian tour of a strange kingdom, one we clearly identify as the United States on the brink of sectional strife. The goddess of the kingdom, slavery itself, wears white robes stained with "great spots of blood." These stains represent violence perpetrated on the enslaved who are hidden beneath the throne of the goddess. The goddess' priests search "their sacred texts," for "it was one of their rites to search them for texts and passages to spread over the stains on her garment." Worshipping, they entreat the embodiment of the slave system, "Thou art the handmaid of Christianity; thy mission is heaven-appointed and divine" (*BCD* 115). Such polemical fantasy restates the more explicit critique of church complicity and rhetorical failure.

Against this backdrop of a corrupt church, the narrator of Harper's "The Triumph of Freedom—A Dream," her patience for the figural distance of parable running thin it seems, introduces a "blood-stained ruffian, named the General Government." The narrator calls this government the "ruffian accomplice" of the goddess of slavery. Amid this pervasive conspiracy, a young man stands resolute, uttering the words, "It is false," to the citizens of the "kingdom." The power of:

> that one word, so sublime in its brevity, sent a thrill of indignant fear through the hearts of the crowd. It lashed them into tumultuous fury. Some of them dashed madly after the intruder, and hissed in his ears— "Fanatic, madman, traitor, and infidel." But the effort they made to silence him only gained him a better hearing . . . [A] number of adherents gathered around the young man, and asked to know his meaning, "Come with me," said he, "and I will show you." (115)

Lest there be any confusion about the nature of the "sublime" word of the heretic, Harper asserts that it has "awakened the spirit of Agitation, that would not slumber." However, even as the young man's words shake the foundation of the goddess' "blood-cemented throne," slavery rallies behind the support of her ruffian accomplice. "Hide me," the goddess pleads, "beneath your constitution and laws." Then, when those inspired to "noble deeds" by the spirit of agitation threaten the authority of the goddess, the "bristling . . . bayonets" of the government intercede (117). If we consider the systematic degradation of the rhetorical culture of the era—gag laws preventing antislavery petitions to Congress, laws banning slave literacy, Southern restrictions on mail hampering the circulation of

abolitionist literature, and the relentless vilification of abolitionist agitation—we can read Harper's parabolic gloss of the slaveholder's accusa-
tions—"Fanatic, madman, traitor, and infidel"—as pedagogical. If hearts
and minds in the racial state needed reform, so, for Harper, did its available pathways of communication.

PEDAGOGICAL CHARACTER AND AFRICAN AMERICAN CHRISTIAN RHETORIC

While it may seem idiosyncratic to make the primary terms of moral character the terms of language itself, Harper's tactics are quintessentially Protestant: the burden of textual interpretation weighed heavily on the subject
of mid-century Protestant morality. In particular, church-based abolitionist
polemic charged its auditors with a hermeneutical ethics of immediatism, in
which the self was the primary figure to be interpreted within the teleological context of emancipation. In this Protestant rhetoric, abolition became
the necessary proof of faith and the world historical future of God's grace.
All of Harper's work takes as axiomatic the notion that the individual is
always in a state of becoming, with the way one speaks, reads, and writes
understood as the primary means of that process of self-formation. If the
individual "heart" bears a "record," it is one that can be both read and
revised. In Harper's abolitionist theory, ethical judgments of the quality
of moral character are always tribunals appraising the powers that have
influenced character, that have imprinted changes on the record of the individual and the national heart. These moments of interpretation are represented as moments of character definition for individuals and for a social
collective that shifted with the dictates of her rhetorical situation.[9]

A good deal of critical attention has been paid to the prophetic strain in
African American political thought and the jeremiad as a rhetorical form
for protest. From the pre-national period on, biblical *topoi* of a sanctified
mission or "errand" provided a hegemonic logic of national exceptionalism
throughout the historical process of nation building. In his influential study
The American Jeremiad, Sacvan Bercovitch identifies the errand rhetoric as
foundational for a unique American ideology incorporating and organizing
social consent. It is thus, for Bercovitch, the great contradiction and lesson
of American hegemony that what began as revolution against the state mor-
phed into a nationalist process of purification serving only to "reinforce the
values that they supposedly speak against" (Glaude 50). Bercovitch's history of the jeremiad, however, as Eddie S. Glaude Jr. argues, ignores racial
meaning as a necessary ground for jeremiad rhetoric and with this omis-
sion misunderstands the structure of nationalism in the United States, the
constitutive exclusions of African and Native Americans in a white republic (52–53). Bercovitch's conception of an overmastering national ideology
is itself a means of eliding protest, one that cannot account for African

American protest, in particular, the "nation language" derived from the Exodus story (49–52). Glaude's analysis of African American cultural politics, by contrast, acknowledges the role of rhetorical action in ideology theory. As he notes, the prophetic rhetoric enabled by Exodus topoi was constitutive for "a national community of persons with the certain moral and civic obligations (to that community)" which took on importance in "efforts to respond to particular problems" (54). The jeremiad form, as typified for Glaude by David Walker's 1829 *Appeal to Coloured Citizens of the World*, challenged "white Americans to humble themselves before God and to live up to the nation's promise" (43). African American prophetic rhetoric inverts white Protestant jeremiads, according to Glaude, "demanding that Pharaoh (white Americans) let God's people go" (62). Throughout, this book underscores Harper's production of non-state principles for reform, and without question, Harper employed a prophetic, Protestant rhetoric, one deployed according to various configurations of audience and occasion.[10] In 1859, Harper repeatedly charged her *Anglo African Magazine* audience with a race-national mission, measuring collective character by the progress attained along that path.

For Harper, as for so many other rhetoricians of her era, the divided, dynamic moral personhood of Protestant theology, that radically contingent will to self-possession, provided an important source for crafting rhetorical pedagogy, specifically, for conceiving of the subject of persuasion. Harper was markedly ecumenical in her own theological thought. The social power of conversion for immediatists was in the renunciation of a secular self imbued with the qualities of self-abasement imposed by the Jacksonian racial state. The challenge was to reinterpret this secular ethics as a barrier to the development of an ethical moral character. Michel Foucault's "archaeology" of the Christian "episteme" provides an important framework for conceptualizing how such subjectivity has historically been produced. Foucault argues that Christian techniques of the self are constituted by "two ensembles of obligation . . . those regarding the faith, the book, the dogma, and those regarding the self, the soul, and the heart [which] are linked together." The secular self is then, for Foucault, "too much real" and needs to be resisted and rejected to fulfill the potential of the Christian self. The double sense of obligation of Christian moral character necessitates "the task of clearing up all the illusions, temptations, and seductions that can occur in the mind, and of discovering the reality of what is going on within ourselves" (242). Foucault argues that the more the good Christian subject discovers the truth of the self, the more he or she must renounce that self (178–179).

The vigilant self-discipline Foucault attributes to Christian practices of selfhood characterizes very well the ethos of Christian reform work, specifically its emphasis on biblical exegesis and, more broadly, the importance of textual instruction. The "spiral of truth obligation" culminates for Foucault in ritual acts and articulations of such self-renunciation, public displays of the killing off of the old self and the performance of self-alignment with Christian dogma (249). This manner of "self govern-ment" established in relation to institutional power or a pastorate marks a great shift for Foucault from Hellenistic practices, which were far more autonomous.[11] Foucault does acknowledge that as the Christian episteme progressed beyond the Middle Ages, various religious groups resisted the centralizing power of the pastorate and its institutionalized dogma. "According to these groups," Foucault writes, "the individual should take care of his own salvation independently of the ecclesiastical institution" (278). The avariciously desiring, accumulative self is the self, as Foucault has it, that the professing Christian must reject, and to be sure, Harper's reform argument always demanded such principled self-denial. The inner conflict generated by the self-sacrificing practice of subjectivity is central to Harper's pedagogy and activist practice. As the teaching heroine would claim in the penultimate lines of "The Two Offers," her first known fic-tion, "[T]rue happiness consists not so much in the fruition of our wishes as in the regulation of desires and the full development and right culture of our whole natures" (313).

The history of antinomian theological rhetoric in the United States con-stitutes a clear instance of the resistant practices of the self that Foucault notes. The antinomian crises of the mid-seventeenth century, which pitted the proponents of "free grace," or direct commune with God, against the legalism of the New England Puritan patriarchy, marks the beginning of the pedagogical rhetoric in which Harper would later participate. Despite the intervening century, Harper's biblical radicalism shares much with that of Anne Hutchinson, who rejected the Calvinism of John Winthrop, James Sheppard, and other church authorities and was banished from the Massachusetts Bay Colony as a heretic. She and her followers rebelled against the rituals of sanctification, the "evidence" deemed necessary to prove individual salvation. Ultimately, the antinomian practice of "asking 'public questions' of the clergy who preached doctrines" was an offense that the pastorate would not tolerate—especially from a woman (Hall 1–10). This antinomian argument that public speech signifies the "evi-dence" of personal sanctification provided abolitionists with powerful arguments for perfectionism. As a pedagogy of character, this ethics of moral perfection finds its most politically radical expression in the praxis of immediatist abolitionism: it was an act of ethical self-regulation to declare one's separation from the corrupt institutions of the Jacksonian racial state, the realm of avarice and compromise. Like Hutchinsonian radicals, immediatists carried out a hermeneutical revolution, taking con-trol, for their own purposes, of divine interpretation. Branded as danger-ous anarchism by church authorities in the Massachusetts Bay Colony, the antinomian belief in a direct relationship with God was still tinged with heresy, even by the mid-nineteenth century. Abolitionist rhetors took up the cause of iconoclasm zealously, thus circumventing a government that placed institutional doctrine in the path of individual freedom. Reading through any abolitionist anthology, it becomes clear that in the abolitionist imagination, Emancipation was as much a matter of converting Northern church folk as Southern planters.

To be sure, Harper's own complicated relationship to theological and civic doctrine places her within an antinomian lineage with the likes of Hutchinson, as well as Phyllis Wheatley and Maria Stewart. "Miss Watkins and the Constitution" ends, as does much of her withering critique of the state, with an optimistic turn, asserting her ultimate faith in the prevailing of a divine will over the uncertain will of "responsible moral character." The "philosophy" of characterological "crimes" is inscribed in Harper's reading of the foundational texts of the nation:

> Is it a great mystery to you why these things are permitted? Wait, my brother, awhile; the end is not yet. The Psalmist was rather puzzled when he saw the wicked in power and spreading like a Bay tree; but how soon their end! Rest assured that, as nations and individuals, God will do right by us, and we should not ask of either God or man to do less than that. In the freedom of man's will I read the philosophy of his crimes, and the impossibility of his actions having a responsible moral character without it; and hence the continuance of slavery does not strike me as being so very mysterious. (*BCD* 48)

Harper's teleological confidence, despite society's moral failings, in an "end" to enslavement highlights unfortunate lessons about humanity even as it inspires faith. The inevitability of corrupt character is as consistent from King David to the brink of the Civil War in the United States as the challenge of moral interpretation itself. For any reader of the *National Anti-Slavery Standard*, the David of the Psalms is an important figure of self-identification. How does the reader interpret the world? How will God's book represent the reality of the secular realm? How can song instruct? This moment of uncertainty or pause before writing—the Psalmist's dilemma—is the discursive moment of crisis and possibility to which Harper's pedagogy attends. Harper's abolitionist hermeneutics—the act of reading ethical selves—registers the element of Protestant doctrine which understood "free will" to be a prerequisite of moral character. The avaricious will is a discernible "philosophy," that of the slaveholder's "crimes" as well as those of the complicit politician or "founding fathers." However, the complexity of such philosophies pales in comparison to the greater mystery of God's unfolding plan, the master text that lends the authority of an infallible interpretation. Such moments of insightful self-interpretation are represented as moments of conversion, when discursive agency liberates providential, which is to say, abolitionist character.

Frances Smith Foster refers to Harper's principled "subordination of literature to serve militant religion she called Christianity," which aptly describes Harper's theological commitment as a matter of teaching the importance of public language (55). This antinomian tradition in Christian theology provided Harper with a holistic frame for her rhetorical pedagogy of character formation. Harper drew broad strokes for the rhetorical theory she identified as intrinsic to Christian faith, careful Bible reading, and the vigilant maintenance of character. Harper culminated her investigation of the rhetorical attributes of Christian doctrine as a historical force with her address titled "Christianity." Harper represents the social force of Christianity as the scene of reading and writing writ large in a world-historical context. "Christianity," Harper asserts,

> has changed the moral aspect of nations . . . Amid ancient lore the Word of God stands unique and pre-eminent. Wonderful in its construction, admirable in its adaption, it contains truths that a child may comprehend, and mysteries into which angels desire to look. It is in harmony with that adaption of means to ends, which pervades creation . . . It forms the brightest link of that glorious chain which unites the humblest work of creation with the throne of the infinite and eternal Jehovah. (34–36)

Insofar as "[t]he Word of God . . . pervades creation," the world is imagined as textual in this passage. As a text, Christianity is the "brightest link" of human achievement within the great chain of being, and through its influence individuals might gain an inspired holistic perspective. In coming to such an understanding, the individual becomes an agent of spirit, to be sure, but more specifically, an agent of the world-historical persuasiveness of spirit:

> Christianity . . . is a system so uniform, exalted and pure, that the loftiest intellects have acknowledged its influence, and acquiesced in the justness of its claims. Genius has bent from his erratic course to gather fire from her altars, and pathos and agony of Gethsemane and the sufferings of Calvary. (33)

Christianity, in Harper's rendering, wields "pathos" as well as the "uniform" systematicity of logos; it works, in short, through the force of rhetoric, the craft of integrating emotion and reason. Mere "[g]enius" proves "erratic" in comparison to the rhetorical power of the Christian mythos. Certainly this balance of rhetorical modes bears out Carla Peterson's claims about the rhetorical practice of Unitarian moral argument. Though religion must "touch the heart," character must be molded by reason. "Unitarians looked to the spoken word in its many forms . . . as an important instrument for evoking those emotions that would elevate moral conscience and bring about social transformation" (*Doers* 124–125).

Echoing the Unitarian view on the spiritual potential held by the written word, for Harper, "Philosophy and science . . . Poetry . . . Music," indeed, "Learning" itself, generally offer roads to truth only insofar as they are divinely inspired intellectual endeavors. Harper clearly comments on her own increasingly popular poetry when she claims that poetry "has culled her fairest flowers and wreathed her softest, to bind the Author's bleeding browe" ("Christianity" 35). Harper claims the perfection of God's "Word" as a transcendental ethical code, to be sure, but she also acknowledges the free will of individual character. The "glorious chain" has a weak link, as it were, that being the self. But this chain, constituted by human character, is maintained through the discipline of reading. As "Christianity" progresses, Harper takes the micrological view within this historical drama and explains how this hermeneutical ethic has subject-forming power in daily life, shaping perspective and even perception:

> As light, with its infinite particles and curiously blended colors, is suited to an eye prepared for the alterations of day; as air, with its subtle and invisible essence, is fitted for the delicate organs of respiration; and, in a word, as this material world is adapted to man's physical nature; so the word of eternal truth is adapted to his moral nature and mental constitution . . . [A]ided by the Holy Spirit, it guides us through life, points out the shoals, the quicksands and hidden rocks which endanger our path. (36–37)

The Spirit-guided word, then, can touch anyone wherever he or she lives, or really, *however* they live, with its elemental force. In the life of the individual, this force means the power of conversion and redemption. Harper's desire for a joining of individual "moral nature and mental constitution" in a faculty that could be exercised as naturally as breathing, assumes that spirit and word might bring us as close as possible to a "natural" morality. Through this practice the subject of conversion can find self-identification in the "company of angels" and thus "renew his nature" (35). Once affected properly by the spirit-guided word, a convert, her character transformed, might perceive the world as was intended, that is, as God's book, a divine reason articulated in the structure of nature and perception.

Though often speaking and publishing journalistic pieces under the auspices of African Methodist Episcopal, Congregationalist, and Baptist communities, Harper would become a Unitarian and was thus a member of a small minority of African Americans within an overwhelmingly white congregation.[12] There is no explicit record of her comment on her own affiliation, its history, or her rationale for choosing Unitarianism. Raised in the African Methodist Episcopal Church in Maryland, Harper would later join the First Unitarian Church when she moved to Philadelphia with her daughter Mary in 1870 (Groshmeyer par. 9). Jane E. Rosencrans suggests the influence of abolitionist Peter H. Clark, whom Harper met when teaching at Union Seminary in Ohio and who would later join a Unitarian Congregation in Cincinnati. She also argues plausibly that Harper was drawn to Rev. William Henry Furness's First Unitarian ministry in Philadelphia and the "eloquence and passion" of his "antislavery preaching" (Rosencrans 3–4, 8–9). Beyond the individual rhetorical skill of Furness, we should note again the consistency of Harper's rhetorical pedagogy with Unitarian theology. As mentioned earlier, Peterson notes, though Unitarians were sufficiently affected by the Second Great Awakening as the demonstration of the social power of emotion, they held strictly to the precepts of moral sensibility as a balance of head and heart. As Peterson argues, "Rather than encourage the free flow of emotions, Unitarians argued that individual 'character' must be attended to in order to create moral beings whose duty it would be to work for social cohesion in a disordered world" (Peterson, *Doers* 125). For abolitionist Unitarians like Harper, Furness, and Lydia Maria Child, the moral sense constituted a higher faculty, a synthesis of right feeling and rationality. Child's own best-known works evince the rational tone of this moral sense, as in the immediatist jeremiad that cemented her reputation in 1833; *An Appeal in Favor of that Class of Americans Called Africans* and its ethos of trained sentiment provided a rhetorical tonic to the evangelical pathos of William Lloyd Garrison. Her "Unitarian-style preaching" proceeds in a "calm, rational tone," and "her method of allowing facts to speak for themselves" assumes a Christian *logos* according to which her audience would read (Karcher 193).

Although Harper clearly intended to inspire readers' ethical identification with the likes of Christ, Moses, and John the Baptist, it is too simple to say that she led people to find themselves in the Bible. It is more accurate, perhaps, to say that her reform argument persuaded readers to find the Bible in their own lives, to discern "an earth poetic with His ideas" (*BCD* 115). Reading well, which is to say living well, is to find one's own rightful place in these scripts. In his account of a radical reformist strain in African American culture in which Harper was a central figure, John Ernest argues that this tradition, strongly rooted in biblical hermeneutics, "looked for the authority of a transcendent author to support their own narratives of progress, hope, responsibility and community." By linking "sacred" and "secular" narratives, rhetors like Harper, Frederick Douglass, Martin Delany, Harriet Jacobs, and others "try to rescript their worlds by referring to a more significant stage of events" (7). For Harper, claims of progress, elevation, retrogression, and descent were not simply claims of ethical distinction, but also the generative site of a new, socially redemptive language of morality. Character served a diagnostic function in Harper's reform rhetoric, revealing how the relationships between prevailing sources of moral authority shape the reader or auditor's place within that confluence.[13]

LITERARY EXPERIMENTS: AFRICAN AMERICAN
WOMEN'S CHARACTER TALK

Harper designed her fictions to unfold as dramas of rhetorical interaction, narrative lectures intended to equip readers with means of judgment and persuasion. They modeled the heuristics of discursive action, including but not limited to spoken and written acts. As argued in detail in subsequent chapters, Harper's fiction as a whole is a text of working rhetorical theory, *a rhetoric* in the ancient pedagogical sense, which maps a set of discursive possibilities for persuasive action. She provided more than advice for living life as a practice of uplift and race pride. The didacticism of Harper's fiction has drawn what John Ernst calls "critical friendly fire" (181–182). Houston Baker, for one, disparages Harper's prose as "creakingly mechanical and entirely predictable" and bemoans the quality of her fiction in which, as Baker quips, "[c]haracters do not act, they talk—endlessly" (33). We could spend considerable time interrogating the implications of such aesthetic judgments, but even in Baker's own terms, Harper's literary characters are far from simple mouthpieces for static positions. Even if we decide to bar her work from a realist canon, or from Baker's lineage of authentic vernacular artists, we should consider the complex rhetorical functions of her heroines, heroes, villains, and dupes. The conceits of literary character allowed Harper to establish, as a point of readerly identification, a heuristic figure of civic morality positioned at the disjunction between public and private spheres. Inasmuch as this dichotomy represents the divergent codes of gendered social spheres, as well, a women's rights idiom emerged in her early fiction that would remain quite consistent for the duration of Harper's career, as would the pedagogical structure of all her subsequent fictions.

The extent to which nineteenth-century literary publics doubled as the scenes of women's political activity is a matter of substantial scholarly record.[14] By the time Harper began writing and publishing fiction, the canon of sentimental literature advocating for women's rights offered a wide variety of narrative devices for the construction of literary character as a point of ethical identification. Harper's conversance with the politics of this genre is evident enough in her poems, including "Eliza Harris," which extends a heroic-mothering plotline from Harriet Beecher Stowe's *Uncle Tom's Cabin.* Indeed, Harper appears to have approached the genre as a collectively composed rhetoric, with plot lines and character sketches offering so many *topoi* from which to choose. Thinking of sentimental literature in this way allows us to conceive of the literary tradition upheld in Harper's work composing what she would call the "ideal beings" of her fiction. The core feminist precepts of Harper's fictitious dramas of persuasion were established in the multiple editions of her first book, *Poems on Miscellaneous Subjects.* The heroines of these poems, who suffer at the hands of men and male institutional authority, suffer very specifically as subjects of state-sanctioned acts of domination, violence, or neglect. Poems, including "The Slave Mother," "The Slave Auction," and "Eliza Harris," confronted readers with the experience of slave women and girls subject to the most abject crimes under the economics of slavery, the *sine qua non* of white sexual mastery. "The Slave Auction" begins with pointed abruptness, "The sale began—young girls were there, / Defenceless in their wretchedness" (*Miscellaneous* 14). The ethical disposition of the slave women for whom Harper advocated would remain the guiding political touch point of her pedagogy into the twentieth century.[15]

Baker's jibes at the conversational quality of Harper's fictions are accurate enough as a comment about narrative structure, even if the accompanying value judgments cut short rhetorical analysis. Her abiding interest as a narrative artist remained focused for the entirety of her career on talk, and more specifically, on conversational interaction and exchange. Written in the context of the *Anglo African Magazine*'s elite exchange of ideas, Harper's juxtaposition of political and literary scripts clearly served a teaching function. By injecting narrative forms into social theory, Harper self-consciously addressed, as an exigency, the ideological forum of the *Anglo African Magazine* itself. The precepts of womanhood Harper delivers in these early fictions function pedagogically in both collective and individual registers, theorizing proper rhetorical action for the promotion of black-nationalist community and presenting commonplace *topoi* for use on the everyday gender lines within that community. Harper stages an anatomy of the gender dynamics of reform discourse in "Chit Chat, or Fancy Sketches," published under the name Jane Rustic in the November 1859 issue of the *Anglo African Magazine*.[16] Therein, we see for the first time the pedagogical character talk that would subsequently come to dominate her fiction. As the sketch opens, a group of guests gathers at a wedding before the ceremony begins and discusses the "condition of our people." In the context of the *Anglo African Magazine*, a forum for black-nationalist thought, the dialogue takes on a self-referential quality, giving voice to different positions on emigration, slave rebellion, and economic ambition, disseminating a vision of a collective future born from debate among the magazine's contributors and readership. "My only hope is emigration," declares one wedding guest, only to draw the response of another man who, pledging loyalty to Southern slaves, would opt for "staying and fighting it out . . . if he will only throw down his sugar knife, cast away his cotton hook and strike for liberty." One of the interlocutors raises again the line of reasoning Harper rejected in "Our Greatest Want": "'Give us wealth,' said he, 'and that will give us position; white men will court our society, and gold, though yellow, will be the most potent whitewash we can find.'" Harper's narrator subtly or not so subtly disparages each proclamation of collective logic. As would become a signature of her fiction, Harper asserts the speaking position of a woman confronting racial and patriarchal abuses, introducing the notion of duty-bound speech. The problems Harper's narrator faces in instructing her people are twofold. First, as the narrator wryly comments, because she is "only a woman," her interlocutors, at least initially, "did not think it worth while" to argue with her or refute the claims she advances (341). Second, the narrator struggles with the problem of instructing people on the very presuppositions to which they are subject.

The bluster continues, and another wedding guest, the emigrationist, makes a case for leaving the United States and finally breaking with the ostensibly inevitable imitation of white society. The narrator, finding this to be a red herring of sorts, makes a finer distinction, between "imitation" and "aping." When asked to explain the distinction, the narrator is at first hesitant to speak, as the first instructive example occurring to her is the wedding party itself, with its conspicuous consumption and the ostentation of the guests' clothes and jewelry. Her observations call into question the true commitments of the wedding guests. No matter their pretensions of speaking on behalf of the people, their characterological weakness makes all their pronouncements suspect. As was so often the tendency in Harper's fiction, the domestic eye of the narrator works to juxtapose sincerity and integrity of expression with hypocrisy and self-serving social posing. "Aping, in short," she states, is "servile imitation" that "leads us to copy the vices and follies of others, because they fill what are called superior stations." As examples, and perhaps as a veiled accusation, the narrator forwards as apish behavior, "a colored man in business for instance, a barber, afraid to shave a respectable colored man, afraid to have an anti-slavery paper in his shop or to take an active part in the anti-slavery enterprise." "Aping," as qualified by the narrator, amounts to the failed racial solidarity that is always held up for rejection in Harper's work, while imitation is presented as a simple "copying or making patterns after an example," which leads the narrator to wonder in what social habits her fellow wedding guests have found their constitutive patterns ("Chit Chat" 341).[17]

The story literally casts a shadow over these interlocutors and their discourse. Despite the bright, midday sun, the shades are drawn and the room is closed off from what lies beyond its walls, evincing an odd preference for gaslight over sunlight and for the "stifled air of the drawing room" over the "balmy breath of spring" (341). Considering Harper's liberal use of sun figures for truth and knowledge, the figurality of light and shadow cues readers to the corrupt communicative site of the wedding celebration. The geography changes in "Town and Country, or Fancy Sketches," the second sketch in the Jane Rustic series, published in the *Anglo African Magazine*'s December, 1959, issue. In this sketch, an outspoken country cousin from the wedding party returns to her rural home, enervated and pale after her sojourn in the city. Harper bids her readers to consider how the social atmosphere, as much as the want of sunlight, has impacted the guests' well-being. After the doting and tender care of her Aunt Melissa and the balm of a family Bible study, the narrator sleeps only to continue the reflection on gender and black-national speech in a fictional dream state.

Dreaming that "a call had been issued for an anti-sunshine convention," the narrator recasts the outspoken men of the wedding party as convention leaders. What the narrator could not publicly pronounce within the society of the conversation and its male guests, finds the following satirical expression. A "rather pompous looking man" makes a series of resolutions that read in part:

> Resolved, That this convention form a society called the Anti-sunshine Society.
>
> Resolved, That it shall be the duty of this convention to send out lecturers, and circulate documents and tracts, to show the superiority of gaslight over sunshine.
>
> Resolved, That no woman shall hold any office in our Society, unless it be to collect funds.
>
> Resolved, That the sun is a bore, because it freckles our faces and tans our complexions. ("Town and Country" 384)

The narrator replays the rebuff of the wedding party, but this time sounding its clear implication for the future of the racial collective that the dream conventioneers claim to represent. Foreseeing the "ruined harvests, blighted crops, and faded flowers" that would be ushered in by the political vision of the Anti-Sunshine Society, the narrator rises in her dream to speak. In the midst of making an "excellent speech," she is shouted down. "Mr. Speaker, Mr. Speaker!" a voice commands, "The lady is out of order." She "appealed to the chair, but in the end," just as she's woken from the dream, the narrator was "forced to take [her] seat" (384). Rustic's satirical dreamscape suggests Harper's cognizance of women's liminal position in the world of African American reform. As Peterson notes, despite the crucial political contributions of African American women, they were "officially excluded from those black national institutions . . . through which men of the elite came together to promote public civic debate," a dialogue devoted to practical matters of activism and "more theoretical considerations of black nationality" (*Doers* 17). Harper's satirical conceit teaches *Anglo African* readers a lesson, questioning the invidious gender politics existing within the African American reform community.

If the narrator of the "Fancy Sketches" confronts male exclusivity as a pedagogical problem to be solved, Harper's earliest experiments in sentimental fiction explore more holistically the devastating will of male privilege in practice. "The Two Offers," published in the *Anglo African Magazine* in May of 1859, is thought to be the earliest short story published by an African American woman. In it, Harper examines the importance of women's rhetoric as a counterforce to the destructive assertion of masculine will over women's fortunes in context of familial relationships and the broader community. This temperance story is a scathing if sentimental indictment of the destructive social power of drunken men and its impact on women and children.[18]

Not surprisingly, a pedagogy of character—of disciplined thought, action, and language—emerges as the remedy for the ethical and political disorder fomented by the "curse" of uncontrolled masculine impulse. The story opens with an instructive conflation of economic and linguistic action as an indicator of character; the scene of moral and political insight is represented as a moment of linguistic indecision. Laura LaGrange begins a letter that she cannot finish as she compares two marriage offers. Her cousin, Janette Alston, offers the advice that "a woman who is undecided between two offers, has not love enough for either . . . lest her marriage, instead of being an affinity of souls or a union of hearts, should be a mere matter of bargain and sale, or an affair of convenience and selfish interests." Alston warns her cousin, in other words, against signing a contract rather than a pledge of enlightened, loving commitment. The fear of being an "old maid" dominates LaGrange's consciousness as an unspeakable possibility "that is not to be thought of." When she finally does make her coerced choice, her husband is said to be "[v]ain and superficial in his character" and to conceive of marriage "not as a divine sacrament for the soul's development and human progression, but as the title-deed that gave him possession of the woman." In the course of the story, indeed in Harper's temperance rhetoric generally, this economic thinking is complexly linked to the more obvious character flaw that drives the temperance plot, that is, male alcoholism. This temperance melodrama brings LaGrange to her deathbed lamenting her inebriate husband who is absent even in the tragic moment, pursuing his "headlong career" in the saloon ("The Two Offers" 288). In a classic sentimental manner, the couple's son and then Laura herself die, of neglect it seems, in the absence of their profligate guardian.

The two women make a comparative, inter-subjective key to virtue and vice, an example of the dyadic structure that would remain central to Harper's pedagogical practice. At the heart of LaGrange's moral failure is her lack of reason. LaGrange's and Alston's divergent practices of literacy provide a stark contrast, as do their ways of being (or not being) with men. LaGrange's indecision at the opening of the story, that literal inability to write, parallels her lack of agency within her marriage and family. LaGrange seems stung by Alston's impugning of her character and responds with a specifically feminized insult:

> Oh! What a little preacher you are. I really believe that you were cut out for an old maid; that when nature formed you she put in a double portion of intellect to make up for a deficiency of love; and yet you are kind and affectionate. But I don't think that you know anything of the grand over-mastering passions, or the deep necessity of woman's heart for loving. (289)

Alston, as it turns out, also had known intense romantic love. However, in learning to live beyond its loss, she gained insight and determination as a public intellectual. LaGrange assumes that Alston, the "preacher" making her stern warning, is de-feminized as she assumes this agonistic role. LaGrange's assertion that Alston had received a "double portion of intellect" and a "deficiency of love" casts her as something of a characterological anomaly in an attempt to expel her from a characterologically bounded feminine sphere. We find more notable, perhaps, LaGrange's assumption that "love" and "intellect" are mutually exclusive. In Harper's telos of moral suasion, love and intellect are mutually reinforcing virtues, the constant balancing of which forms the very essence of morality. The implications here are quite radical, as Harper's narrative logic suggests that marriage and the domestic sphere sequester "heart support" away from a larger social collective. Thus, as the division of social spheres entraps women, it also denies the world their political contributions. Like the narrator of the Jane Rustic sketches, Janette Alston is depicted as having paid a heavy emotional and social cost for speaking and acting according to the duty of character.

In providing a set of contrasting family histories, Harper further implicates the domestic, familial sphere as a site of political economic agency, one exercised either rightly or wrongly as a matter of character development. Alston is the child of parents "rich only in goodness." After her father's death, the family sinks deeper into poverty as "hungry creditors" pursued "their claims." After the mother's death, Alston is too "self-reliant to depend on the charity of relations" and so supported herself "by her own exertions," which would win her a place "in the literary world." LaGrange, by contrast, "was the only daughter of rich and indulgent parents, who had spared no pains to make her an accomplished lady." The drunken husband LaGrange would marry, and who would destroy the family, grew up in a home that was "not the place for the true culture and right development of his soul." His father is said to have been "too much engrossed in making money" and his mother too focused on "spending it" to "give the proper direction to the character of the wayward and impulsive son" (289). In the end, Harper figures the intersection of public and private spheres, demonstrating how even domestic affections fall victim to the corrupting force of a barbaric economy.

The characterological investigation of "The Two Offers" reveals the economic-familial systems that hold the fictional characters together. The drunkard, raised in a home in which character developed through the "administration of chance" as opposed to parental guidance, inherits his father's avariciousness and his mother's penchant for reckless consumption. He exercises these character traits in his relationship to LaGrange, whose own character has been warped by her family's economy, in which reckless spending and desire for wealth's social distinctions replaced the moral training privileged by the story's narrator. While readers are not privy to the source of LaGrange's family wealth or that of the drunkard husband's, the Alston family's economic ruin suggests the destructive agency of accumulation. LaGrange claims that Alston cannot understand the "grand over-mastering passion" that characterizes a woman in love, but in actuality, she understands it very well as an economics of character. Alston's preceptive statement—"true happiness" derives from "the regulation of desires and the full development and right culture of our whole natures"—evokes Protestant self-discipline as a guard against the destructive, accumulative economics, in which a lack of temperance wreaks havoc as a negative force repressing moral development.

This regulation of desire and characterological self-mastery evinces the qualities of self-determination required in both Protestant and civic republican moral codes, and these precepts governing Harper's familial instruction frame Alston's identity as a public intellectual. Alston's literary work, it seems, no less than Harper's, is of a political nature:

> She would willingly espouse an unpopular cause but not an unrighteous one. In her the down-trodden slave found an earnest advocate; the flying fugitive remembered her kindness as he stepped cautiously through our Republic, to gain his freedom in a monarchical land . . . Her life was like a beautiful story, only it was clothed with the dignity of reality and invested with the sublimity of truth. (313)

The abolitionist gesture in this penultimate moment of narrative omniscience is an important point of orientation for the women's rhetorical ethic of the story, merging narratives of privatization—that of the economics of the slave system and of male ownership of women as domestic workers. Alston's advocacy for "the down-trodden slave" and the indictment of "our Republic" links the political logic of this temperance polemic with the cause of antislavery. To marry intemperately is to become property and to thus embody the subjectivity of unfreedom; familiarity with Harper's oeuvre should help us discern the figure of the fugitive in this passage, fleeing in an act of heroic self-determination that contrasts tellingly with LaGrange's voluntary entry into bonds. Alston, who bears the characterological sign of self-reliance and rhetorical action, chooses not to enter the economy of marriage or participate in the political-economic common sense of the Fugitive Slave Law, a decision she is able to make through "the regulation of desires." As Peterson argues, it is Alston's voice that merges with narrative omniscience to thus "enter into history" Harper's own voice (*Doers* 172). Despite her certain reputation within the discursive circulation of the *Anglo African Magazine*, Harper introduces herself here in a bold signature of principle and intention.

The "offers" extended in the title of the story are LaGrange's matrimonial options, but are also juxtaposed options for the reader as well, as the didactic structure bids women readers to chose between two examples of femininity. Alston's assertion that one should live one's life like a "beautiful story" locates the agency of the self-reliant character within the realm of literary production. The fiction ends with Alston's contemplation of her own life and how it might unfold as a reformist pedagogy that would stand in opposition to her cousin's example. Janette Alston is the first in a long line of fictional heroines who carry the rhetorical signs of Harper's reform work. In the fictions that would appear with increasing frequency in the decades to come, we repeatedly encounter these heroines at interpretive crossroads, inventing self-definition in relation to the signs of cultural power in the nineteenth-century United States.

2 Reconstruction and Black Republican Pedagogy

It would be difficult to overemphasize the degree to which African American writers and orators represented the period following the Civil War as a moment of historically unprecedented hope. Initially heralded as the practical extension of democratic principle, and later harkened back to as a truncated experiment with democracy, Reconstruction's lost promise continues to reverberate in the political imagination of African American culture. Then-presidential candidate Barack Obama's March 18, 2008, speech serves well as a contemporary exemplar of this conflicted and ongoing legacy. In response to criticisms raised about his former pastor, the Reverend Jeremiah Wright of Trinity United Church of Christ in Chicago, Obama condemned Wright's provocative racial comments and yet affirmed a black-national historical memory traced back to the failures of Reconstruction. He acknowledged the anger and frustration of African Americans and the enduring racial hierarchies of twenty-first-century United States. Stepping into a role many African Americans might recognize, Obama served on this day as a race teacher, asking a nation to remember that

> so many of the disparities that exist between the African-American community and the larger American community today can be traced directly to inequalities passed on from an earlier generation that suffered under the brutal legacy of slavery and Jim Crow. (*New York Times*, 18 March 2008)[1]

Just as Obama straddled the line between hope and censure, African American post–Civil War commentators were watchful and qualified their praise from Emancipation through each hard-won political battle of the Radical Republican reform era. For Harper, the initial years of Reconstruction were a time of great productivity and experimentation. Despite continued misgivings about the intrinsic corruption of government, Harper, like the great majority of African American abolitionists, actively supported the so-called Radical Revolution of the 39th Congress of 1865. Led by a coalition of abolitionist Republicans and free labor advocates whose commitment to civil rights of a more utilitarian quality, this initiative would ultimately result in the passage of the Thirteenth, Fourteenth, and Fifteenth Amendments and other major civil rights legislation. Southern Democrats of the planter class derisively termed the emergent Radical agenda "Black Republicanism." From the beginning of Reconstruction, it was clear to African American abolitionists that "emancipation" was not the realization of a new age of freedom. Like her Radical colleagues Frederick Douglass and Republican majority leaders Massachusetts Senator Charles Sumner and Pennsylvania Representative Thaddeus Stevens, Harper argued that to the extent that the war had been about reforming the racial state, that project was still perilously incomplete. In her writing and oratory throughout Reconstruction, Harper returned to the preceptive *topoi* of love and care, now as the source of arguments for the necessity of African American women's leadership and judgment in a moment of profound political uncertainty.

Michael Omi and Howard Winant characterize this crisis of state as a historic shift in the "racial formation" of the United States, structural changes amounting to a dismantling of the "racial dictatorship" of the slavery era (65-66). Throughout the early years of Reconstruction, Harper worked in concert with the Congressional Republicans, but often taught as a dissenter within that general project. The political potential of race loyalty had definite limits for African American women, as did the loyalty of the white leadership of early feminist organizations. The coalition of reformers re-organizing the racial state who sought also to extend political rights and protections to women had less immediate impact, though the political networks established among women's groups in this era created the ground of future success in the process of state reformation. Carla Peterson theorizes the institution building of African American women like Harper as the creation of liminal discursive sites around which a politics of African American womanhood could be constructed (*Doers* 18-19). This chapter charts the pedagogy and instructional presentation of Harper's organizing rhetoric within this conflicted context.

Alongside Frederick Douglass, Harper was the most high-profile African American spokesperson for the Radical agenda (McPherson 398). Her explicitly Republican oratory and writing are politically ambivalent and feature carefully made criticisms of Republican pretensions to democracy, even as she advocated for suffrage rights and legal protections, and praised Lincoln's historic wisdom and the commitment of Congressional leaders. As the century progressed, the free labor promise of self-determination and dignified work did not materialize for the majority of African American laborers. From the perspective of countless African American reformers throughout the rest of the century, a moral accounting was necessary of the failure of the state to protect African American labor rights or to secure anything that could fairly be called widespread liberty.

As subsequent chapters argue, the creed of free labor could all too easily be turned on African American workers as an accusation of characterological failure, a failure to embody the republican virtues of productive citizenship. African American free labor rhetoric, therefore, must be distinguished from the dominant free labor platform of the Civil War and Reconstruction era insofar as its critical commonplaces, of which Harper was a prominent architect, held the state accountable for defending the ground of free labor self making.

This chapter considers Harper's Reconstruction writing and oratory as a response to the contradictions of the Republican platform and as a rhetorical act of affiliational politics. During the initial years of Reconstruction, Harper came to the national stage as a women's rights reformer. Of political necessity, she developed a rhetorical stance that this study, adapting the critical language of Kimberle Williams Crenshaw, calls an intersectional ethos.[2] Throughout her work in this period, Harper was constrained to reconcile what many held to be mutually exclusive political goals—civil rights both for women and for African Americans. Like many neo-immediatists, Haper understood Reconstruction as an opportunity for comprehensive social reform. As Melba Joyce Boyd has demonstrated, Harper's Reconstruction years were taken up with a Mosaic politics of nation building in her poetics and rhetoric (119–120). In her speeches on Reconstruction politics and her first pedagogical novel, *Minnie's Sacrifice*, serialized in the *Christian Recorder* in 1869, Harper mapped a course of state reform in which the judgment, leadership, and rhetorical action of African American women were essential. Taking up the rhetorical sign of Laura LaGrange in "The Two Offers," the novel's heroine Minnie models reform practice for the Afro-Protestant press audience. From *Minnie's Sacrifice* on to the end of the century, Harper would extol the world-changing force of African American women's rhetoric.

FREE LABOR RHETORIC AND THE ETHOS OF SELF-DETERMINATION

Like many African American abolitionists, Harper grappled with the fraught, often contradictory relationship between free labor and civil rights politics. Speaking in the flush of Radical hegemony in 1866 on the New York stage of the National Women's Rights Convention, Harper signaled her Radical alliance through her harsh words for President Andrew Johnson, who after succeeding the assassinated Lincoln almost immediately positioned himself in opposition to the Radicals.[3] Harper thought Radical politics important enough to take partisan shots at the President, but more crucial to understand is the characterological pedagogy of her disparagement. In one of her most expansive extant commentaries on her family life, Harper positions her own moral character in opposition to that of Johnson, and in so doing, merges the suffragist agenda with that of Radical Reconstruction. We can think of her stance as a performance of sorts, an intentionally failed attempt to claim a civic republican ethos that was not available to her as a political reality. The 1866 address is a pageant of the political concerns and rhetorical tactics that would characterize all of Harper's post-Emancipation work:

I am feeling something of a novice upon this platform. Born of a race whose inheritance has been outrage and wrong, most of my life had been spent in battling against those wrongs. But I did not feel as keenly as others, that I had these rights, in common with the other women, which are now demanded. About two years ago, I stood within the shadows of my home. A great sorrow had fallen upon my life. My husband had died suddenly, leaving me a widow with four children, one my own, and the others step-children. I tried to keep my children together. But my husband died in debt; and before he had been in his grave three months, the administrator had swept the very milk-crocks and wash tubs from my hands. I was a farmer's wife and had made butter for the Columbus market; but what could I do, when they had swept all away? They left me one thing—and that was a looking glass! Had I died instead of my husband what would have been the result? By this time he would have had another wife, it is likely; and no administrator would have gone into his house, broken up his home, and sold his bed, and taken away his means of support . . . I say then that justice is not fulfilled so long as woman is unequal before the law . . . We are all bound up together in one great bundle of humanity, and society cannot trample on the weakest and feeblest of its members without receiving the curse in its own soul. You tried that in the case of the negro . . . When the hands of the black were fettered, white men were deprived of the liberty of speech and the freedom of the press . . . At the South, the legislation of the country was in behalf of the rich slaveholders, while the poor white man was neglected. What is the consequence to-day? From that very class of neglected poor white men, comes the man who stands to-day with his hand across the helm of the nation. He fails to catch the watchword of the hour, and throws himself, the incarnation of meanness, across the pathway of the nation. My objection to Andrew Johnson is not that he has been a poor white man; my objection is that he keeps "poor whits" all the way through. That is the trouble with him. (*BCD* 217–218)

The image of Harper alone with the "looking glass" is striking. To what self-knowledge had the aftermath of her husband's death brought her? Many of the 1866 conventioneers would likely have rallied around such language, recognizing the sentimental narrative, even if they found the class critique jarring. Those familiar with the work of Harper, Harriet Jacobs, Harriet Beecher Stowe, and Lydia Maria Child, among other writers of domestic abolitionist narratives, will recognize the economics of a particular domestic rhetoric in this passage. The *topoi* of an immoral national jurisdiction of law that disrupts the home, scattering children and leaving women destitute, pervade the work of all these abolitionists.[4] In these texts, the trope of being left in the "shadows" appears again and again as husbands and other male guardians die, and black women are forced into a realization of their status as property.

Without the legal right of ownership, Harper could not prevent the liquidation of what had been her home—though not her property—and the tools of her livelihood. Tempering her "great sorrow" is her recognition that it is her husband's debt, his misfortune, to which she is the paradoxical heir. She is far from the mouthpiece of a retrograde "true womanhood" as she notes her husband's participation in a patriarchal economy in which wives are domestic workers, and as such, essentially replaceable. Indeed, it is her agency as a worker that has been censured in this self-portrait. Stripped of property and the means of economic self-determination—"the administrator had swept the very milk-crocks and wash tubs from my hands"—Harper is sent wandering, a feminine Mosaic figure and a vivid example of how the patriarchal limits of republican nationalism excluded African American women from the rights and the protections of the state. Central to this ethical disposition are the republican criteria of individual liberties as the freedom to work and profit from one's own labor, to purchase and develop one's own land, and to be free of government tyranny. Protestant and republican ideologies converge in this ethic; the spiritual and civic space of struggle—the exercise of free will and economic self-determination—is the requisite proving ground of moral character.

Harper's heuristic use of her own disenfranchisement is further elaborated as the autobiographical narrative shifts, and the disjuncture leads her to a declaration of universal belonging in "one great bundle of humanity." Though institutionalized gender or racial distinction would ostensibly be absent in this ideal collective, they are still the divisions that are most marked in this passage. All African Americans, like all women, lacked agency within a violent and divisive system "trampling on the weakest and feeblest of its members." Harper makes the transition from the ideal to the actual with an accusation of her audience's participation in this oppression: "You tried that in the case of the negro," she asserts, and while it is impossible to know exactly who is included in the second-person address, this rhetorical tactic throws into question the ethical authority of the National Women's Rights Convention itself, the very auspices under which Haper spoke. She registers the contradiction of working-class racism, identifying the "rich slaveholder" as the antagonist of both blacks and "poor whites." Both of the latter groups, like Harper herself, were marginalized within the Jacksonian compromise, what she calls "legislation on behalf" of the interests of the slavocracy. In the wake of the 1866 Civil Rights Act veto, this was a common enough charge against Johnson, and as an agent of the Congressional and neo-abolitionist efforts to change the course of state, Harper did not pass up this opportunity to publicly impugn the moral character of the president.[5] Johnson embodies the "consequence" of the neglect of "the poor white man." Somehow, Johnson's life experience, it seems, unfit him "to catch the watchword of the hour," by which Harper refers to the Radical Republican agenda.

The 1866 Women's Rights Convention carried on amid a racial controversy that would mark the shift in the allegiances of women's rights reform. The New York convention gathered after months of suffragette lobbying and recriminations of Radical Republican leaders over the crafting of the Fourteenth Amendment and the manifest abandonment of the women's rights cause by former abolitionist allies. In light of this split, we can more fully understand the challenging nature of Harper's staunch insistence on complicating the question of women's rights by framing it as an issue of Reconstruction. The pedagogical impetus that underwrites Harper's disparagement of Johnson's character is her historical model of ignorance. She understands his failure to develop morally or intellectually as the consequence of an underdeveloped culture of literacy in the South—the same "depriv[ation] of the liberty of speech and the freedom of the press," which was enforced to impede slave literacy.[6] Therefore, Johnson is "the incarnation of meanness," a subject of the vicious economic system no less than Harper herself; Johnson, however, has no looking glass and thus acts the part of his racialized class consciousness. Almost seventy years later, W. E. B. Du Bois would describe Johnson's inability to challenge the imperatives of his working-class Tennessean identity as "the transubstantiation of a poor white." Du Bois painted a satirical picture of the rube president as the mouthpiece of Southern planter lobbyists maneuvering their hegemonic recovery through political means, seduced by visiting Southern ladies and the praise of the Democratic press. Johnson is, in Du Bois's text, the Judas figure who sold out the coalition of black workers and Radical Republicans (237–322). Du Bois is nowhere more directly the descendant of nineteenth-century African American reform writers than in his penchant for lecturing on character. Johnson could not exercise a Protestant free will, victim as he himself was of economic privation, without the social ground to develop reason and other qualities of moral character.

Eric Foner places Reconstruction within a general context of the history of capitalism, describing the era as a "period of unprecedented economic expansion presided over by a triumphant industrial bourgeoisie" (*Reconstruction* 460).[7] Even as the Republican promise of free labor seemed to be in reach, legal limits on white women and all African Americans put the lie to civic republican universalism. Without land, the assurance of a fair contract, or the right to work unmolested, the "freedmen" did not find themselves in the position to work out their own destiny in ideal republican fashion with any more certainty than white or African American women. Among the ranks of the Anti-Slavery Society, Frederick Douglass used the Radical platform to caution against rising triumphalism. What was widely known as the "free labor experiment" in the postwar South, in which the freed slaves began to receive wages for their work, quickly devolved into the racial and gender oppression of emerging state capitalism. When the group met in May of 1865, William Lloyd Garrison moved to disband the Anti-Slavery Society given the ratification of the Thirteenth Amendment.

Presumably for Garrison, the Society's functional purpose had ended. This put Garrison at odds with many other members of the Anti-Slavery Society, Wendell Phillips most notably (McPhereson 303–305). Douglass dissented strongly, as he did not share Garrison's confidence. He argued that the Black Codes, state laws that eclipsed the promise of free labor for black workers, could prove "a mockery and a snare," returning the slave oligarchy to power and African Americans "to a condition similar to slavery" (Douglass 4: 82).

Harper too posed fundamental questions about both the quality of freedom achieved through emancipation alone and the duty of abolitionists after the outlawing of slavery. Her advocacy of the historical healing power of free labor would ultimately place Harper at cross purposes with her larger vision of civil rights, as the self-making agency of black labor became increasingly coerced and exploited. Through her extensive lecture schedule and wide variety of journalism, poetry, and fiction, Harper publicized the Radical agenda and its progress, imbuing Reconstruction with a Mosaic promise exceeding even her eulogizing of John Brown and his fellow martyrs. With actual legal emancipation accomplished, Harper traveled among the recently "free" and overwhelmingly disadvantaged people for the first time, becoming more invested in theorizing the connections between moral character and economic practice. Like Douglass and a number of neo-abolitionist women, she found in the language of moral character a conflicted set of rhetorical resources.

Amid Reconstruction's unprecedented crisis of state, and its attending vagaries of allegiance and commitment, Harper grounded her rhetorical pedagogy in black-nationalist precepts consistent with those of her abolitionist writing and oratory, as is evident in her epic poem *Moses: A Story of the Nile*, published in 1869. Echoing her essay, "Our Greatest Want," discussed in Chapter 1, the poem reworks the biblical story of Exodus and casts Moses as a pedagogical model for practical politics, one designed for the Reconstruction moment. In keeping with the biblical story, Harper's Moses commits to national race solidarity, a loyalty to his mother's slave lineage. As the poem opens, Moses declares his intention to Pharaoh's daughter, the princess who raised him, to renounce his Egyptian inheritance as Pharaoh's heir and turn instead to "the paths of labor" (139).

Moses responds to his surrogate mother's incredulity with a richly pedagogical explanation, one consistent with the rhetorical theory of republican motherhood. Moses recalls the force of the national-historical storytelling practiced by his Hebrew mother, whom the Pharaoh's daughter unknowingly chose to be Moses's nurse, remembering how with "kindling eye and glowing cheek, forgetful / Of the present pain, she would lead us through / the distant past." Insofar as it takes the form of a drama of persuasion, the poem is of a formal piece with the novels that would take prominence in Harper's writing, specifically in her use of characterological binaries to contrast opposing principles of social and economic morality. By comparison,

Pharoah's daughter is "eloquent," employing "words of tenderness" that "breathed / Her full heart into her lips"; this characterization or persuasive appeal is juxtaposed to that of Moses, who "was slow in speech." However, in the "calm / Grandeur of his will," Moses resists the Princess's claim to his loyalty, remembering the teachings of his mother. Her lessons of history and heritage recounted the story of Abraham, "The father of our race" who stood God's test and earned for future generations "a promise . . . That God, the God our fathers loved and worshiped, / Would break our chains, and bring to us a great / Deliverance." Moses tells the Princess, "I feel the hour / Draws near which brings deliverance to our race." Still unbelieving, the Princess dismisses Moses's prophetic stance as a "young fancy" and says she's "Never hear[d] of men resigning ease for toil" or of "casting down a diadem / To wear a servile badge." Moses never vocalizes a response, but Harper's depiction of his countenance demonstrates the constitutive pedagogical bond of mother and child: the face of Moses is "lit with lofty / Faith and high resolves," and his "dark prophetic eyes" like his mother's, "look beyond the present pain / Unto the future greatness of his race" (143–144). It is from his mother, then, that he has learned race-national loyalty.

Such precepts of race loyalty and the historical mission of racial uplift predominate Harper's writing and oratory in this period, texts that endorsed with careful qualification the Radical Republican agenda. Published in 1871, Harper's poem "Words for the Hour" addresses in refrain the politicians and generals of early Reconstruction, charging them with the moral obligations of state within an urgent crisis moment. Urging a discipline of character at a dangerous moment of truth, the poem imagines the progress of just policy—of suffrage, legal protection, and education:

> Men of the North! It is no time
>   To quit the battle-field
> When danger from your rear and van
>   It is no time to yield.
> . . . .
> Oh Northern Men! Within your hands
>   Is held no common trust;
> Secure the victories won by blood
>   When treason bit the dust.
>
> 'Tis yours to banish from the land
>   Oppression's iron rule;
> And o'er the auction-block
>   Erect the common school.
>
> To wipe from labor's branded brow
>   The curse that shamed the land

And teach the Freedman how to wield
  The ballot in his hand.

This is the nation's golden hour
  Nerve every heart and hand
To build on Justice, as a rock,
  The future of the land.

Exactly which "hour" Harper found "golden" is not entirely clear, and as Frances Smith Foster notes, the poem was likely written earlier than its publication date.[8] Judging from the evoked vanquishing of "treason" and the considerable agency Harper grants the Northern men thus addressed, men invested with the power to "banish . . . Oppression," it seems likely that this is at least as recent as Emancipation. Though it is clear that Harper's poem attempts to "Nerve every heart and every hand," the address of the poem attributes the much-needed rhetorical agency to the powerful Northern men. The poem declares it their duty to embolden "heart and hand" in the constructing of future "Justice."

This call to political action compares interestingly with Harper's speeches in 1865 at the close of the war. As reported in the *Liberator*, during a speech in Providence, Harper told her audience that African Americans should have more than "only bare freedom" but "the rights that are necessary to a complete citizenship." Arguing for universal male suffrage, Harper held up slavery as the "the great mistake of the early founders of the Republic" and argued that in Reconstruction, the nation should "build, not upon the shifting sands of policy and expediency, but upon the granite of eternal justice" ("Mrs. Frances E. W. Harper on Reconstruction," par. 4). Harper remained duty-bound in addressing the political betrayals of ostensible emancipation even at the very moment legal freedom was conferred.

THE CHARACTER OF LABOR: THE LABOR OF CHARACTER

When Harper impugned Andrew Johnson's intelligence at the National Women's Rights Convention in 1866, she asserted the president's character flaw as a way to raise larger questions about the importance of economic opportunity and free speech in the republic. Through the pedagogical referent of Johnson's character, she impugns the political intelligence of impoverished white Southerners as a function of the slave system and Northern capitulation to that system. Harper argues that when "the hands of the black were fettered, white men were deprived of the liberty of speech and the freedom of the press . . . At the South, the legislation of the country was in behalf of the rich slaveholders, while the poor white man was neglected" (*BCD* 217–218). Johnson is simply the "consequence" of this system in

Harper's characterological history lesson, the subject of a corrupt cultural pedagogy, a lack of intellectual nurture.

Like many African American abolitionists, Harper was drawn to a Republican Party that increasingly defined itself against the economic agenda of the Southern slave economy. Through the agency of abolitionist Republicans including Charles Sumner, Thaddeus Stevens, and Salmon Chase, among many others, arguments for civil rights were integrated with more purely market-based arguments for free labor. Even with the rise of market culture and the subsequent decline of independent small production, the precepts of classical republican citizenship were gaining momentum. Leading up to the war and through Reconstruction, this republican construction of economic individualism was publicized by the Republican Party as a foil to the culture of compromise, which characterized Jacksonian politics. Eric Foner argues that

> the Republican party before the Civil War was united by a commitment to a free labor ideology, grounded in the precepts that free labor was economically and socially superior to slave labor . . . [T]he definition of free labor depended on juxtaposition with its ideological opposite, slave labor. (*Free* x)

As mentioned previously, the espousal of free labor pedagogy or her disparagement of President Johnson circulated widely in neo-aboloitionist circles. In "A Family Talk on Reconstruction" (1869), Harriet Beecher Stowe also casts Andrew Johnson as a politician at world-historical crossroads, who must choose a national path of progress toward a democratic free marketplace or retreat back to the aristocratic nepotism of the past. In Stowe's text, the moral character of President Johnson is caught between two narratives of class interpolation:

> If Andy Johnson is consistent with himself, with the principles which raised him from a tailor's bench to the head of a mighty nation, he will see to it that the work that Lincoln began is so thoroughly done, that every man and every woman in America, of whatever race or complexion, shall have exactly equal rights before the law, and be free to rise or fall according to their individual intelligence, industry, and moral worth. So long as everything is not strictly in accordance with our principles of democracy, so long as there is in any part of the country an aristocratic upper class who despite labor, and a laboring lower class that is denied equal political rights, so long this grinding and discord between the two will never cease in America. It will make trouble not only in the South, but in the North,—the trouble between employers and employed,—trouble in every branch and department of government of labor,—trouble in every parlor and every kitchen. (*Household* 294)

Johnson's own paradigmatic success as a free labor subject, who "raised" himself from humble beginnings to the presidency, is shown to be contingent on moral character, which itself depends on whether the economy nurtures or degrades it. What is most striking here is Stowe's configuration of racial difference as essentially a matter of class conflict, which she locates at the heart of all institutional violence in the U.S. body politic. In a similar account of racism as a product of class conflict, Lydia Maria Child also argued for the inherently pedagogical importance of free labor as a school for character development in a multiracial society. In a letter to the *National Standard* in 1870, she wrote, "For my own part, I consider the workingman the privileged class . . . It develops the powers of mind and body . . . Honest labor strengthens the muscles far more than any gymnastic exercise; while it has the double advantage of being useful to others, as well as to one's self" (qtd. in Karcher 568). Child's statement makes a fair example of the economic utilitarianism that made neo-abolitionism, as Louis S. Gerteis understands it, palatable for a growing middle class (21–22).

As an unprecedented and far-reaching reform effort, the pedagogical precepts of "freedmen's education" held literacy to be a cornerstone for republican citizenship. Viewed as a prerequisite of the free labor ideal, only education could assure the exercise of an informed free will and the ability to participate in public discourse, which as we saw in the last chapter were held to be essential elements of the republican character. And yet, political and pedagogical debates within the freedmen's education movement were trenchant. Many of the schools and publications organized by the American Missionary Association (AMA) remained detached from Radical politics, serving instead as loci of "social discipline" aiming to "create a neutralized, pliant black race bound to the dominant society and culture" (Butchart 51). The American Tract Society, publishing organ of the AMA, produced the *Freedmen's Reader* series, which included *John Freedmen and His Family* and *Plain Counsel for Freedmen*, texts that stressed modest aspirations, bourgeois domesticity, the Protestant work ethic, and a route to citizenship through laborious diligence and faith in god. According to Saidiya V. Hartman, the pedagogical hypocrisy of most freedmen's education occurred in the service of the post-Emancipation racial control of labor. American Tract Society pedagogy offered contradictory definitions of freedom, encouraging "both a republican free labor vision in which wage labor was the stepping stone to small proprietorship" and, in denial of the coercive contract arrangements of the postwar South, "a liberal vision in which freedom was solely defined by the liberty of contract." According to Hartman, "emergent forms of domination . . . intensified and exacerbated the responsibilities and afflictions" of the emancipated-slave-become-caste-laborer. This notion of "burdened individuality" captures well the discursive position constraining African American subjects of so-called free labor discourse (117).

Not all of the pedagogical projects of Reconstruction were as coercive. As Ronald E. Butchart demonstrates, neo-abolitionist and Radical Republican sponsorship of Southern schools and texts offered a more liberatory alternative (10). In opposition to AMA pedagogy, the American Freedmen's Union Commission (AFUC) stressed political-economic empowerment for African Americans and strenuously promoted Radical politics through its journal *The National Freedmen*. As a featured author in Lydia Maria Child's *The Freedmen's Book*, published by Ticknor and Field in 1865, Harper was quite literally a civic, intellectual, and moral exemplar held up to the newly freed people. In her editor's introduction, Child addresses "the Freedmen" as "your old friend":

> I have prepared this book expressly for you, with the hope that those of you who can read will read it aloud to others, and that all of you will derive fresh strength and courage from this true record of what colored men have accomplished, under great disadvantages. (i)

Historian Jacqueline Jones notes that Child, who had the ear of all the leading Radicals, presented in *The Freedmen's Book* a progressive pedagogy written in opposition to the limiting social vision of the AMA, which would go on to disseminate a pedagogy of "industrial education" designed to produce the subjects of the New Southern agrarianism (109–166). Child's biographical character sketches of African American luminaries promoted race pride, and like Harper, Child supported Representative Stevens's land reform initiatives and the growing lobby for a Fifteenth Amendment (Karcher 487–495). Child included Harper's poem, "President Lincoln's Proclamation of Freedom," written to commemorate the Emancipation Proclamation of 1863. In this poem, the light of Lincoln's Proclamation washes over the South like sunshine, a "dawn of freedom" obliterating the shadows of "Oppression, grim and hoary." The light of Lincoln's action has transformative power also with regards to the labor relations of slavery:

> It shall flood with golden splendor
>   And the huts of Caroline,
> And the sun-kissed brow of labor
>   With a lustre new shall shine. (qtd. in *Freedmen's Book* 250)

Harper layers figural intensities of perception, as Lincoln's voice mingles with the sunlight on the South. In this poetic endorsement of the inherent dignity of human labor, the voice of reform is fully integrated with the administrative voice of the martyred president.[9]

The labor politics of Radical Reconstruction pervade the rhetorical drama of Harper's most ambitious pedagogical fiction to date, her first known novel, *Minnie's Sacrifice*, serialized in the *Christian Recorder* in 1869. The novel tells the story of two Southerners who grow to adulthood without knowing they are the children of slave mothers, and as such, legally slaves themselves. Louis LeCroix, the son of a slave woman and her master, is raised as an "adopted" brother after Camilla, the planter's daughter, intercedes on his behalf. On another plantation, Minnie, also the child of a planter and his slave, is sent North by her father, where she is raised in the Quaker home of Josiah Strong. Both characters echo Harper's poetic Moses; both are rescued from slavery, but upon learning of their heritage, make the choice of racial solidarity and leadership. Louis, on the brink of joining the Confederate army, is told of his true heritage, and resolves that he "can never raise [his] hand against his mother's race" (*MS* 60). He subsequently makes his way North as a fugitive of both slavery and military duty and finds a place in the Union army. Minnie and Louis marry and return South to teach in the Freedmen's School and promote the Republican agenda. In response to their efforts, the Ku Klux Klan threatens Louis with death, but it is Minnie who is murdered.[10] The conclusion of the novel, as discussed in the Introduction, presses the lesson of racial solidarity for those of the *Christian Recorder* readership who are possessed of economic and intellectual resources, but who might choose to ignore the struggle of the newly emancipated slaves. Melba Joyce Boyd is right to claim that the novel is a challenge to "the political apathy of the black reading public" (130).

Among its other grounding Republican precepts, *Minnie's Sacrifice* teaches the superiority of free labor culture through the perspective of Camilla, Louis's Southern belle sister; the characterization of Camilla's rhetorical dynamism provides a receptive frame for Harper's pedagogical articulation of moral character. Camilla ultimately exerts the familial influence, which challenges Louis's commitments as a Confederate firebrand. Camilla, herself the pedagogical subject of radical abolitionism, is the persuasive agency which effects Louis's critical consciousness. As a girl, Camilla had gone North with LeCroix and Louis in order to secure the boy a position in a Northern school. Camilla undergoes her own crisis of subjectivity when she attends, at her father's whim—perhaps he was expecting a minstrel show—an "Anti Slavery Meeting" at which the girl hears the personal narrative of a fugitive slave. The stories he tells "make a deep impression on the audience," not least of all Camilla. Her crisis of consciousness registers the contrasting economic systems of North and South and their effects on individual workers. The precocious Camilla is "much pleased with the factories; and watched with curious eyes the intelligent faces of the operatives, as they plied with ready fingers their daily tasks." For the girl raised in the midst of slave-produced luxury and leisure, the intelligence and eagerness of the free laborers are a curiosity. When she "contrasts their appearance" with the enslaved workers of her own

experience, Camilla becomes "sober even to sadness" (11). Clearly there
is hope for Camilla's moral reformation, and as the novel progresses, she
herself becomes an agent of reform and a Southern Unionist supporting of
the Republican agenda.

In addition to members of the slavocracy, the novel's pedagogy takes
into account Northern proponents of exclusive white labor, who found
strong philosophical support among slavery ideologues in the South.
George Fitzhugh's notorious philosophical treatise *Cannibals All! Or
Slaves Without Masters* (1857) suggests the degree to which the free
labor ideology presented itself as a threat to both defenders of the slave
system and of the Northern economic hierarchy. Fitzhugh identifies the
social tenets of free labor to be the "false philosophy of the age," tracing this philosophy from the anti-institutionalism of the Reformation:
"The right of Private Judgment led to the doctrine of Human Individuality . . . Hence, also, arose the doctrines of Laissez Faire, free competition, human equality, freedom of religion, of speech and of the press,
and universal liberty" (53). We should recognize this as a comprehensive
dismissal of republican virtues; for Fitzhugh, the flaw in such doctrines
is their ostensible tendency toward anarchy and the cruelty of the powerful few into whose hands power would surely fall once loosed from
governmental adjudication. Sounding the popular Confederate argument
for the slave system's benevolence, Fitzhugh claimed that as a naturally
inferior people, African American slaves were in need of the patriarchal
"care" of their masters. Fitzhugh stressed the cruelty of Northern capitalism, arguing that white industrial workers were materially worse off than
African American slaves in the South. In his dismissal of the republican
creed, Fitzhugh makes his own pedagogical assertion regarding African
American labor:

> There is one strong argument in favor of Negro slavery over all other
> slavery: that he, being unfitted for the mechanic arts, for trade, and all
> skillful pursuits, leaves those pursuits to be carried on by the whites;
> and does not bring all industry into disrepute, as in Greece and Rome,
> where the slaves were not only the artists and mechanics, but also the
> merchants. (201)

Fitzhugh's imagination of the white artisan slaves of antiquity contrasts
tellingly with his assessment of the African intellect. His assertions regarding a classical citizenship that *a priori* excludes African-descended people
relies on a theory of intrinsically debased character in which the inability
to labor skillfully serves as the crucial proof in his argument for the moral
superiority of slavery. Here Fitzhugh appeals to the growing antebellum
resistance to an integrated labor movement in the North, wherein emancipation came to be viewed by rank and file Democrats as a betrayal of

"white labor" organized conspiratorially by abolitionists and capitalist Republicans (Roediger 171).

Fitzhugh's theory of race is only a rarified example of the general racial common sense that held African American free labor to be an impossibility based on the ostensible characterological deficiency of African American laborers. The free labor experiment was constructed as a radical historical break, a chance for African Americans to withstand the test of character inherent in the myth of republican self-reliance.[11] Through travel and writing in the South, Harper, like other Radical operatives, sought evidence of the success of this so-called experiment. Two such reports are Carl Schurz's *Report on Conditions in the South* and Whitelaw Reid's *After the War: A Tour of the Southern States, 1865–66*. Schurz, a Union general, and Reid, a literary journalist, were both Radicals, and both made appeals to President Johnson to reconsider his political course. Schurz and Reid argued that the president's actions had emboldened the neo-Confederate influence within the Southern Democratic Party. In strict accordance with Radical policy, Schurz and Reid supported a continued occupation of the South and a provisional disenfranchisement of formal rebels. Schurz used the status of the free labor experiment as proof for this argument. "The facts enumerated in this report," he asserts, "must make it evident to every unbiased observer unadulterated free labor cannot be had at present, unless the National Government holds its protective and controlling hand over it." In particular, Schurz cited lynching and the "Black Codes" debarring equitable labor contracts as primary impediments to "the spirit of free labor" (359).

Harper participated in the journalistic effort to generate persuasive evidence of a successful free labor experiment even as she taught the precepts of free labor virtue lecturing in the South between the years of 1867 and 1871 (*BCD* 122). This evidence, of course, was characterological, and across contexts and genres Harper worked to reverse the ethical burden of the "experiment," so that the test subject was, rather than the laborer, the state itself.[12] Harper addressed mixed audiences, many of which she notes included a dangerous element of unrepentant "rebels." She spoke also to audiences constituted exclusively of African American women. Like Sumner, Stevens, and Schurz, Harper advocated key components of the Radical Republican platform: the need for legal protection of Southern African Americans, suffrage as a necessary extension of emancipation, and the reforming powers of free labor culture.

Throughout her Southern tours, Harper reported evidence of free labor culture taking hold among the emancipated people. In this 1871 letter written to Still while she was a lodger in the "Reconstructed" plantation of Jefferson Davis, Harper documented the "strange" transformation of the slavocracy—its domestic embodiment—as black free labor thrived. In her narrative, the slave family is replaced by the free labor family:

My Dear Friend—It is said that truth is stranger than fiction; and if ten years since some one had entered my humble log house and seen me kneading bread and making butter, and said that in less than ten years you will be in the lecture field, you will be a welcome guest under the roof of the President of the Confederacy, though not by special invitation from him, that you will see his brother's former slave a man of business and influence, that hundreds of colored men will congregate on the old baronial possessions . . . that labor will be organized upon a new basis, and that under the sole auspices and moulding hands of [Mr. Montgomery] and his sons will be developed a business whose transactions will be numbered in hundreds of thousands dollars, would you not have smiled incredulously? Every hand of his family is adding its quota to the success of this experiment of a colored man both trading and farming on an extensive scale . . . The business of this firm of Montgomery & Sons has amounted, I understand, to between three and four hundred thousand dollars in a year. (qtd. in Still 774–775)

Harper's portrait of the successful black business is cross-generational, projecting into the future a thriving culture of black family and business. She stresses the freedom of racial self-determination that potentiates such success, created "under the sole auspices and moulding hands" of a black man. In the new free labor version of the former lynchpin of the slave system— the plantation—we find the synecdoche for the transformative power of economic and political agency. Also from Alabama in 1871, Harper wrote of her interview with a man who as a slave-mason had labored seven years without compensation. "Now mark the contrast," she writes, "That man is now free, owns the home of his former master, has I think more than sixty acres of land, and his master is in the poor-house" (776). Tempering such success stories were more sober accounts of how the promise of free labor could be so easily thwarted. One "tale of wrong" recounts a man who "worked a whole year . . . and now he has been put off with fifteen bushels of corn and his food; yesterday he went to see about getting his money, and the person to whom he went, threatened to kick him off, and accused him of stealing" (768).

The same point is made in the preceptive script of *Minnie's Sacrifice*. In documenting the struggle for the right to a republican way of life in the South, the novel demands that the *Christian Recorder*'s middle-class African American readership consider its own place in the struggle as a question of moral character. In the "Conclusion" to the novel, Harper offers an interpretive frame, one that would allow readers to find their own uplift obligations in the novel:

The lesson of Minnie's sacrifice is this, that it is braver to suffer with one's own branch of the human race—to feel, that the weaker and the more despised they are, the closer we will cling to them, for the sake of helping them, than to attempt to creep out of all identity with them in their feebleness, for the sake of mere personal advantage, and to do this at the expense of self-respect, and a true manhood, and a truly dignified womanhood, that with whatever gifts we possess, whether they be genius, culture, wealth or social position, we can best serve the interests of our race by a generous and loving diffusion, than by a narrow and selfish isolation which, after all, is only one type of the barbarous and anti-social state. (91)

In Minnie's pledge to racial solidarity upon learning of her slave heritage, Harper clearly distinguishes her novel from the popular "tragic mulatta" novel in which African American women "pass" in white society until their parentage is discovered.[13] Continuing her abolitionist charge to the black middle-class of the North, Harper asks her readers to examine their own complicity in these racialized scenarios that play out on a daily basis, rejecting "mere personal advantage" for identification within "our race." Such solidarity is the requirement of "a true manhood and a truly dignified womanhood."

Harper's exhortations avoid the privatizing logic that characterizes the more individualist strain of reformism, the "burdened individuality" Saidiya V. Hartman identifies as the position of African American laborers in the wake of Emancipation. In Harper's political-economic reform ethic, the possibility of self-help does not place the full burden of self-determination on the subject of free labor but serves instead as an index of institutional values. Louis articulates this vision in the language of the self-made man as the best argument for equal rights and protections under the law, the denial of which *Minnie's Sacrifice* so thoroughly documents:

> We are going to open a school, and devote our lives to the up-building of the future race. I intend entering into some plan to facilitate the freedmen in obtaining homes of their own. I want to see this newly enfranchised race adding its quota to the civilization of the land. I believe there is power and capacity, only let it have room for exercise and development. We demand no social equality, no supremacy of power. All we ask is that the American people will take their Christless, Godless prejudices out of the way, and give us a chance to grow, an opportunity to accept life, not merely as a matter of ease and indulgence, but of struggle, conquest, and achievement. (73)

By advocating the economic system's inclusion of black interests and acknowledging white anxieties about black political power, Harper operates in accordance with Republican ideologues, who stressed a strong black workforce whose material success was in the best interest of the national economy. As a teacher in the school, Louis's pedagogy is characterized as rational, not "inflame[d] [with] passion," as Harper has it. Louis's monologue recounts Harper's own views on Reconstruction economics as stated in a letter to William Still from South Carolina in 1867: "I hold that between the white people and the colored there is a community of interests, and the sooner they find it out, the better it will be for both parties" (qtd. in Boyd 123). Harper's preceptive statement posits social progress as a matter of productivity within a web of mutual economic dependence.

The degree to which Harper's theological orientation was integrated with the free labor platform can be determined by considering the work of a contemporary who likely influenced her economic and rhetorical thought. As mentioned in Chapter 1, the Reverend William Henry Furness was the minister of the First Congregational Unitarian Church in Philadelphia, the church that Harper joined in 1870. Furness was a staunch antislavery theologian, and the Unitarian ethic he preached, with its "social gospel" precepts, resonated strongly with the reformist agenda of the African Methodist Episcopal Church in which Harper was raised. Furness's address "The Blessings of Abolitionism," delivered at the First Congregational Church on July 1, 1860, stands as an exemplar not only of the antislavery sermonizing Harper practiced as well, but also of the blurred line between theology and economics that characterizes much of her reform work. As Furness framed the situation, "the great problem to be solved" required the transformation of "some four millions of imbruted, objectless human beings into free and active laborers" (5). Suggesting how racial barriers to the labor contract can be overcome, Furness asserts that whenever people engage in "common transactions so that each is profitable to all the rest what fast friends do they soon become, intimate as brothers, ready to serve one another in emergencies each with his whole fortune!" (8). Furness holds up emancipation as the realization of theological principle, arguing that "the bare act of Abolition would be only another name for a new and rich experience of Vital Religion, the experience of a whole great people" (21). Furness's address seems one likely source of Harper's "community of interest" precept, to which she returned repeatedly throughout Reconstruction, especially with regard to land reform and the pursuit of African American male suffrage. In her commentary on land reform, the most controversial and ultimately unsuccessful Radical initiative, Harper fuses the Moses story (a quest for a promised land and race-national destiny) with the republican ethics of self-determination.

HARPER AND THE PROMISE OF RADICAL LAND REFORM

The ethical *topoi* Harper navigated at the 1866 National Women's Rights Convention was one of a Mosaic people, wandering in search of a home

and denied the right to property ownership. Just as crucial in the republican civic mythos as free speech and the right to work was the notion that
only the ownership of land assured the liberty of citizens. Free labor, even
as its ideologues tried to construct it as a practice of freedom, still retained
the taint of "wage labor" and social dependency (Roediger 65–72). In the
popular imagination, only land ownership allowed the mythic freedom of
the family farm that could operate independently, yet within a network of
similarly situated families. Despite Harper's documentation of successful
African American landowners, it is the unfortunate truth that such ownership was the exception and not the rule. Pennsylvania Representative and
Joint Committee on Reconstruction leader Thaddeus Stevens proposed a
"confiscation" policy by which the land of former slaveholders would be
redistributed so that every male former slave would receive forty acres. In
1865, Stevens argued for the confiscation of 400 million acres to be taken
from the wealthiest ten percent of the planter class (Foner, *Reconstruction*
235). Eric Foner argues that confiscation generated a great deal of anxiety among potential Northern investors, who sought to accumulate extensive tracts of land in the South and required a ready workforce of African
American wage laborers, rather than a new class of landowning competitors (*Politics* 128–149). To be sure, in the agricultural consolidation of the
new national economy, a republican yeomanry was obsolete, an obstacle
to the consolidation of capital.[14] In republican fashion, Harper held land
ownership to be as important as suffrage for political freedom: "A man
landless, ignorant and poor may use the vote against his interests, but with
intelligence and land he holds in his hand the basis of power and elements
of strength" (qtd. in Still 770). Harper's hope not only for the acquisition
of these "elements," but also for a multiracial recognition of common interests, was a key precept in her Reconstruction pedagogy.

Despite the political-economic barriers, the promise of land ownership
was claimed as the *sine qua non* of race-national development by many
reform rhetors. Harper herself takes on faith the transformational potential
of owning land in *Minnie's Sacrifice*, when Louis advises students in his
freedmen's school

> to be saving and industrious, and to turn their attention towards be-
> coming land owners. He attended their political meetings, not to array
> class against class, nor to inflame the passion of either side. He wanted
> the vote of the colored people not to express the old hates and animosi-
> ties of the plantation, but the new community of interests arising from
> freedmen. (*MS* 74)

For Louis, African American land acquisition is itself an act of multiracial
democracy, a fulfillment of the social contract in which productive independence contributes to the collective "community of interests."

From Harper's Radical perspective, the republican ethos of the self-determining, productive citizen was not habitable as a material result of black landlessness. In the following passage from *Minnie's Sacrifice*, Josiah Collins, a Quaker abolitionist, speaks of "free blacks" in the North, but the relevance of this polemic in the context of land reform is unmistakable:

> This generation has known him as being landless, poor, and ignorant. One of the most important things for him to do is to acquire land. He will never gain his full measure of strength until (like Anteus) he touches the earth. And I think here is the great fault, or misfortune of the race; they seem to me to readily accept their situation, and not to let their industrial aspirations rise high enough. I wish they had more of the earth hunger that characterizes the German, or the concentration of purpose which we see in the Jews . . . for more than two hundred years his history has been a record of blood and tears, of ignorance, degradation, and slavery. And when nominally free, prejudice has assigned him the lowest positions and the humblest situations. (30)

Hercules was only able to crush Anteus once he had lifted him off the ground; this classical myth becomes the figure of Radical land reform. The desire to become landowners, "earth hunger," is constitutive of a collective political interest, or "concentration of purpose"; conversely, the lack of property ownership engenders a culture of excessively modest "industrial aspirations." Thus the Quaker Collins points up precepts of race-national economic duty.

AFRICAN AMERICAN WOMANHOOD
AND THE AMBIGUITIES OF SUFFRAGE

Perhaps no endeavor more clearly illustrates the challenges Harper faced in crafting pedagogy at the intersection of her race and gender loyalties than her writing and oratory within the suffrage debates of Reconstruction. At the 1866 National Women's Rights Convention, held to draw up a post–Civil War agenda for what we now refer to as first-wave feminism, the formidable Susan B. Anthony made the ostensibly egalitarian declaration that with slavery abolished, "the negro and the woman now hold the same civil and political *status*, alike needing only the ballot . . . [T]he time has come for an organization that shall demand UNIVERSAL SUFFRAGE" (Stanton 171). Anthony made this declaration of universality through a representational strategy relying on the supposed political equivalence of "woman" and "negro" and the supposition that voting rights would secure citizenship for both groups. However, the unstated analogy of "woman" as essentially white and "negro" as essentially male effaces the specificity of African American women, just as it effaces the white privilege of the suffragists. Insisting in this moment on racial distinctiveness to counteract the exclusionist logic of the white suffragist argument, Harper's 1866 address returns to her Mosaic *topos* in her characterological praise of the great Underground Railroad hero, Harriet Tubman:

> We have a woman in our country who has received the name of "Moses," not by lying about it, but by acting it out—a woman who has gone down into the Egypt of slavery and brought out hundreds of our people into liberty. The last time I saw that woman, her hands were . . . all swollen from a conflict with a brutal conductor, who undertook to eject her from her place. That woman, whose courage and bravery won a recognition from our army and from every black man in the land, is excluded from every thoroughfare of travel. (*BCD* errata 1)

For Harper, Tubman's work highlights divergent paths both politically and spacially in the society of the racial state. Despite praiseful recognition from the African American community, Tubman is "excluded" from official lines of travel in the United States. Harper recounted her own experience of being physically removed from train cars in Maryland, Pennsylvania, and Washington, D.C., to publicize the courage African American women showed on a daily basis in confronting contingencies of the racial state unacknowledged by Anthony. Shirley Wilson Logan's analysis of Harper's means of address in 1866 points out its "continuous shifts and adjustments," identifying a tense coalitional rhetoric deployed at a political crossroads (*We Are Coming* 58–59). Before her New York audience, Harper was careful to affirm her women's rights resolve while also demanding a hearing for African American women, for whom the question of political rights was far more complicated.[15]

At the contentious Equal Rights Association Convention of 1869, where the women's rights group became divided over the issues of black male suffrage and support for the Republican Party, Harper was at the center of the dispute. *The Revolution* reported Harper as saying that "she would not have the black woman put a single straw in the way, if only the men of the race could obtain what they wanted," in this instance favoring her race affiliation over gender solidarity, a choice which set her at odds with the mainstream suffragists (qtd. in P. Foner 36). In November of 1869, Lucy Stone and Henry Blackwell formed the American Woman Suffrage Association (AWSA) to support the passage of the Fifteenth Amendment, which would secure the vote for African American men. At the same time, Elizabeth Cady Stanton and Susan B. Anthony headed up the National

Women's Suffrage Association (NWSA), which, seeking a constitutional amendment to secure women's franchise, condemned the Fifteenth Amendment as an injustice to women (P. Foner 36–37). Harper allied herself with the AWSA, which supported Radical Reconstruction. The NWSA and AWSA functioned separately until 1890, when they merged to form the National American Women's Suffrage Association (NAWSA), in which Harper was active.

Prior to this splintering of the neo-abolitionist and white suffragette coalition, Harper had geared her pedagogical address to white women whose character, in Harper's estimation, lacked the critical intelligence necessary for progressive politics and the efficacious exercise of the ballot. At the 1866 National Women's Rights Convention, she had juxtaposed the determined and sacrificing character of African American women, Tubman's and her own example serving in illustration, to the character of white women in a manner that was untenable in the estimation of the NWSA leadership. As Nell Irving Painter notes, this address is auspiciously absent in Elizabeth Cady Stanton and Susan B. Anthony's *History of Women's Suffrage* (225). Harper told her audience,

> I do not believe that giving the woman the ballot is immediately going to cure all the ills of life. I do not believe that white women are dew-drops just exhaled from the skies. I think that like men they may be divided into three classes, the good, the bad, and the indifferent. The good would vote according to their convictions and principles; the bad, as dictated by prejudice or malice, and the indifferent will vote on the strongest side of the question, with the winning party . . . You white women speak here of rights. I speak of wrongs. I, as a colored woman, have had in this country an education which has made me feel as if I were in the situation of Ishmael, my hand against every man, and every man's hand against me. (*BCD* 218)

In the juxtaposition of her own political situation with that of "white women," Harper demystifies the efficacy of the vote. The vote is an expression of character in her argument; only those removed from the civil rights struggle in a way that Harper or Tubman could not be might cast votes based on "prejudice or malice" or "indifference." In Harper's construction, the politics of suffrage involve more than the right to cast a ballot, an act too easily corrupted by lack of "principles and convictions." Offering a pedagogical frame, Harper goes so far as to assert that suffrage is "a normal school, and the white women of this country need it" for their own moral development. Only this will assure that "the white women of America" will "be lifted out of their airy nothings and selfishness" (116). Harper's challenging racial characterization disrupts the ease of Anthony's coalitional universalism.

Minnie's Sacrifice appeared in 1869, the same year Harper made her controversial choice of affiliation with American Woman Suffrage Association. In a characteristic manner, Harper worked portions of her suffrage oratory into the preceptive script of her fiction, giving the task of restatement to her heroine, Minnie, but this time directed at the African American reform audience of the *Christian Recorder*. In a dialogue between Minnie and Louis, Harper delivers a lesson on the coalitions and divisions within the suffrage movement. When Minnie and Louis argue about the relative importance of black males' and black women's suffrage, Minnie mouths Harper's own 1869 Equal Rights Association Convention address, but with a clearer qualification of her support of black male suffrage. "And while I would not throw a straw in the way of the colored man, even though I know that he would vote against me as soon as he gets his vote, yet I do think that woman should have some power to defend herself from oppression, and equal laws as if she were a man" (78). Just as Harper distinguished her position from the white suffragists in New York in 1866, here she seeks to maintain the distinctiveness of African American women's political position within the broader, masculinist African American reform community. When Louis claims that in the struggle for suffrage the "hour belongs to the negro," Minnie asks, "But, Louis, is it not the negro woman's hour also?" Louis attempts to sidestep this claim by asserting "you cannot better the condition of the colored men without helping the colored woman. What elevates him helps her."

Through the pedagogical means of the drama of persuasion, Harper offered *Christian Recorder* readers a precept by which staunch support for the Fifteenth Amendment need not preclude women's suffrage. Minnie questions the public-private logic by which women are ancillary to men. Louis continues with equally domesticating reply. "But, really," he says, "I should not like to see you wending your way through rough and brawling mobs to the polls." Minnie's response turns the patriarchal propriety of this argument about separate spheres to her political advantage. Women's suffrage, by Minnie's argument, would serve as a feminine reform agency that would "bring into our politics a deeper and broader humanity" (78). Louis apparently rethinks some of his own assumptions as Minnie's persuasive force gains his concurrence. In the most powerful premise, Minnie argues that "basing our rights on the ground of our common humanity is the only true foundation for national peace and durability." According to Minnie, a "strong and enduring government" should be entrenched "in the hearts of both the men and women of the land" (79).

In *Minnie's Sacrifice*, Harper revisits the crucial state elections of 1867 in which black suffrage was on the ballot and was overwhelmingly rejected. As Xi Wang argues, this rejection of black suffrage by white Northerners made Republican suffrage policy ideologically inconsistent (41). In dialogue between Minnie and Louis, Harper acknowledges the fragile and merely nominal existence of the multiracial Republican alliance. The moral integrity of race character once again comes to the fore:

> Louis has just returned from a journey to the city, and has brought with him the latest Northern papers. He is looking rather sober, and Minnie, ready to detect the least change of his countenance, is at his side.
>
> "What is the matter?" Minnie asked, in a tone of deep concern.
>
> "I am really discouraged."
>
> "What about?"
>
> "Look here," said he, handing her the *New York Tribune*. "State after state has rolled up a majority against negro suffrage. I have been trying to persuade our people to vote the Republican ticket, but to-day, I feel like blushing for the party. They are weakening our hands and strengthening those of the rebels." (*MS* 75)

When Minnie reminds him that "they were not Republicans who gave these majorities against us," Louis counters that "if large numbers of these Republicans stayed at home, and let the election go by default, the result was just the same," noting how any weakness in the interracial Radical alliance supplies neo-Confederates with an arsenal of polemical barbs. Harper registers the venom in Democratic papers when Louis complains that "every rebel can throw it in our teeth and say, 'See your great Republican party; they refuse to let the negro vote with them, but they force him upon us. They don't do it out of regard to the negro, but only to spite us'" (75–76).

As Louis's lament continues, it is punctuated by a knock at the door. Mr. Jackson enters, and in this character, Harper offers a pedagogical figure of suffrage, one just as apt as Louis for representing the movement to pass the Fifteenth Amendment. Mr. Jackson's story counters the white supremacist legitimations of disenfranchisement based on degraded African character, and in offering this vignette, Harper partook in what had become a standard feature of an emerging racial discourse, the polemical representation of black workers and (potential) voters. Thus, the results of disenfranchisement are connected causally to the ambivalence of the Republican Party during the state elections of 1867, as well as during the failed 1869 Fifteenth Amendment vote. In a novel whose hero and heroine are mulattos raised as white man and woman, Harper pointedly notes that Jackson is a "dark man," and she quickly repeats this racial detail, explaining that "nothing in his appearance . . . showed any connection with the white race." There is almost a redundancy here, as if Harper feels it necessary to establish a purity of African heritage. This is a reversal of the lowest common denominator rhetoric of Whitelaw Reid's Southern documentary.[16] Louis's whiteness, which makes visible his blushing, is thus a marker of the political complicity he feels, a shame over the very auspices of Republican power that authorize his political speech and pedagogy. Jackson's story of his thwarted attempt at free labor piques Louis's embarrassment over his own political and cultural affiliations. Jackson is denied the republican right to practice his trade for aligning himself, Harper's fiction stipulates, with the Republican Party. His unwillingness to sacrifice his political affiliation is constructed carefully. Countering the public perception that African Americans would only, if given suffrage, sell or squander their vote, Harper stresses Jackson's right economic morality by having him refuse the $500 bribe of Southern Democrats. He has done everything the republican ideology holds to be requisite and still he is denied the rights of citizenship.

Other literary experimentation allowed Harper to argue for universal suffrage from the moral authority of African American women's character. *Sketches of Southern Life*, published in 1872 after the ratification of the Fifteenth Amendment, introduces Aunt Chloe, the narrator of a group of poems specifically treating Reconstruction politics. Frances Smith Foster says of the poems' narrator,

> Aunt Chloe is a significant contribution to African-American written literary expression. She is probably the first black female protagonist, outside the tragic mulatta tradition, to be presented as a model for life . . . Barely literate and unsophisticated, Aunt Chloe is a folk character, a no-nonsense woman of moral strength and great common sense. (137)

Smith Foster is correct in her estimation of Aunt Chloe as a pedagogical "model," and the "common sense" of this character's preceptive script assumes a Radical Republican sense of the Reconstruction moment. Criticizing Johnsonian policy, praising then-President Grant for his crackdown on the Ku Klux Klan, commenting approvingly on the establishment of schools for African Americans, and again endorsing black suffrage, Aunt Chloe espouses a mother wit of political specificity.

In the poem "The Deliverance," Chloe recounts a community of African American women whose characterological qualifications for citizenship exceed those of their husbands. Chloe stipulates that she "would not have you think / That all our men are shabby; But 'tis said in every flock of sheep / There will be one that's scabby." By contrast, she asserts that "Curnel Johnson" was unseated in the presidential election of 1868 due to the disruptive moral agency of "women radicals" who "got right in the way." The source of this moral disruption is the influence of African American women's politicization of the home:

> And if any man should ask me
>   If I would sell my vote,
> I'd tell him I was not the one
>   To change and turn my coat.

. . . .
I do not think I'd ever be
    As slack as Jonas Handy;
Because I heard he sold his vote
    For just three sticks of candy.

But when John Thomas Reeder brought
    His wife some flour and meat,
And told her he had sold his vote
    For something good to eat,

You ought to seen Aunt Kitty raise,
    And heard her blaze away;
She gave the meat and flour a toss,
    And said they should not stay.
. . . .
Day after day did Milly Green
    Just follow after Joe,
And told him if he voted wrong
    To take his rags and go. (*Complete Poems* 124–126)

Although the political rationale of casting such aspersions on African American men can be questioned as an untimely intervention in light of the racialized debate surrounding the Fifteenth Amendment, Aunt Chloe's argument about African American women's character ground necessary lessons in Harper's pedagogy. Aunt Chloe's sense of her female compatriots posits the dedicated Radical Republican political disposition of African American women. By establishing African American women as both a force of reform within institutional politics and a potentially important Republican constituency, Harper seeks to build on the political success of African American men. Like Harriet Tubman and Harper herself, Aunt Chloe is represented as having stood the test of character in the crucible of racial and gender oppression.

    If Harper tread carefully when making women's rights arguments in the context of Radical politics, biblical remove from the scene of contemporary politics allowed a more aggressive pedagogical means for teaching against patriarchal state mechanisms. While the pathos of these poems served a clear persuasive function, one resonating across the sentimental tradition in which reform literature circulated, the pedagogical force of her poems requires attention to the manner in which Harper *staged* her appeals. "Vashti," first published in the 1871 *Poems*, retells a story from the Book of Esther in which Vashti, the queen of Persia, refuses King Ahasuerus's command that she display her beauty and "'mid my lords and mighty men, / Unveil her lovely face.'" The queen's attendants wait to hear her reply, which, in keeping with the text of Esther, comes in the form of an indignant refusal. Harper's Vashti offers as rationale her concern that should she yield to the indecency of the king's proposal, "Persia's women all would blush." Vashti thus takes her bold stance in unequivocal terms:

> "Go back!" she cried, and waved her hand,
>   And grief was in her eye;
> "Go tell the King," she sadly said,
>   That I would rather die.

The king is made furious by the report of Vashti's disobedience, and upon asking his "wily counselors" for guidance in his response, the king is reminded of his dominion and reputation and the stakes of maintaining them:

> Then spoke his wily counselors—
>   "O King of this fair land!
> From distant Ind to Ethiop,
>   All bow to thy command.
>
> "But if, before they servant's eyes,
>   This thing they plainly see,
> That Vashti doth not heed thy will
>   Nor yield herself to thee,
>
> "The women, restive 'neath our rule,
>   Would learn to scorn our name,
> And from her deed to us would come
>   Reproach and burning shame. (*Complete Poems* 98–99)

The counselors urge the king to "sign with [his] hand" an edict stripping Vashti of her royal position and casting her out. Vashti is subject, then, not simply to the king's authority, but to a network of patriarchal counsel coextensive with the authority of the state itself, mapped as the dominion of his reputation—"from Ind to Ethiop"—which the counselors are committed to protecting. The anxiety of the counselors is telling; they fear specifically what here we call the preceptive force of the symbolic act, its instructive function. The counselors' fear is not unfounded: the political danger rests not in the defiant act itself but in the audience it might be given. Despite her subordination within this power system, Vashti's resistance to the exercise of patriarchal state power holds the potential for dangerous disruption.

The poem, framing Vashti's rhetorical action as witnessed with anticipation by all Persian women, raises the queen's refusal, again, in keeping with the biblical text, to the status of history-making language. Despite the king's decree that Vashti "lay aside her crown," the poem ends, making reference to Vashti's own sense of having maintained the reputation of her "womanhood"—she leaves her "high estate . . . Proud of her spotless name"—with the suggestion that despite her loss of official, state-recognized honor, her symbolic act on behalf of all women wields still a persuasive force. Her willingness to sacrifice position in the name of solidarity serves "restive" women as a precept for action. As a pedagogical text, "Vashti" teaches a practice of resistance to patriarchal state power, staging the imperative of rhetorical action as the necessary work of teaching a nation about the power of its women. As a rhetorical strategy, invoking a biblical ethic enabled Harper to sidestep the factional rift in the public discourse of suffrage politics.

THE LIMITS OF REPUBLICANISM

Harper's poetic eulogy, "Lines to Hon. Thaddeus Stevens," elevates the Radical Republican architect within the community of abolitionist martyrs. The poem laments that Stevens did not live long enough to see the postwar nation reach the "fullness of its time" as a project of reform, and evokes the continued millennial "justice" of a warlike God who "hath bathed his sword in judgment" (167). Likely written within a year of this poem, *Minnie's Sacrifice* also represents Reconstruction as imperiled amid the danger of racial violence. The invisibility of the Klan, its approximation as "the spirit of the lost cause," is embodied as well by Northern voters who rejected the Radicals' civil rights agenda:

> In the evening Louis called the people together, and talked with them, trying to keep them from being discouraged, for the times were evil, and the days were very gloomy. The impeachment had failed. State after State in the North had voted against enfranchising the colored man in their midst. The spirit of the lost cause revived, murders multiplied. The Ku Klux spread terror and death around . . . Ballot and bullet had failed, but another resort was found in secret assassination. (85)

Louis glimpses the horizons of his Republican affiliation as he addresses the black community in which he is the voice of political leadership. Through Louis, Harper throws into question the viability of the state as a protectorate for African Americans. He tells the people gathered,

> "Defend your firesides if they are invaded, live as peaceably as you can, spare no pains to educate your children, be saving and industrious, try to get land under your feet and homes over your heads. My faith is very

strong in political parties, but, as the world has outgrown other forms of wrong, I believe that it will outgrow this also. We must trust and hope for better things." What else could he say? And yet there were times when his words seemed to him almost like bitter mockery. Here was outrage upon outrage committed upon these people, and to tell them to hope and wait for better times, but seemed like speaking hollow words. Oh he longed for a central administration strong enough to put down violence and misrule in the South. If Johnson was clasping hands with rebels and traitors was there no power in Congress to give, at least, security to life? Must they wait till murder was organized into an institution, and life and property were at the mercy of the mob? And, if so, would not such a government be a farce, and such a civilization a failure? (86)

Louis's bitter sense that he speaks "hollow words" to the crowd strongly suggests how Harper qualifies her own ironic position as a disenfranchised Republican operative. The indefinite pronoun "this" in the second sentence could refer to either white supremacist violence or the very political system in which Louis expresses his grudging "faith." Read the first way, the polemic suggests that official political means will not lead to an extension of freedoms, and read the second way, "political parties" are themselves a "form . . . of wrong," an essentially flawed system which is itself the major impediment to liberation.

The Johnsonian return to Jacksonian politics, the "clasping [of] hands with rebels and traitors," leads Louis to wonder if even the Radical Congress offered coalitional possibilities. Here the hopes, aspirations, and intelligence of an alternative politics are articulated by the Mosaic figure of Louis, and the ineffectual pronouncements of Republican policy are supplemented with the counsel of armed resistance. Late in the novel, the character Louis, who like Minnie is literally a mouthpiece by which Harper re-disseminated her political speeches, lectures, and essays, receives a secret missive from the Ku Klux Klan: "Louis LeCroix, you are a doomed man. We are determined to tolerate no scalawags, nor carpetbaggers among us. Beware, the sacred serpent has hissed" (81). The "anonymous letters" of the Klan are antithetical to Harper's ethics of free speech. Just as surely as authentic, abolitionist speech builds coalition publicly, secret speech signifies, here heralds, physical assault. But when Minnie rather than Louis is murdered by the Klan, her sentimental death draws the community of freed people together, thus bearing up the grieving Louis and sealing his political resolve.

Louis's struggle with the morality of Republican authority figures Harper's own highly contingent status as a "black Republican." Insofar as her work during Reconstruction sought to de-privatize the material needs of African Americans, *Minnie's Sacrifice* chronicles as well the relative success and failure of such efforts by the Radical Republicans and their supporters. Minnie's death is evidence that black Republicanism was as of yet an ethos African American women could embody only at great peril. Harper's own perilous experience on the Southern lecture circuit no doubt provided the inspiration for the lesson of Minnie's death.[17] In the end, the pedagogical character of Minnie and of Louis emerges as an agency that exceeds the limits of institutional politics, even that of the Radicals. For the remainder of her career, institutional politics, though never abandoned, would occupy a conspicuously ancillary position in relation to the non-state politics of the reform organizations for which Harper would become a prolific spokesperson. But if Harper ultimately found the black Republican position untenable, she retained the republican ethics of economic and discursive self-determination as a variety of political language to be taught. Nevertheless, we see in the frustration of characters like Louis that Harper's often-idealistic articulations of republican principles were tactical rather than naive.

3 Temperance Pedagogy
Lessons of Character
in a Drunken Economy

> And again the injured negro
>> Grind the dreadful mills of fate
> Pressing out the fearful vintage
> Of the nation's scorn and hate?
>> "Lines to the Hon. Thaddeus Stevens"

It would be easy to read past the complexity of Harper's poetic image, in particular, to miss the temperance figures amid the more obvious race-national jeremiad in her poetic eulogy for the late Radical Republican leader. "Lines to the Hon. Thaddeus Stevens" afforded Harper the opportunity not only to mourn the death of her political ally, but also to gauge the political promise of the Radical Revolution of 1865, in which an uneasy interparty hegemony was formed around an agenda of national free labor and civil rights for African Americans. The poem poses a series of questions to the deceased. Evoking the postwar ethos of a nation obliterated by "the cinders of God's wrath," Harper asks Stevens's ghost if it is possible that, despite the ruination, the nation might not have learned the lesson of millennial democracy. Stevens's "bright and glowing visions" of civil rights were stifled, in Harper's phrase, by the "timid counsels" of a Republican Party (*Complete Poems* 81), which was, as historian Sean Wilentz has phrased it, "veering ever rightward" (120). In her address to Stevens's transcendent consciousness, the penultimate inquiry casts the "negro question" in a didactic figuration of production and consumption. This ambiguous image of black labor, paradoxically producing "the nation's scorn and hate," suggests the uncertainty of Reconstruction's legacy. This makes a stark contrast with the celebratory poem "President Lincoln's Proclamation of Freedom," in which the legislative power of the 1863 Emancipation Proclamation, figured both by Lincoln's voice and sunlight, transforms the state of Southern labor: "And the sun-kissed brow of labor / With lustre new shall shine" (*Poems* 104). By contrast, "Lines to the Hon. Thaddeus Stevens" recognizes a bitter irony, one acknowledged among abolitionist rhetors: African American labor continued to empowered a nation seemingly bent on the disenfranchisement of African Americans. The synecdochal conceit of the poem, which figures the "national scorn and hate" of the post-Reconstruction moment as the distillation of liquor itself, a "fearful vintage" with destructive effects, provides a key to Harper's synthesis of free labor and temperance reform agendas in the second half of her career.

At the reform podium and as a matter of pedagogical drama in her fiction, Harper addressed the crises of race and leadership that beset the national temperance effort. Harper's position as an African American woman within the Woman's Christian Temperance Union (WCTU) represents one of her great challenges as an integrationist and theorist of political affiliation. She was active for decades in the WCTU, one of the largest and most influential voluntary organizations in the history of the United States. Harper was an officer in the Philadelphia and Pennsylvania state WCTU chapters beginning in 1875. WCTU president Frances Willard formally introduced Harper at the 1876 national convention.[1] At the 1889 meeting, by which time she had been selected as the Superintendent of Work among Colored People, Harper made a formal recommendation that "in dealing with colored women . . . Christian courtesy be shown" (qtd. in Mattingly 86). As Carol Mattingly suggests, the fact that Harper needed to make this kind of recommendation indicates the racial conflict within the WCTU, and her ambivalence regarding the organization's capacity to "promote the cause of women and her people." Willard was all too ready to compromise and use the national visibility of the WCTU to send dangerously mixed racial messages to constituents. Mattingly argues that for all her rhetoric of racial openness, Willard continued to appeal to white racial hatred and to marginalize the concerns of African American WCTU members like Harper (87–88). Anti-lynching reformer Ida B. Wells condemned Frances Willard's comments about the problem of black drunkenness in the South, which Willard characterized as a kind of plague endangering the "safety of women, of childhood, [and] of the home . . . in a thousand localities" (qtd. in Mattingly 75–76). Wells would continue to critique Willard's racial politics for the remainder of her life. Willard's responses to Wells ran a gambit of denial, careful qualification of previous comments, further demonstrations of racial prejudice, and the marginalization of Wells within the WCTU (Mattingly 76–81).

Throughout the second half of her career, Harper experimented teaching rhetoric in the public sphere at the intersection of temperance activism and the neo-abolitionist struggle for civil rights. For Harper, this was an opportunity to reconfigure the masculine commonplaces of the suffrage debate, which were motivated by political and economic expediency rather than social reform. In the following passage from the essay "Temperance," published in the *African Methodist Episcopal Church Review* in 1891, Harper repeatedly digresses to the "failures and crimes of the reconstruction period," with an obviously economic sense to the recurrence. After alluding to the business alliance of North and South and its utilitarian commitment to the black suffrage initiative, Harper offers this further comment on African American prospects for party politics:

As a race, we have a right to be interested in the success of the temperance movement. The liquor power is too strong and dangerous for us to give it aid or countenance. We are too poor to be moderate drinkers, and in part of the country too much of political nonentities to clasp hands with a power which can dictate its terms to the two great parties, and awe one into silence and entice the other into alliance. (qtd. in Boyd 201)

The "liquor power" takes on an important double valence here, as a reference to both the business interests of the liquor industry *and* to the power of alcohol over the will of the individual citizen. Addressing a collectively configured African American community, Harper claims, "[W]e are too poor to be moderate drinkers." Harper's quintessential uplift precept casts African American poverty as a burden of self-determination shared collectively across class lines. In this temperance context, Harper repeats the imperative of ethical consumerism that oriented her public career as a "free produce" activist in the 1850s. As then, Harper's logic here is that an oppressed people should not patronize a business that holds in its pocket political parties which have failed that people. By Harper's estimation, the Republican Party had been "entice[d] . . . into alliance" with the liquor power.[2] With the unfortunate situation of a government "too weak or too vicious to place protection to human life at the basis of its civilization," Harper advises that "the colored" should "abate somewhat of his political zeal." As Harper has it, "Man cannot live by politics alone." As a prescription for reform and collective rhetorical action, Harper charges her audience to "form themselves into reading clubs" and to "unite with the great moral and philanthropic movements of the day" in order to "throw light on the unsolved problems of modern civilization." In the process, argues Harper, they might further the "progress and development of the country" (qtd. in Boyd 200–201). Harper's prescription charts a political future that diverges from the path of runaway capitalism followed by a corrupt state.

Harper's temperance pedagogy constituted a cross-genre narrative running the better part of her career. Challenging the masculinist economic ethos of reunification, the primary texts of this ongoing rhetorical drama make a claim for the rights of women as being fundamental to any just society. The characterological precepts of temperance, specifically the figure of the drunkard, provided the pedagogical means of teaching against this laissez-faire legitimization of an unjust economy. Harper's rhetoric, then, disrupted the pretensions of economic privilege as a mark of citizenship, rearticulating the immediatist rejection of market values in which political access and white masculinity imply one another. The pledge rhetoric of temperance provided the platform for a more general call to collective justice and self-determination, one consistent with the black nationalism of the African American press but now fundamentally qualified by Harper's women's rights vision. Common precepts of collective fealty and duty integrated these political efforts. In her temperance fiction, characters imagine, foolishly, drunkenly, that any one person could truly act in social isolation from others. The irrational pretension of independent economic agency characterizes the didactic fictional drunkards, who serve as foils for Harper's reform rhetors.

The next section continues the discussion of Harper's coalitional politics and takes up the critical debate about racial representation in African American temperance writing, focusing on *Sowing and Reaping*, a temperance novel serialized in the *Christian Recorder* in 1876 and 1877. In a satirical turn, representing the crisis-ridden U.S. economy of the late 1870s and early 1880s as *the whiskey business*, Harper once again theorizes moral society as an alternative economy and public alliance, in this case, the boycott culture of the temperance movement. Teaching the reform idiom of non-participation, Harper wrote pedagogical characters whose moment of reformation comes in taking the pledge of sobriety, uttering the temperance commonplaces of discipline, inter-subjectivity, and rejection of capitalist monadism—what she called the "narrow and selfish isolation . . . of the anti-social state" (*Minnie's Sacrifice* 91).

RACIAL AMBIGUITY AND HARPER'S TEMPERANCE RHETORIC

The two national referents of *Sowing and Reaping* are economic depression and temperance activism, and in didactic conjunction, these competing interests configure the dynamic of opposing rituals of speech. As these discursive patterns come into conflict in Harper's pedagogical drama, intersecting uneasily at mutual, if irreconcilable, points of interest, they inevitably modify one another. It is through this discursive interaction that Harper saw the world both divided up and potentially healed together by the word, which is to say, the public agency of rhetorical pedagogy realized in the form of properly instructed character. Recalling the "Crusade of 1873" in her *African Methodist Episcopal Church Review* essay, "The Woman's Christian Temperance Union and the Colored Woman," Harper assessed the ongoing work of the WCTU in the context of the racial state. For Harper, the WCTU, like the entire nation, was under the thrall of racial prejudice no less than a drunkard was controlled by alcohol.[3] Harper's pairing of the "twin evils of slavery and intemperance" suggests something of the abolitionist roots of temperance reform (*BCD* 281). Belle Gordon, the heroine of *Sowing and Reaping*, marks the limits of association, proclaiming, "[T]here are two classes of people with whom I never wish to associate, or number among my especial friends, and they are rum sellers and slaveholders" (110).

Despite her use of the slavery–intemperance analogy, Harper seems to have arranged her temperence fictions avoiding the racial specificity of abolitionist discourse. In these texts, racial descriptors are almost entirely under erasure. By the time of *Sowing and Reaping*, Harper was the most well-known African American writer in the United States, and her reputation as a spokesperson for her race was well established. Thus, it seems safe to say that Harper, even had she wished to, would have been unable to extract her texts from the national discourse of racial politics. Critics including Carla Peterson and Debra J. Rosenthal have noted that given its appearance in the African American press, the novel, like the short story "The Two Offers," is most certainly addressed to an African American audience (*Doers* 209; Rosenthal 155). This generic anomaly nonetheless merits critical attention.

For Rosenthal, "deracialized discourse" cues multiracial audiences along racial lines, addressing African American audiences while providing white readers with "interpretive dilemmas" as they fall into their own assumptions "that characters are white unless otherwise indicated." However, insofar as racial ambiguity refuses to perform the pervasive cultural logic of racial separation, we might simply take Harper at her word and assume this as a universalizing gesture (154). Intemperance, she argued, was "an enemy, old and strong . . . warring against the best interests of society; not simply an enemy to one race, but an enemy to all races" (*BCD* 281). This was a functionally integrationist precept for an African American woman attempting to navigate institutionally within a racially hierarchical reform movement.

In terms of its pedagogy and its fictional delivery, we should consider the continuities between the explicitly racialized ethos of Harper's abolitionist work and the "deracialized discourse" of her temperance writing, specifically, the common pedagogical character for which her fictional heroines serve as instructional figures.[4] Another constant between Harper's temperance rhetoric and her earlier writing is her use of sentimental fictional forms to posit marriage and the home as both emblem and operation of nationalist political economics. Given Harper's general pedagogical contstruction of domesticity, it is possible to understand how Harper used "coupling conventions," to borrow Anne duCille's phrase, to highlight the economic basis of racial and gender oppression. Though Harper spoke harshly about the mulatta plot, she retained it as a rhetorical structure for the rest of her writing life. For Harper and her literary predecessors, this popular narrative form served as a genre of access for an important ideological innovation: presenting the seduction of black women by white men as evidence in the argument for political-economic justice for African American women.[5] The similarities between Harper's representations of the tragic mulatta and the drunkard's wife are striking. Both enter relationships with men and, as a result of political-economic powerlessness, die, lose their children, and suffer various forms of subjugation. The tragic mulatta plot is itself an innovation of abolitionist polemic, which raged against the sex crimes of slavery and the powerlessness of slave mothers to stop the sale of their children or themselves. As a comment on economic systems, this is of a piece with Harper's warning against entering into a marriage "transaction" without careful consideration, a didactic positioning of masculinist desire as the fuel for an immoral and destructive economy.

The absence of an explicitly racialist ethos tells us the most, perhaps, about Harper's understanding of the economic link between racial and gender oppression. And yet, in privileging *Sowing and Reaping* in isolation from her other work, critics risk a rhetorically insensitive critical approach. In fact, a good deal of Harper's temperance rhetoric was very carefully situated within a racialized discourse, as evidenced by two essays written under the auspices of the temperance movement, both of which move inexorably to questions of racial politics after Reconstruction.

To be sure, whatever ambiguities contemporary readers identify, Harper's participation in the WCTU must have been an experience of acute racial consciousness, given her need to negotiate the organization's own segregationist tendencies. In her 1888 essay "The Woman's Christian Temperance Union and the Colored Woman," addressing an Afro-Protestant press audience, Harper chose to stress the "hopeful results" of increasing integration in the WCTU, noting that Northern chapters had "met the [race] question in a liberal and Christian manner." Of Southern chapters, however, Harper notes, "[O]thers have not seemed to have so fully outgrown the old shards and shells of the past as to make the distinction between Christian affiliation and social equality" (*BCD* 282). Southern Democrats had long warned white audiences about the perils of social equality as an appeal to white racial solidarity and racial dread, and neo-immediatists had always been quick to reject the rhetorical force of such tactics. At a mass meeting in Washington, D.C., immediately following the 1883 Supreme Court nullification of the 1875 Civil Rights Act, Frederick Douglass made a show of constrained frustration with the "spirit of caste" and "racial prejudice," which had clearly trumped the law and its intent. Douglass's address is clearly constrained by the racial intolerance that would brand his or anyone's dissent against the 1883 decision as tantamount to "denouncing the Court itself." This rhetorical strategy is analogous with the "persistent effort to stigmatize the 'Civil Rights Bill' as a 'Social Rights Bill.'"[6] For Douglass, the conflation of social and civil equality, which in practice would remain a matter of voluntary association, was a "perversion of the truth" (5: 121–122).

Harper argued in a very similar vein in her 1888 essay. "Social equality," she suggests, "if I rightly understand the term, is the outgrowth of social affinities and social conditions, and may be based on talent, ability or wealth, on either or all of these conditions" (283). She rejects, in other words, the premises that African Americans desired social affiliation with whites and that racial mixing was an inevitable result of civil equality. Thus Harper qualifies her integrationist precepts by distinguishing civil equality as a moral imperative, a natural-rights absolute akin to "Christly affiliation." The rest of the essay, like all Harper's work, stresses the "talent" and "ability" of "the race," but also characteristically brings the question back around to "wealth"—the basis of all "social conditions" and, of course, the distinctions among them. And here she makes the connection between civil inequality and the curse of intemperance, "an enemy that . . . entrenched itself in the strongholds of appetite and ava- rice, and was upheld by fashion, custom and legislation" (281). Harper indicts the moral failure of the state and the reproduction of those failures within temperance reform and the WCTU.

In an essay titled simply "Temperance," delivered to an African American reform audience in 1891, Harper seems singularly unable to stay focused on her ostensible topic. By this time, lynching campaigns in the South had begun in earnest, a violence she compares to the "liquor power": "Men of my race look at the dead who have fallen basely and brutally murdered since the war in Southern lands. See the liquor traffic, sending its floods of sorrow, shame and death to the habitations of men." Harper takes this latter sentence directly from the text of *Sowing and Reaping*: "Perhaps the white race have just as much or more reason to be anxious about their future in the South as we have, just so long as it shall be written, 'As ye sow, so shall ye reap'" (qtd. in Boyd 201).

TOWARD A TEMPERATE PUBLIC

In his reading of her last novel, *Iola Leroy, or, Shadows Uplifted* (1892), Kenneth W. Warren argues that Harper rejects "the values of the Gilded Age" (111), and the same claim can be extended to her earlier novel *Sowing and Reaping*. That rejection orients the political economics of the temper- ance pledge articulated repeatedly in *Sowing and Reaping*. John Anderson, the anti-hero of the novel, for all his capitalist bravado, is an anxious char- acter. When his wife asks for money for shopping and "to engage a sempt- ress,"[7] the wealthy saloon owner demurs, claiming that the "money market is very tight" and that he has "very heavy bills to meet." Mrs. Anderson is angry and disbelieving, and her husband replies:

> "Well you may believe it or not, just as you choose, but I tell you this crusading has made quite a hole in my business."
> "Now John Anderson, tell that to somebody that don't know. I don't believe this crusading has laid a finger's weight upon your business."
> "Yes it has, and if you read the paper you would find that it has even affected the revenue of the state." (167)

Harper's readers would have recognized the self-referentiality of such a passage. By the time Harper wrote *Sowing and Reaping*, she was among the WCTU leadership, and the organization had established itself as a force of cultural politics. The "crusade" to which John Anderson refers is the temperance movement itself, which began in Ohio in 1873 and, spreading nationally, had significant impact on local economies. Temperance historian Ruth Bordin argues that the curtailment of liquor sales was not nearly the most significant outcome of the crusade, which "touched off a mass movement of women that resulted in a nationwide organization with units in thousands of cities and towns, attracting tens of thousands of women members" (33). Bordin's research suggests that the participants themselves, in the words of one crusader, gained "broader views of women's sphere and responsibility" through the experience of temperance work (32). Through an extensive network of journals, meetings, conventions, fliers, correspondence, and public demonstrations, the WCTU's efforts in community mobilization challenged, to an unprecedented extent, the "doctrine of spheres," as a practice of rhetorical organization. Confronting saloon owners, accosting patrons, blocking entryways in praying, hymn-singing ranks, these women, even more so than their abolitionist predecessors, used the grounds of motherly influence as a justification for public action. By moving into market spaces and disrupting activity in the name of domestic purity, these women began what would by the end of the century become the most powerful women's organization in the nation's history.

Bordin argues that women found such a compelling field in temperance work because the general state of women's political-economic disenfranchisement was illustrated so dramatically by the "curse of intemperance." "The drunken husband," she argues, "epitomized the evils of a society in which women were second-class citizens." As late as 1900, in a majority of the United States, women possessed no rights to property, or to the guardianship of their own children. Wages earned by women were subject to the economic fortunes of their husbands. This was a particular problem for working class families positioned already in dangerously close proximity to economic ruin.[8] Widespread also were wife battering and child abuse at the hands of drunken husbands and fathers. Bordin notes that the letters and diaries of many women of the 1870s suggest "it was as victims of alcohol abuse that women were attracted to the temperance movement" (6–9). Harper repeatedly asserts the injustice of those of such degraded character possessing the right of suffrage, while "Christian women" were disenfranchised and thus denied a political agency that would allow them to protect their property, their earnings, and their children. Because reformers understood the government to be in thrall of liquor interests, temperance rhetoric represented women as entering the ranks of the enfranchised not merely as voters but as reformers of the political process itself. Thus, the temperance community not only called attention to the consequences of liquor consumption, but also demanded a reversal of deeply ingrained cultural practices, which operated within a system of mutual exclusivities: the separation between private, familial affairs and concerns of the public good; between the workings of the economy and the institutions of government.

Nancy Fraser's conceptual framework for analyzing resistant rhetorical practices within the stratified communicative networks of "late capitalist society" works well for a discussion of the nineteenth-century Afro-Protestant press. Fraser argues that "family and official economy are the principal de-politicizing enclaves that needs must exceed in order to become 'political' in the discourse sense in male-dominated, capitalist societies" (*Unruly Practices* 169). In the figure of the inebriate popularized through temperance narratives, the spheres of economy, family, and government collide. Without explicitly using the terms of rhetorical criticism, Fraser's general theory holds that such discursive transgressions are at the heart of counter-publicity (171).

Temperance arguments for women's political rights challenged the same pervasive assumptions about separate gendered spheres as Harper's broader work within women's rights organizations. Jane Flax offers a complementary account in her reading of the categorical foundations of modern conceptions of the public sphere. Flax makes a persuasive case for the domestic sphere as a feminized *other* against which a masculine public is defined, arguing that a key aspect of modernity is the "emergence of a distinctive ideology of family as the world of love / family / dependence / women and children" (78). This undifferentiated mass of familial inter-subjectivity remains a rhetorical point of masculine distinction, an ostensible force of irrationality from which they must escape, "walking alone" as rational subjects (77–78). Similarly, in Fraser's account, capitalist institutions "de-politicize certain matters by economizing them; the issues in question here are cast as impersonal market imperatives, or as 'private' ownership prerogatives . . . in contradistinction to political matters" (168). Thus the economy is posited as a network of private interests, which, according to the myth of the liberal public sphere, must be kept separate from discussion of the public good. For Harper and her temperance allies, male drunkenness proved the perfect issue for challenging such distinctions.

Harper signals the national implications of her rhetorical lessons by self-referentially setting the plot of her fictions within WCTU and American Women's Suffrage Association reform networks. The temperance idiom Harper taught linked the commonplace values of temperance, women's rights, and African American civil rights, weaving these different threads of rhetorical politics together to demonstrate all the inter-causalities within the systematic overlapping of public and private spheres. Just as the coalitional address of *Minnie's Sacrifice* negotiated factionalism within the Radical Republican initiative, *Sowing and Reaping* negotiated the split between temperance suffragettes and those women who viewed their temperance work as a strictly domestic reform. It was during the years Harper wrote *Sowing and Reaping* (1876–1877) that this split within the movement reached its most divisive point. In 1876, Frances Willard, then secretary of the WCTU, requested permission of president Annie Wittenmeyer to speak in favor of women's suffrage at the organization's Centennial Conference. Wittenmeyer refused, and Willard acquiesced but only temporarily, speaking for suffrage later that year and winning enthusiastic support from WCTU locals. Over the course of the next three years, Willard and Wittenmeyer fought for control of the organization, and in 1879, Willard unseated Wittenmeyer for president. Willard framed the women's suffrage initiative as a push for the "home protection ballot," a strategy Ruth Bordin calls "a master stroke of public relations." Lucy Stone, longtime women's rights activist, editorialized in the *Women's Journal* in 1879 that Willard's rhetoric articulated a crucial synthesis of women's domestic and political roles, one which constituted a definitive response to those who objected to women's suffrage on the basis of separate-spheres ideology. Bordin argues that it was without question the temperance movement that provided the grassroots support that would make the eventual passing of the Nineteenth Amendment possible (52–58).

Sowing and Reaping taught a suffrage lesson much in keeping with Harper's late-century writing and oratory assessing the state of civil rights for African Americans. Suffrage, while a clear right of citizenship, was but one means of affecting political change, a means entirely beholden to the more fundamental quality of character. In one of the novel's dialogues taking place in the home of Mrs. Gladstone, Harper once again articulates the political-economic imperatives of coalitional politics, negotiating the Willard–Wittenmeyer split that kept suffrage on the sidelines of temperance politics. Mrs. Gladstone argues for the centrality of women's suffrage as a counter-measure to the legal inequities that oppressed women: "I hold . . . that a nation as well as an individual should have a conscience, and on this liquor question there is room for woman's conscience not merely as a persuasive influence but as an enlightened and aggressive power" (161). Harper's readership would have recognized in the distinction between "influence" and "power," two schools of political thought.[9]

While few could deny women's domestic "influence," the politics of women's suffrage was a matter that had to be negotiated more carefully with the readership of the *Christian Recorder*. Advocacy of women's suffrage, not simply for temperance legislation, but as a part of political-economic enfranchisement, was considered to be the position of the radical fringe. While this was in fact Harper's position as well, she chose a more elliptical approach in *Sowing and Reaping*, employing a tactic of inter-publicity as a way of including and paying respect to the two different validations of women's suffrage represented by the Willard–Wittenmeyer rift. The more "radical" position is reserved for Miss Tabitha, who is the most negligible character in the novel. In the installment following Mrs. Gladstone's case for women's rights, she appears exactly long enough to deliver these lines:

"Why Mrs. Gladstone," said Miss Tabitha, "you are as zealous as a new convert to the cause of woman suffrage. We single women who are constantly taxed without being represented, know what it is to see ignorance and corruption striking hands together and voting away our money for whatever purposes they choose. I pay as large a tax as many of the men in A.P., and yet cannot say who shall assess my property for a single year."

Noting Gladstone's politicization, Tabitha likens her to a women's suffrage activist, the comparison intended by Harper to highlight the existing disconnect between women's domestic roles and radical women's politics. And yet Harper suggests the possible coalition of these women as a foil to an oppressive political economy, figured as "ignorance and corruption striking hands together." Even after this double removal of the women's suffrage issue from the sentimental economy of the novel's marriage plot, Harper was constrained to re-emphasize the "home ballot" rhetoric. Gladstone replies to Tabitha, saying that there is "another thing . . . They refuse to let us vote and yet fail to protect our homes from the ravages of rum" (162). No other character in the novel so explicitly speaks the language of "taxation without representation," that radical redeployment of republican rhetoric in a revolutionary key.

By contrast, heroine Belle Gordon articulates the temperance argument in the idioms of Christian charity, civilization, and individual character, the constitutive precepts of Protestant reform language. But it is crucial to understand that as an unmarried property holder, Miss Tabitha speaks to the broader political-economic concerns of the Willardian temperance women, drawing the inexorable connection between home and market. Harper and the temperance activists constructed a rhetorical causality from individual character—the acknowledged province of maternal concern—to the workings of the economy, what had been assumed as a masculine realm. Along this gendered axis of inter-publicity, temperance women won political recognition for issues including wife battering, child abuse, and women's suffrage (Bordin 145–148). Through Belle Gordon, Harper shows how temperance activists who might appear "softer" on suffrage were working toward the same ends of liberating women's agency as the more vocal temperance activists.

PEDAGOGICAL CHARACTERS AND DRUNKEN INDIVIDUALISM

In *Sowing and Reaping*, as in all her fiction, economic activity serves as the index of character. Belle Gordon and Paul Clifford, heroine and hero of the novel, insist on responsible business conduct. More specifically, they insist that the language of civility and the language of business be the same language. The dialogue of the novel constructs public scripts to which characters adhere. This pledge language of Gordan and Clifford serves as the primary point of constitutive identification meant to cultivate the communal inter-subjectivity of the temperance public.

Anti-hero John Anderson is the only businessman in the fictional town of A.P. who does not struggle during the "general depression in every department of trade and business," which, along with temperance activism, provides the political-economic frame of the novel (104). The reasons for Anderson's success, Harper stresses repeatedly in her temperance polemic, are his utter lack of ethical concern and the inability of addicted "customers" to resist the product. One who is a "slave to the cup" cannot resist *consumption*, neither the expenditure nor the liquor it affords. As we will see, the inebriate exists for Harper in a state of coerced abjection. As a proponent of frugality and careful investment—this being central to her steadfast commitment to free labor ideology and to the uplift of an impoverished people—she espoused non-participation within the cycle of personal accumulation and consumption encouraged by corrupt economic interests.

The most repeated question in the novel's dialogue—"How is business?"—is not simply a question of the bottom line. It is, in fact, a question of civic morality that drives Harper's polemic, with the problem of inter-subjective influence informing its ontological perspective. The novel opens with a dialogue between Anderson and Paul Clifford, the only son of a widow "whose young life had been overshadowed by the curse of intemperance." Her husband, "a man of splendid abilities and magnificent culture . . . was laid away the wreck of his former self in a drunkards grave."[10] The opening dialogue between these moral antipodes establishes the political opposition that constitutes the ethos of the novel. John Anderson is the mouthpiece of the opposing script of drunken individualism. He chides Clifford, who has refused to foreclose on a mortgage he is owed and thus lost a substantial sum, for his "moonstruck theories, some wild visionary and impracticable ideas." Clifford's generosity, which he sees as an "investment," flies in the face of Anderson's constitutive rationale, which rests on such tautologies of the market as "'business is business.'" Many of Anderson's platitudes appear in quotation marks, highlighting the cultural commonsense text of laissez-faire liberalism from which he cites, what Harper named at the close of *Minnie's Sacrifice* "one type of the barbarous and anti-social state" (92). Harper frames Anderson's language as espousal of the capitalist creed, highlighting the way those of Anderson's ilk employ their own constitutive precepts to rationalize self-serving economic behavior; thus we can detect the defensiveness in the satirical exaggeration of his character. Within a page, Anderson justifies his actions repeatedly—"business is business" and "My motto is to look out for Number One" and "I believe in every man looking out for himself." As if this were not a clear enough emphasis on the interpolating ideology producing Anderson's language, Harper's narrator stresses that Anderson is a subject of belief, asserting that "there is one article of faith that moulds and colors all his life more than anything else, it is a firm and unfaltering belief in the 'main chance.' He has made up his mind to be rich, and his highest ideal of existence may be expressed in four words—*getting on in life*" (96–99).

Harper taught against the social isolationism of this economic rationale in her earlier fiction as well. In the "Fancy Sketches" published in the *Christian Recorder* from 1871 to 1874, the character of Aunt Jane delivers the preceptive script of uplift economics as a practice of daily life. Aunt Jane, like many of Harper's pedagogical heroines, speaks against the tide of prevailing custom and opinion, adhering to a creed of non-conformity. In the 1873 sketch "Dangerous Economies," Aunt Jane harangues her niece Jenny, who is on her way to a dressmaker, one, Jenny notes, who "works very cheaply [because] she is quiet, poor, and very anxious for work." Aunt Jane suggests that both Jenny's adherence to fashion and her desire to give the dressmaker even "25 cents less than her work was worth" are an ethical failure. Aunt Jane must argue carefully, though, before Jenny takes her words to heart. "I don't know what you mean," Jenny tells her aunt, "your words are a riddle to me." This confusion, represented as an undeveloped political literacy, is typical of the subjects of persuasion represented in Harper's rhetorical dramas. Aunt Jane's lesson continues as the recalcitrant Jenny continues to attempt rationalizations for her errant economic behavior:

> "But Aunty, doesn't everybody try to have their work done as cheaply as possible?"
>
> "No, Jenny, not everyone. I have given a number of times a larger sum for work than was demanded, because I thought the work was worth more."
>
> "Well, Aunty, I guess that you are an exception."
>
> "I hope not, Jenny. I am not conceited enough to think that I am better than my neighbors."
>
> "But Aunty, are not such people the best judges of their own business? I should think that Mrs. Anderson knows better than I do on what terms she can afford to make dresses."
>
> "I suppose she does, but Mrs. Anderson has too many hungry mouths to feed to run the risk of losing her work by chaffering about prices."

According to her aunt's preceptive script, Jenny's economic assumptions are an ethical failing in need of reform. Jenny's petitions to her aunt attempt to normalize the creed of economic individualism, but Aunt Jane's responses make it clear that poverty negates such agency in actual practice. She ultimately suggests a different configuration of social responsibility, asking, "[W]ouldn't we better serve humanity by striving to save women from falling?" (1).

As in "Fancy Sketches," the character talk of *Sowing and Reaping* foregrounds questions of self-control and collective responsibility derived from the Protestant practices of self-management. In the following passage, Harper constructs familial and civic causalities surrounding the actions of uncontrolled inebriates. Thomas Cary has just explained how drink has ruined not only himself, but also his son who "drank himself into the grave"; this plot line, in which alcoholism is a paternal "curse," proliferates in the novel:

> By this time two or three loungers had gathered around John Anderson and Thomas Cary, and one of them said, "Mr. Cary you have had sad experiences, why don't you give up drinking yourself?"
>
> "Give it up! Because I can't! To-day I would give one half of my farm if I could pass by this saloon and not feel that I wanted to come in. No, I feel that I am a slave. There was a time when I could have broken my chain, but it is too late now, and I say young men take warning by me and don't make slaves and fools of yourselves."
>
> "Now, Tom Cary," said John Anderson, "it is time for you to dry up, we have had enough of this foolishness, if you can't govern yourself, the more's the pity for you." (134)

Liquor tycoon John Anderson's exhortation regarding the "foolishness" of drunkard Thomas Cary is characteristic of the defensiveness with which Harper consistently marks the character's speech. To let Cary's figurative lament go unchallenged would place Anderson in the position analogous to a slave trader. Seeking to deflect such associations, Anderson shifts the burden of agency to Cary himself, ascribing the fate of a drunkard to an individual failing—"if you can't govern yourself, the more's the pity for you." Harper's pedagogy demands a pledge of duty to the very social values of commonality and interconnectedness rejected by Anderson.[11]

This anatomy of individual will and economic force is punctuated tellingly by the intrusion of a news seller carrying a paper with the sensationalist headline, "LOVE, JEALOUSY, AND MURDER," a story about John Coots's murder of a rival suitor vying for the affections of Lizzie Wilson. Several patrons of Anderson's saloon note that Coots has "been here a half dozen times today." But Anderson does not want to acknowledge that the drunkenness Coots purchased in his establishment "nerv'd the hand" of the murderer. When he reads the headline, Anderson, "looking somewhat relieved," says, "The old story . . . A woman's at the bottom of it" (145). He classifies this violence as a domestic issue, relegating it to the private sphere to mask his complicity. Cary reiterates his critique of liquor's influence when he says in response, "And liquor . . . At the top of it." A scowling Anderson replies defensively, "I wish you would keep a civil tongue in your head." By offering the newspaper account instead of a fuller narration of the story of the murder, Harper eschews the "mainstream" of sensationalist temperance literature[12] and, in the process, represents the death and immorality associated with intemperance as a matter of public debate, forcing her readers to understand themselves as participants in the production of social knowledge.[13]

As in all her fiction, Harper here juxtaposes divergent practices of moral character. Clifford, Harper's antipode to the "barbarous" circularity of Anderson's worldview, "believes in lending a helping hand . . . [and] was the only son of a widow, whose young life had been overshadowed by the curse of intemperance." Clifford's mother was widowed when her husband died of alcoholism, "victim to the wine cup," and with "the remains of what had been an ample fortune," she moved to "an unpretending home" and "watched over and superintended the education of her only son." This is the first of many such scenarios presented in the novel; in the representation of motherly anxiety, we see how the "curse" of drunkenness is a paternal lineage in Harper's polemic. Clifford's mother has this perspective on her son's character as he grows to manhood:

> He was a promising boy, full [of] life and vivacity, having inherited much of the careless joyousness of his father's temperament; and although he was the light and joy of his home, yet his mother sometimes felt as if her heart was contracting with a spasm of agony, when she remembered that it was through that same geniality of disposition and wonderful fascination of manner, the tempter had woven his meshes for her husband, and that the qualities that made him so desirable at home, made him equally so to his jovial, careless, inexperienced companions. Fearful that the appetite for strong drink might have been transmitted to her child as a fatal legacy of sin, she sedulously endeavored to develop within him self control, feeling that the lack of it is a prolific cause of misery and crime, and she spared no pains to create within his mind a horror of intemperance, and when he was old enough to understand the nature of a vow, she knelt with him in earnest prayer, and pledging him to eternal enmity against everything that would intoxicate, whether fermented or distilled. (98–99)

There is, then, something of a thorn in the rose regarding the characterological disposition of the potential drunkard. It is, paradoxically, the very disposition that makes a boy "the light and joy of his home" that fits him for alcohol addiction as he moves out of the domestic sphere and away from the influence of the home. This charm was also that of the father who had devastated the family. Therefore, the temperance pledge, as a coming-of-age rite, guards against further generations of drunkenness and its terrible costs. Clearly this is a pledge against outside influence, one of characterological intentionality. In this generational narrative, the notion of "self-control" mediates the very relationship between individual and society.

Self-control is always performed through a double renunciation of both liquor and the logic of laissez-faire in Harper's temperance writing. In this paradigm, then, John Anderson is out of control on both fronts, and this reversal of expectations (given his wealth, Anderson would seem to be the most self-determing of all the novel's characters) hinges on the representation of Anderson's speaking style. Harper impugns his ability to participate in rational discussion. Readers are cued to this subtle bit of satire by Anderson's position as the dupe in another dialogue with Clifford. Upon their second meeting, Anderson offers as salutation, "How is business?" and Clifford, noting the national economic crisis, responds, "Very dull, I am losing terribly . . . Confidence has been greatly shaken, men of . . . business have grown exceedingly timid about investing." Anderson, who still has not gleaned Clifford's ethical business philosophy and his staunch position on temperance, makes him a proposition:

> "Now Paul will you listen to reason and common sense? I have a proposition to make. I am about to embark in a profitable business, and I know that it will pay better than any thing else I could undertake in these times. Men will buy liquor if they have not got money for other things. I am going to open a first class saloon, and club-house, on M. Street, and if you will join with me we can make a splendid thing of it. Why just see how well off Joe Harden is since he set up in the business; and what airs he does put on! I know when he was not worth fifty dollars, and kept a little low groggery on the corner on L. and S. Streets, but he is out of that now—keeps a first class Cafe, and owns a block of houses . . . Of course I mean to keep a first class saloon. I don't intend to tolerate loafing, or disorderly conduct, or to sell to drunken men. In fact, I shall put up my scale of prices so that you need fear no annoyance from rough, low, boisterous men who don't know how to behave themselves. What say you, Paul? (104–105)

Anderson's observation, that "[m]en will buy liquor when they have not got money for other things," identifies the drunkard's lack of agency as an article of faith for the capitalist; the drunkard's unwitting participation in his own exploitation is borne out as a sad truth by the rest of the novel. As in their first meeting, Anderson builds his argument on the logic of economic privacy, upholding the precept of the fundamental separation between capitalist enterprise and the public good. Clifford, in his vociferous refusal, negates the basic assumption of Anderson's logic, asserting, "I wouldn't engage in such business, not if it paid me a hundred thousand dollars a year."

In her preceptive delivery, Harper further demonstrates the debasement of Anderson's character by endowing him with a conformist rhetorical style that seeks self-justification in the like behavior of others. Anderson uses, as a means of persuasion, the story of Joe Harden's accumulation of wealth and property, and he assures Clifford that his too will be a "first class saloon," one which will prohibit "rough, low boisterous men who don't know how to behave themselves." Clifford dismisses the idea that bourgeois punctiliousness justifies unethical business, calling the liquor trade a "conspiracy of sin against the peace, happiness and welfare of the community." In this way, he shifts the terms of the disagreement from those of profit to those of civic good in order to expose the relation of whiskey interests to the interests of citizens. While Harden's success takes him from ownership of a "little low groggery" to a "first class saloon," the "demoralizing influence" of such a business within a community is stressed repeatedly in Harper's work. Harper's narrator disrupts the dialogue to frame with authority the characterological underpinnings of the communication gap between these two antipodes:

> You may think it strange that knowing Paul Clifford as John Anderson did, that he should propose to him an interest in a drinking saloon; but John Anderson was a man who was almost destitute of faith in human goodness. His motto was that "every man has his price," and as business was fairly dull, and Paul was somewhat cramped for want of capital, he thought a good business investment would be the price for Paul Clifford's conscientious scruples. (105)

Harper emphasizes again Anderson's logic as a learned set of platitudes— "every man has his price." We see also that in his skeptical estimation of Clifford's ethics, Anderson understands the other man in the narrow terms of his own megalomaniacal greed. For Anderson, a man's character is merely the embodiment of a certain economic worth; like every "man," Anderson reasons, Clifford will have "his price." Thus, Anderson is simply unable to take Clifford at his word. Anderson is both villain and fool in Harper's novel, a mean dupe whose folly jeopardizes his own well-being and degrades the public good. The irrationality, then, of greed and drunkenness becomes a liminal zone between public and private, driven by a reckless consumption ethic masked as the "personal interests" running the liquor trade. Anderson, the powerful but vapid capitalist drone, operates outside the classic republican rhetoric of a rational and democratically deliberated public good, an isolation that eventually ruins his family, cuts his own life short, and jeopardizes the well-being of citizens at large.

Harper constructs her equation of individual will as both cause and effect of civic reality, and suggests that it is the regulation of desire that can counteract the effects of the drunken economy. Harper makes this point in further characterizing Clifford's business ethics. In the eighth installment of *Sowing and Reaping*, Clifford's grocery business is about to be foreclosed on and liquidated by the bank. The resolve of his temperance economics is put to the test, as "less than an hour" before foreclosure, Clifford recalls Anderson's proposal, only to dismiss it in principled pledge language— "[Anderson's] money is the price of blood." In a moment of didactic coincidence, the son of Charles Smith, the man whose debt Clifford previously forgave, arrives fifteen minutes before the close of the business day. In fact, the revelatory conversation between the two must wait for Clifford to return from making the bank deposit where he is told that he is "just in time." The coincidence deepens as they talk. When Clifford expresses his surprise over Smith's newfound resolve in paying the family debt, he credits "the blessed influence of my sainted mother." Thus Harper gives another instantiation of how the maternal pedagogy produces the self-control required for ethical personal conduct in the public sphere.

In this chapter's final section, we see how Harper further dramatizes the interdependence of domestic affairs and economic behavior, as she elaborates her broadly humanizing pedagogy through her representation of marriage. Maintaining a pedagogical distinction between the public and private spheres, *Sowing and Reaping* was Harper's most concentrated lesson on the difference between market-based marriage contracts and the bonds of affection pledged by committed reform partners.

SENTIMENTAL INEBRIATION: A POLITICS OF MARRIAGE

The "ideal beings" of *Sowing and Reaping*, like those of *Minnie's Sacrifice*, prove their worth through skill as moral suasionists and thus serve the pedagogical function of exemplifying reform rhetoric as a way of life. The structure of the novel itself, as it brings heroine and hero together, encourages readers to compare their complementary, if traditionally gendered, pedagogical characters. The first four installments alternate between the Anderson–Clifford plot line and the relationship of heroine Belle Gordon to her cousin Jeanette Roland. The first installment, governed by the ethically inflected question "How is business?" positions the circular privatizing logic of Anderson against the de-privatizing pledge language of Clifford. In the second installment of the novel, titled "The Decision," Harper introduces Gordon and Roland in a characterological juxtaposition that compares tellingly with Clifford and Anderson. Gordon, like Clifford, is the child of a drunkard, a woman who through experience has become unwavering on the temperance question. Both speak from the script of pledge language in memory of a history of loss, and each strictly refuses to adhere to the "common sense" of the social dilemmas with which they are presented. Just as Anderson accused Clifford of "visionary and impracticable ideas," Roland accuses Gordon of being a "monomaniac on the temperance question," asserting that her political-ethical position "is very fine in theory . . . but you would find it rather difficult if you tried to reduce your theory to practice" (103).

This same ethical disconnect appears repeatedly in Harper's texts, as characters attempt to explain their beliefs to one another. In fact, Gordon has just so recently put her "theory to practice" in making her decision not to marry Charles Romaine, whom she admittedly loves. Jeanette Roland asks incredulously if the gossip is true, if Gordon has rejected Romaine because of "some squeamish notions on the subject of temperance." Gordon confirms this, saying, "I feel that the hands of a moderate drinker are not steady enough to hold my future happiness." Roland is bewildered by her cousin's "release" of Romaine, calling her "an enigma." Her inability to understand Gordon's rejection of the wealthy Romaine's "excellent offer of marriage," what amounts to a "splendid opportunity," is analogous to Anderson's confusion over Clifford's unwillingness to foreclose. Roland, like Anderson, cannot think outside the terms of the market. It is also clear that she inhabits her inscribed gender role through both her understanding of marriage as an economic contract and her own negligible agency within that contract. "My dear cousin," she informs Gordon, "it is not my role to be a reformer. I take things as I find them and drift along the tide of circumstance." She is incredulous at Gordon's assertion that "God never made one code of ethics for a man and another for a woman," an assertion consistent with Clifford's own professions of gender equality. While Gordon vows her life will be one of "consecration, endeavor and achievement," Roland, on the other hand, claims she would rather "be a butterfly born in a bower," offering a sentimental and de-humanizing self-representation, one which figures a lack of any will to resist and thus provides a characterological counterpoint for Harper's non-conformist ethos. Roland ends the conversation speculatively: "Well, Belle, should we live twenty years longer, I would like to meet you and see by comparing notes which of us shall have gathered the most sunshine or shadow" (99–103).

This narrative is a recasting of Harper's first known fiction, the short story "The Two Offers," published in the *Weekly Anglo African Magazine* in 1859 and discussed at length in Chapter One. As we first saw, in this story Harper introduced the satirical dialogue that came to characterize her novels and "sketches." Melba Joyce Boyd characterizes this polemical fiction as one employed "in an integrative capacity with the women's movement through the Woman's Christian Temperance Union" (202); it is through the *topoi* of the drunken economy that Harper performs this particular negotiation of agendas. As we know, "The Two Offers" opens with Laura LaGrange comparing the merits of two marriage proposals. Her cousin, Janette Alston, offers the advice that "a woman who is undecided between two offers, has not love enough for either . . . lest her marriage, instead of being an affinity of souls or a union of hearts, should be a mere matter of bargain and sale, or an affair of convenience and selfish interests." Her story becomes yet another refrain in Harper's portrait of the victimhood of intemperance: Laura's fear of becoming an "old maid" propels a doomed marriage to a man whose "headlong career" in the saloon figures Laura as the quintessential neglected wife, even while on her deathbed. The narration is dominated by the preceptive logic of Janette, an unmarried woman in the prime of her life who, by the end of the story, has become, like Harper herself, a successful writer dedicated to progressive causes including abolitionism:

She would willingly espouse an unpopular cause but not an unrigh-
teous one. In her the down-trodden slave found an earnest advocate;
the flying fugitive remembered her kindness as he stepped cautiously
through our Republic, to gain his freedom in a monarchical land . . .
Her life was like a beautiful story, only it was clothed with the dignity
of reality and invested with the sublimity of truth. True, she was an old
maid; no husband brightened her life with his love, or shaded it with
his neglect . . . she learned one of life's most precious lessons, that true
happiness consists not so much in the fruition of our wishes as in the
regulation of desires and the full development and right culture of our
whole natures. (313)

Through her commitment to "the regulation of desires," Janette embodies Harper's ideal moral character; conversely, it is the unregulated desire
of the market that generates the tragedy of Harper's fiction. For women,
as legal and political appendages of men, the marriage contract requires
complicity with the "barbarous and anti-social state." Laura, like Roland
in *Sowing and Reaping*, can only see marriage in market terms, "a mere
matter of bargain and sale, or an affair of convenience and selfish interest"
(109). For his part, Laura's husband, like John Anderson, "looked upon
marriage not as a divine sacrament for the soul's development and human
progression, but as the title-deed that gave him possession of the woman he
thought he loved" ("The Two Offers" 290).

In both fictions, these coercive economies of marriage end in sentimental tragedy. Laura LaGrange dies of a "sickness of the soul," the result
of the "unkindness and neglect of her husband" and grief at their child's
death, a scene in which Harper recasts her poem of 1854, "The Drunkard's Child." In both texts, the drunken father returns from the saloon just
in time for the sentimental death of the child, and this conceit is repeated
a third time in *Sowing and Reaping* when the Romaines' child dies. In
the progression of this rewriting, Harper rejects sentimental conversion in
favor of a more skeptical scenario. In "The Drunkard's Child," the power
of the sentimental death wins the father back to temperance, but in "The
Two Offers," LaGrange is only temporarily stayed from the path of familial destruction, which eventuates the death of his wife. By the time of
Sowing and Reaping's treatment of this plot line, the drunkard, Romaine,
returns from the saloon in time to simply witness the death helplessly. The
child is not, as was the case in the two previous texts, given final words
that rationalize the tragedy toward persuasive ends; there is instead mute-
ness as Harper suspends all redemption. The increasing skepticism suggested by the revision of the sentimental trope, is a function of the more
fully elaborated ethos of economic causality, which underwrote Harper's
rhetorical pedagogy for the entirety of her career. As we have seen, drunkenness is a paternal curse, with upper-class drunkenness an "inheritance"
just as surely as is paternal privilege.

Pursuing her long-standing project of training parents as themselves trainers of character, Harper crafted *Sowing and Reaping* as a characterological pedagogy of domestic influence and familial culture. We learn of LaGrange's father that he

> had been "too much engrossed in making money, and his mother in spending it, in striving to maintain a fashionable position in society, and shining in the eyes of the world, to give the proper direction to the character of their wayward and impulsive son. . . . [I]n his home, a love for the good, the true and the right, had been sacrificed at the shrine of frivolity and fashion. That parental authority which should have been preserved as a string of precious pearls, unbroken and unscattered, was simply the administration of chance. (110)

Harper's construction of the Romaines' paternal line posits the drunkard's curse as a matter of improper familial economics and affections. Romaine and his father are literally business partners, and Romaine senior, aghast at his son's erratic behavior and fiscal irresponsibility, resolves to "dissolve partnership with Charles," vowing, for the sake of his business, "our reputation has been unspotted and I mean to keep it so, if I have to cut off my right hand." Putting on a brave face, Romaine junior replies, "Whenever the articles of dissolution are made out I am ready to sign." After assuring his son that the papers will be ready the next day, he leaves the room, and Romaine junior collapses in shame and anger:

> Charles sat, burying his head in his hands and indulging bitter thoughts toward his father. "To-day," he said to himself, "he resolved to cut loose from me apparently forgetting that it was from his hands, and at his table I received my first glass of wine. He prides himself on his power of self-control, and after all what does it amount to? It simply means this, that he has an iron constitution, and can drink five times as much as I can without showing its effects, and to-day if Mr. R.N. would ask him to sign the total-abstinence pledge, he wouldn't hear to it. Ye[t] I am ready to sign any articles he will bring, even if it is to sign never to enter this house, or see his face." (146)

Here the temperance pledge is starkly juxtaposed with the papers of dispossession—the divergent social scripts that structure the novel as a whole. Charles must sign as his father uses the authority of legal business contracts even in his family relations. His son understands it as banishment. Romaine senior has chosen the contractual text of unbridled capitalism over the pledge language of temperance reform.

The power of pledge language to stem such unregulated desire and to organize the subaltern counter-public is most dramatically illustrated through *Sowing and Reaping*'s story of Josiah and Mary Gough. The story

of the redemption of Josiah Gough is the archetype of the pledge confes-
sional disseminated by the temperance counter-public.[14] Far and away, the
most well known of these narratives was John Bartholomew Gough's *Autobiography*. It seems likely that Harper chose the name of her own character to evoke the celebrity of the preceding text, so that the reader might
understand her own participation in a long-standing cultural movement.
Whatever the politics of citationality here, it is the way in which (Harper's) Gough, the very figure of abject drunkenness, enables the economic
pedagogy of the novel that is here most noteworthy. Indeed, the generic
structure is tellingly different from Washingtonian temperance narratives
such as Gough's *Autobiography*, which are characterized by their sensationalism and histrionics.[15] It takes more than an overwhelming emotional
experience to save the drunkard in Harper's text: the redemption of Josiah
Gough depends on an entire reordering of political economy.

We are introduced to the Gough home through the temperance relief
work of Belle Gordon. Gordon ministers to Mary Gough, who has col-
lapsed on her way home from work. "It all seems like a dream to me,"
Gough recalls from her sickbed: "I was carrying a large bundle of work to
the store . . . my employer spoke harshly to me and talked of cutting down
my wages, my eyes were almost blinded with tears, and I felt a dizziness in
my head" (127). This woman has worked for a cruel boss to the point of
exhaustion, we are told, because her husband is a drunkard who is unable
to find work amid the depression and spends every cent his wife makes in
"Jim Green's saloon." Upon a return visit, Gordon is shocked by a change
in Mary Gough's appearance. "Do tell me what has happened and what has
become of your beautiful hair, oh you had such a wealth of tresses." Mary
Gough relays her story of subjection:

> Last night my husband, or the wreck of what was once my husband,
> came home. His eyes were wild and bloodshot; his face as pale and
> haggard, his gait uneven, and his hand trembled . . . He held in his
> hand a pair of shears, and approached my bedside. I was ready to faint
> with terror, when he exclaimed, "Mary I must have liquor or I shall go
> wild," he caught my hair in his hand . . . and in a few minutes he had
> cut every lock from my head . . . (131)

This shocking image of violence casts drunkenness as the disposition of
wanton consumption, one that necessitates an avaricious accumulation and
directly impacts women's lives and well-being. This private shame and the
economy that supports it are posited as evidence in the case for the reconstruction of the public good as Mary Gough's lament closes the installment.
"Oh, Miss Gordon, do you think the men who make our laws ever stop to
consider the misery, crime and destruction that flow out of the liquor traffic? I have done all I could to induce him to abstain" (132).

Mary Gough's plight, of course, is meant to elicit the reader's sympathy and outrage, but the rhetorical drama as a whole offers readers heuristics for making economic sense of those sentiments. What is perhaps most striking in Harper's portrayal are the pains she takes to put the woman's fate in an economic context. Readers are reminded of the depression through reference to Joe Gough's unemployment, and we are led to believe that anxiety over her to-be-reduced wages has attributed considerably to her collapse. Also, it is her meditation on the civic destruction of the "liquor traffic" that leads her to understand the limits of her own individual powers of matronly persuasion. When Gordon suggests that Mary Gough might find extra work as a seamstress working for one "Mrs. Roberts," Gough explains that she has worked for the woman in the past and that the experience was "unprofitable." Gordon defends Roberts, with whom she is acquainted through their mutual middle-class milieu: "But Mrs. Gough, the times are very hard; and the rich feel it as well as the poor." Gough makes short work of refuting this rather naïve assumption, noting that different versions of privation exist in different economic classes; it is the difference between doing without "luxuries" for Roberts and "necessities" for Gough. Gough recounts that Roberts, seeing that she was desperate for income, drove an excessively hard bargain, according to the logic of supply and demand: "I can get it done for one dollar . . . and I am not willing to give any more." Gordon is surprised by this news, noting, "I know [Roberts] pays her dressmaker handsomely." Gough replies,

> That is because her dressmaker is in a situation to dictate her own terms; but while she would pay her large sum for dressmaking, she would screw and pinch a five-cent piece from one who hadn't power to resist her demands. I have seen people save twenty-five or fifty cents in dealing with poor people, who would squander ten times as much on some luxury of the table or wardrobe. I . . . often find that meanness and extravagance go hand in hand. (129–131)

Gough's explanation recapitulates almost identically the economic morality tale of "Dangerous Economies." Just as Aunt Jane instructs Jenny, Belle Gordon surmises, "I think people often act like Mrs. Roberts more from want of thought than want of heart" (131). Thus, in spite of Gough's indictment, Harper provides pathways of sensibility and change for readers who might identify their own unjust economic actions in the novel. While more than one critic has taken Harper to task for what could be taken as capitulation to middle-class sensibilities, we might note the degree to which Harper disrupts the readerly expectations of the genre in which she works. Gordon, clearly marked as the sentimental heroine, is not, in fact, the voice of moral authority in this instance. It is rather the impoverished Mary Gough who teaches the younger woman that her laissez-faire script

has very definite ethical limits. Ironically, the "want of thought" Gordon
ascribes to Roberts is, in fact, her own. The sentimental subjectivities of
the Goughs provide Harper with the teaching figures for the temperance
counter-public and teach the precepts of economic morality as a *sine qua
non* of unconstrained civil rights. Clifford, coincidentally, is a grocer near
the Gough's neighborhood, and is enlisted by Gordon in her redemptive
efforts. As we have seen, Clifford, literally, *speaks for* the possibility of
ethical business, and in keeping with this promise, he offers Joe Gough a
position once the latter has taken "the pledge."

Affections between Clifford and Gordon grow as the moral character of
each proves the natural compliment of the other.[16] Clifford, it is apparent
to all onlookers, quickly falls in love with Gordon, who represents the ideal
of his mother's own pledge morality. The night Joe Gough takes the pledge,
as Clifford leaves the Gough's tenement, Gordon bids him goodbye, saying,
"This is glorious work in which it is our privilege to clasp hands." The love-
struck man responds,

> "It is and I hope," but as the words rose to his lips, he looked into the
> face of Belle, and it was so radiant with intelligent tenderness and joy
> that she seemed to him a glorified saint, a being too precious for com-
> mon household uses, and so the remainder of the sentence died upon
> his lips and he held his peace. (144)

The decision to marry is fraught in Harper's fiction, and the pedagogical
script of this ambivalence carries pedagogical force, grounding the instruction on the commonplace language of critical courtship. Harper's temperance fiction represents a moment of social fidelity infinitely more expansive
that the romantic love among individuals. Much rides on the negotiation of
men and women entering into a marriage contract. After all, that all men
are potential drunkards, which in the rhetoric of the coalitional address
means that all men are potential abusers and economic subjugators. Eventually, however, Clifford does propose, and in subsequent conversations,
Gordon tells Clifford that she has learned to live without the "daydream"
of romantic love since the pain of Charles Romaine's descent. Clifford
assures Gordon that he would be happy without "the first love of a fresh
young heart" (159). When finally married—the courtship is narrated in less
than a paragraph—their relationship is articulated in terms, still, of moral
education. "[Gordon] taught her sons to be as upright in their lives and as
pure in their conversation as she would have her daughters, recognizing for
each only one code of morals" (175).

This philosophy of parenting clearly runs counter to the domestic world
of the Andersons, in which desire and the exercise of character go unregulated. Thomas Cary's story of the ruination of father and son, a narrative
Anderson sought to censure, proves prophetic as the lesson promised by
the novel's title arrives. Harper offered readers of the final installment this

way back into the story. A doctor lectures Anderson, who has taken to his sick bed: "I cannot ensure your life a single hour, unless you quit business. You are liable to be stricken with paralysis at any moment, if . . . subject to the [least] excitement. Can't you trust your business in the hands of your sons?" (170). Harper's didactic plotting pursues this question dramatically. Before Anderson can respond, even to bemoan his son Frank's drunken irresponsibility, a servant calls from the younger man's room: "Mr. Frank's acting mightily queer; he thinks there are snakes and lizards crawling over him." Within moments of each other, the Anderson men die, the younger of drink and the older, literally, a victim of his drive to profit. The reversal of fortunes between Anderson and Gough witnesses not only the respective demise and redemption of two characters, but also vindicates the alternative economics espoused by Harper's community of temperance reformers.

Harper shows us that Anderson is himself subject to the barbaric economy he propagates. For Gough, the impoverished worker who is "true to his pledge" of citizenship within the alternative institutions of temperance reform, "plenty and comfort have taken the place of poverty and pain" (174). Gordon and Clifford's marriage alliance, consummated in community activism, signal Harper's hope for the generational continuance and growth of the temperance public, which is to say, the reformation of the state through the efforts of women's ethical judgment and leadership.

4 Black Ireland

The Political Economics of African American Rhetorical Pedagogy after Reconstruction

In *Race Adjustment,* his landmark 1909 assessment of the so-called "negro question," African American social critic Kelly Miller cites British historian Edward A. Freeman's comment that in the "Aryan country" he saw about him, "very many approved when I suggested that the best remedy for whatever was amiss would be if every Irishman should kill a negro and be hanged for it" (139). Freeman recorded this in his 1883 travel narrative, *Some Impressions of the United States,* and the genocidal logic of his witticism registers in race-national terms Freeman's antipathy toward the rebellious Irish under British colonial rule. Freeman's comment is a fair sample of the white nativism that confronted both African and Irish Americans as the groups vied for employment, housing, and other resources made scarce by economic competition and racial-ethnic discrimination. By the time Miller and Freeman wrote, the precedent of Irish American violence against African Americans was tragically well established.[1] Competitors for economic and social status throughout the nineteenth century, African and Irish Americans were famously hostile to one another, vying perhaps as trenchantly for the rhetorical resources of characterological virtue within the processes of race and class distinction. Inciting riot mobs and racial exclusion in the labor market, Irish American workers policed the color line claiming white privilege and racial superiority For their own part, African American rhetors defamed Celtic character in the most disparaging terms.

The record of mutual character assassination should be read in all its rhetorical complexity. After Reconstruction, Harper found in the Irish a versatile didactic tool with resonant heuristic force. Reference to the Irish, to their resistance to British colonialism and their fortunes as immigrants in North America, established a set of comparative precepts by which Harper could teach what Eddie Glaude calls "nation language" (79–81). The drama of persuasion unfolding in *Trial and Triumph* represents character talk in its day-to-day function as the constitutive discursive practice of social commitment and racial uplift. Set in the northern city of "A.P.," and published serially in the *Christian Recorder* in 1888 and 1889, the novel tells multiple, intersecting stories of the color line in which the Irish and other immigrant groups figure prominently. Like her earlier fictions, this novel consists of a series of arguments that model the crucial, quotidian rhetorical practices meant to sustain African American nationhood amid the broader political and economic contingencies of the late century. Each installment of the novel, which as a whole can fairly be called meandering, finds its drama in the "trials" of African American characters who struggle to succeed economically and ethically in their commitments to each other despite the compressed opportunities of the post-Reconstruction racial state.[2]

The precepts of committed character talk are most often articulated through the character of Mrs. Lasette, whose readiness to instruct nearly anyone she encounters on a range of topics makes her the figure of mother wit and wisdom in A.P. It is said of Lasette that she "is true as steel, the kind of woman you can tie to." Her virtues as an advocate for the poor, for women's education, for race pride, and for temperance lead her neighbors to wish for "ten thousand like her" (232). To be sure, this wish announces the race-national intentionality of the narrative as a work of rhetorical pedagogy, a mechanism for reproducing from subject to subject the virtues meant to serve as bonds of collectivity. The many dialogues in the novel put Harper's precepts in the mouths of characters facing dilemmas of race and gender oppression in everyday contexts. These rhetorical devices for delivering social messages of uplift, race pride, and protest function to situate knowledge that could ground further rhetorical action. More pointedly than any of her other fictions, *Trial and Triumph* aims at teaching conversation as a rhetorical craft, and it is Lasette who Harper constructs with consistant pedagogical intention.

> Mrs. Lasette was a fine conversationalist. She regarded speech as one of heaven's best gifts, and thought that conversation should be made one of the finest arts, and used to subserve the highest and best purposes of life . . . "Speech," she would say, "is a gift so replete with rich and joyous possibilities," and she always tried to raise the tone of conversation at home and abroad. (199–200)

In this pedagogical statement, the power of conversational "possibilities" is understood to be persuasive and, to be sure, the great common source of a constitutive racial solidarity. To be a "fine conversationalist" entailed using a pledge language intended to be circulated and shared. The art of conversation as practiced by the eloquent rhetors of the novel opens possibilities for employment and education on the color line and ultimately serves the moral and economic interests of the community, uplifting and uplifted as a collective. Harper's didactic fiction teaches readers of the *Christian Recorder* how they ought to receive the fiction as a matter of race-national discipline.

Trial and Triumph continues the progressive historicism of her temperance work surveyed in the previous chapter, promoting the vision of a progressive era inspired by women's judgment and rhetoric as a world-reforming force within the racial state. Advocating the most crucial means to this end, Mrs. Lasette's promotion of female education as essential politically. The character of Mr. Thomas also advocates for this cause. The preceptive script of Mr. Thomas, Lasette's masculine counterpart, is a model of knowing what to say and when to say it. Rhetorical skill is the core of Harper's pedagogical characterization that ranks these figures among her pantheon of heroes and heroines. Thomas is, no less than Lasette, an integrative, persuasive force within A.P. and by extension within a national African American community. Trained as both a teacher and a carpenter, Thomas plies both crafts in the construction of African American A.P. This pair of preceptive characters echo the preceptive statements of Harper's oratory and essay. Together, they constitute a pedagogy that, while seemingly assigning traditionally gendered rhetorical duties, serves more to blur the hegemonic binary of male (public) persuasion and female (private) influence. In the political imagination of African American women's writing in the North, the progress of nationhood relies equally on a range of discursive practices as "the public comes to infiltrate and inhabit the domestic" (Peterson, *Doers* 126).

With Lasette and Thomas, a third character completes the matrix of the novel's rhetorical pedagogy, Annette Harcourt, and the way she is received serves as an index of race-national feeling, a prototype of the characterological geography that underlies the process of uplift. Harcourt, the young heroine of the novel, is burdened, like all of Harper's teaching heroines, with the bias, obstructionism, and discouragement of masculine society as well as with the responsibility of the duty-bound language of racial solidarity. An orphan being raised by her grandmother, Harcourt acts and speaks in ways both laudable and wayward, making her behavior and prospects the primary subject of debate among the novel's many characters, including her teachers, neighbors, and classmates. To them, Harcourt's promise holds potential consequences for the community of A.P. and the racial progress of the post-Reconstruction state. We learn of Harcourt that she "early developed a love for literature and poetry" and "would sometimes try to make rhymes and string verses together," compositions that in Mrs. Lasette estimation revealed "talent or even poetic genius." The latent worth and utility of Harcourt's talent is not lost on Lasette who "ardently wished that it might be cultivated and rightly directed"—trained, in other words, to "set young hearts to thrilling with higher hopes and loftier aspirations." The instruction of Harcourt in this constitutive manner, her incorporation into the intersubjective chain of edifying influence, is the primary point of pedagogical identification in the novel. However, even in the society of her own family, Harcourt's potential languishes unrecognized. Harcourt's "grandmother and aunts" were, we learn, oblivious to the fact that "in their humble home was a rarely gifted soul destined to make music," which could teach and inspire (185). This encouragement of literary activity, as the novel as a whole illustrates, amounts to an *ars rhetorica* of discursive race-nationalism.

These characters and their linguistic interactions serve as a gauge of race-national language and its function within the social "trial and triumph" to which Harper's pedagogy was calibrated. Despite the aspirations of the racial nation, the political trajectory of the state into which Harper's fiction narrates the future of the race is indeterminate. In one typically self-reflective dialogue, Thomas speaks presciently of collective destiny within this dispensation: "We are now passing through a crucial period in our race history and what we so much need, is moral earnestness, strength of character and purpose to guide us through the rocks and shoals on which so many life barques have been stranded and wrecked" (205). Lasette concurs and calls for an "esprit de corps," of racial solidarity, "which shall animate us with higher, nobler and holier purpose in the future than we have ever known in the past" (205). This historical arc of progress and the will of collective character to which Harper attributes its movement constitute a counter-narrative to the prevailing racial common sense of the post-Reconstruction nation.

Choosing an exemplar of the multivalent racial mythmaking of the era, one could do worse than the speeches of *Atlanta Constitution* editor Henry Grady, perhaps the single greatest popularizer of the "New South" creed. Grady heralded a world-historic ascension of the United States as the dominant political and economic power globally, a feat preordained in the blood of "Puritan and Cavalier," racialist terms that denoted the common Anglo-Saxon origin of Northerners and Southerners, respectively (84). As a myth of origins, this narrative of white race-national reunification found its literary expression in the "Plantation Romances" of Thomas Nelson Page and Thomas Dixon, among others. In *Trial and Triumph*, the black–white and North–South binaries of these race-national romances are circumvented, thus destabilizing the racial geography of the New South itself. While white politicians of nearly all stripes heralded a new age of national unity and strength, the *topoi* of "black Ireland" were inveighed to instruct a variety of audiences that a different modern age of race-ethnic conflict might emerge. The lessons of character talk in Harper's *Trial and Triumph* deliver narrative heuristics for making persuasive sense of social progress for African American women, the broader racial community, and the modern state itself.

A CENTURY OF AFRO-IRISH RHETORIC

More than a century before race historian Theodore Allen prescribed it, African American and neo-abolitionist commentators understood that in order to write the history of labor politics in the nineteenth-century United

States, we must "take a long look in the Irish mirror" (Allen 22). Prominent early African American convention leader Hosea Easton found proof of racial prejudice as the peculiar burden of African Americans in comparison to the successful integration of Irish immigrants. Reverend Easton's ambitiously titled *Treatise on the Intellectual Character, and Civil and Political Condition of the Colored People of the U. States; and the Prejudice Exercised Toward Them: With a Sermon on the Duty of the Church to Them* was published in Boston in 1837. Easton overall finds great racial progress despite the plight of Northern "free Negroes" whose "intellectual character" is continually thwarted by the "malignant exercise" of racial prejudice that constrains opportunities for advancement and self-development. For Easton, prejudice's social function—impeding African American self-reliance—emerges "the moment the colored people show signs of life" and of "being possessed with redeeming principles." A sardonic Easton finds this timing of prejudice to be "remarkable" in its racial utility. It is through the Irish turn that Easton more fully elaborates his theory of the social power of ignoble distinctiveness. "The moment an Irishman adopts the maxims and prevailing religion of the country," Easton assured his audience, "he is no longer regarded an Irishman, other than by birth" (36).[3]

Other commentators more aggressively exploited racial sentiment surrounding the Irish, insinuating a host of characterological vices.[4] The Rev. Samuel Ringgold Ward assessed rural Irish workers disparagingly, attributing to them an essential animality and lack of self-making discipline. For Ward, the depth of Irish vice was made evident by the ostensible prevalence of beggars in the Irish countryside, "the abominable profession of a very great number of hale, strong, Irish men, women, and children." Recalling his experience on the abolitionist lecture circuit in Ireland in his 1855 *Autobiography of a Fugitive Negro: His Anti-Slavery Labours in the United States, Canada and England*, Ward scarcely tried to contain his contempt for the poor Irish Catholic farmer "who on his native bog is unwashed and unshaved a fellow lodger with his pig in a cabin too filthy for most people's stables or styes" (383). The Rev. Ward offered damning lessons about the Irish, characterological scorn over the "air of neglect," for example, which ostensibly "frowned on every hand upon us and around us, with the rarest exceptions" (374). This inability to master resources and cultivate the land became the material sign of degraded character, a lack of will in developing an ethic of productivity, progress, and utility.

Afro-Irish comparative rhetoric in antebellum black-nationalist publicity appears prominently in Frederick Douglass's address of May 15, 1863, "The Present and Future of the Colored Race," presented less than a year after the issuance of Abraham Lincoln's Emancipation Proclamation. At the podium, Douglass offered his New York audience guarded if optimistic predictions of African American integration into the polity and into the manifest history of democratic progress. International precedent provided Douglass with a means to argue outside the binaries of late Jacksonian racial constraints and also to shame and disparage the character of those claiming the ethical authority of whiteness in itself. Addressing the political power of "the Irish element in this country," Douglass addressed the persistence of Irish mob violence perpetrated against African Americans in Northern cities, New York among them. Douglass proceeded according to his perpetual ambivalence regarding the Irish, rejecting the commonplace that Irish antipathy toward "the colored race" would always prevent "equal political footing with white men":

> Well, my friends, I admit that the Irish people are among our bitterest persecutors. In one sense it is strange, passing strange, that they should be such, but in another sense it is quite easily accounted for. It is said that a negro always makes the most cruel negro driver, that a northern slaveholder the most rigorous master, and the poor man suddenly made rich become the most haughty [and] insufferable of all purse-proud fools.
>
> Daniel O'Connell once said that the history of Ireland might be traced like a wounded man through a crowd—by the blood. The Irishman has been persecuted for his religion about as rigorously as the black man has been for his color. The Irishman has outlived his persecution, and I believe that the negro will survive his. (2: 581)

The passage typifies the diversity of ethical claims derived from both sameness and difference, which vie for priority in this address and in Afro-Irish rhetoric generally. In the New York of May 1863, the "purse-proud fools" Douglass has in mind, those who have been "suddenly made rich," were Irishmen. Disparaging the character of Irish immigrants was a common ethical proof in his writing and oratory, one exceeded, however, by praise of the social virtue of Irish self-determination. Douglass's praise for Irish Catholic "patriot" and abolitionist Daniel O'Connell served as an important point of orientation for the defense of African American manhood.[5]

The rhetorical circulation of Afro-Irish *topoi* increased after the 1883 repeal of the 1875 Civil Rights Act, a shift allowed in part by the historical course of de-colonization in Britain. In the second half of the nineteenth century, the movement for national self-determination became a force to be reckoned with. The "Home Rule" movement grew tremendously in strength in these years and witnessed fractious protest on Irish soil and political schism in British Parliament. The vitriol expressed in Edward A. Freeman's *Impressions of the United States* could be classified as the kind of white reaction to reform that Michael Omi and Howard Winant trace in their Gramscian analysis of hegemonic flux in the racial state (66–67). Freeman's resentment over rising Irish political power elides the crimes of British colonial power and of the American racial state. Freeman wrote his account in 1883, the very year of the repeal of the Civil Rights Act, one of the most devastating occurrences ushering in the post–civil rights era of Jim Crow.

THE IGNORANT VOTE—HONORS ARE EASY.

Figure 4.1   In this *Harper's Weekly* cover from 1876, Thomas Nast's drawing expresses equal disdain for the quality of African and Irish American political intelligence. The bigotry of the image is a fair sample of a widespread race-ethnic disparagement in this comparative mode. Picture Collection. The New York Public Library, Astor Lenox and Tilden Foundations.

It would be difficult to overstate the outrage and protest elicited in African American political circles by the repeal. The Civil Rights Act of 1875 could be viewed as a high-water mark of Reconstruction and Radical Republicanism. The act had legislated that "[a]ll persons within the jurisdiction of the United States" would be "entitled to the full and equal enjoyment of the accommodations, advantages, facilities, and privileges of inns, public conveyances on land or water, theaters, and other places of public amusement . . . regardless of any previous condition of servitude." Wendell Phillips declared that the act "washed color out of the Constitution" (Bennett 260). As the century progressed, however, and governmental support for African American civil rights waned, and in the wake of the "Compromise of 1877," equal protection under the law proved to be a fiction. When the Supreme Court ruled the act unconstitutional in 1883, the logic of states' rights held sway, and segregation laws began to proliferate. Thomas Fortune, perhaps the most influential African American journalist of the century, wrote that African Americans felt they had been "baptized in ice water" (263).

Fortune indicted the hegemony of states' rights as the new juridical means of upholding the racial caste system. In *Black and White: Land, Labor and Politics in the South*, published in 1884, he surveyed the Southern peonage system in the wake of the Civil Rights Act repeal:

> [Black workers] are more absolutely under the control of the Southern whites; they are more systematically robbed of their labor . . . and they enjoy, practically, less of the protection of the laws of the State or of the Federal government . . . they are told by the Supreme Court to go to the State authorities—as if they would have appealed to the one had the other given them that protection to which their sovereign citizenship entitles them! . . . He is, like the Irishman in Ireland, an alien in his native land.

Just as Harper would, Fortune finessed the question of revolutionary black labor through comparison and historical reference, conjecturing that the "American negro is no better and no worse than the Haytian revolutionists headed by Toussaint l'Overture, Christophe and the bloody Dessalaines" (34).[6]

This reversal of Reconstruction's gains had particular impact, in Frederick Douglass's estimation, on black workers whose "cause is one with the laboring classes all over the world" (96). Days after the repeal, Frederick Douglass used the Irish example to make sense of the legislative decision, which ran counter to the progressive history of liberty of which Douglass often spoke with such confidence:

> Perhaps no class of our fellow citizens has carried this prejudice against color to a point more extreme and dangerous than have our Catholic Irish fellow citizens, and yet no people on the face of the earth have been more relentlessly persecuted and oppressed on account of race and religion, than the Irish people. But in Ireland, persecution has at last reached a point where it reacts terribly upon her persecutors. Ask any man of intelligence today, "What is the chief source of England's

weakness? What has reduced her to rank of a second-class power?" and the answer will be *"Ireland!"* Poor, ragged, hungry, starving and oppressed as she is, she is strong enough to be a standing menace to the power and glory of England. Fellow-citizens! We want no black Ireland in America. We want no aggrieved class in America. (5: 119)

Comparisons of African American and Catholic Irish labor are, of course, implicitly a comparison of a "democratic" United States with a de-colonizing England, one nation ostensibly on the rise and one whose national power was waning. As Harper would in *Trial and Triumph*, Douglass represented this culture of oppression as a self-destructive force threatening the state. One of the most outspoken critics of inequitable labor relations in the United States, Douglass poses the threat of black class violence in European terms: "Out of the misery of Ireland comes murder, assassination, fire and sword . . . The woe pronounced upon those who keep back wages of the laborer by fraud is self-acting and self-executing and certain as death. The world is full of warnings" (5: 101).

AFRICAN AMERICAN RHETORICAL
PEDAGOGY AFTER RECONSTRUCTION

Trial and Triumph was for the duration of its run a front-page feature in the "Communications" section of the *Christian Recorder*, as were novels *Minnie's Sacrifice* and *Sowing and Reaping*. Recall here Frances Smith Foster's argument regarding the broad and influential instructional mission of the *Recorder* and Harper's work published therein ("Gender, Genre" 54–55). While the installments certainly cohere as a story, each one has its own didactic objective. Following the "sketch" form of the earlier novels and short fictions, *Trial and Triumph* was clearly, like its predecessors, written for the diverse political forum the *Recorder* provided. In addition to her abiding focus on the roles of the church and education in the life of the individual and the community, Harper editorializes about a wide range of issues presented as crucial matters of uplift, such as school de-segregation; the continued poverty among Southern African Americans and the support of Northern relief efforts; relations between the sexes; the "progress" of African American politics and culture; and increasingly by the late 1880s, racialist hiring practices and segregated labor unions in the North. Joining the question of labor to the question of civil rights, Harper was well within the editorial purview of the *Christian Recorder*. In "A National Shame: Closing the Doors of Various Trades Against Colored People," published in the June 28, 1888, issue of the *Recorder*, Rev. R. C. Ransom offers a biting reference to the New South: "Although we have had emancipation proclamations, constitutional amendments, civil rights bills, and that hotbed of oppression now popularly called the 'new South', the colored race in America has never yet been accorded a full and equal chance in the race of life." Ransom's great concern, like that of Harper's Thomas, is for the progress of the race against the tide of the prevailing racial sentiment of the labor market and its "crushing effect against the progress of the colored race" (Ransom 5)

Trial and Triumph documents such segregation, and like Ransom's text, argues that it has the potential to destroy the republic. Ransom warns, "Do not think that colored men are satisfied with the position they are forced to occupy in this country. They are not. They are growing restive, discouraged, disheartened." The reverend warns against the same assumptions of black complacency that the character of Mr. Thomas was designed to dispel by fictional word and deed. Mr. Thomas speaks the preceptive script of Ransom, Douglass, and Fortune and is Harper's ideal figure of masculine, self-making virtue. Thomas is always at once a persuasive force and a force of unification within the black community. As mentioned earlier, Thomas's occupations as a teacher and a carpenter are literally generative of the African American community. The most crucial of his constructive efforts are rhetorical, which becomes clear as Harper's didactic drama of persuasion unfolds. When his friend Charley Cooper, a light-complected African American, relays his experience of being fired upon the discovery of his heritage and his subsequent plans to quit A.P. and "start life afresh," passing as white, Thomas intercedes. Speaking Harper's characteristic sanction against passing, he convinces Cooper to stay, promising to assist him in his search for employment. Thomas delivers his call to race solidarity as a matter of filial loyalty. "I know you could pass as a white man," Thomas tells Cooper, "but, Charley, don't you know that to do so must separate from your kindred and virtually ignore your mother?" Thomas's appeal to a familial ethic gives over immediately to race-national concern as he presses Cooper to "stand in your lot without compromise of concealment, and feel that the feebler your mother's race is the closer you will cling to it" (212).

Through Thomas's assessment of the prevailing common sense, Harper asserts characterological disparagement as pedagogical precepts. Of the white man who dismissed Cooper, Thomas says, "I think there never was slave more cowed under the whip of his master than he is under the lash of public opinion" (214). With characteristic attention to pedagogical cause and social effect, Harper has Thomas warn that "men cannot sow avarice and oppression without reaping the harvest of retribution." This comment presages his conversation with Mr. Hastings, the white shop owner to whom Thomas has appealed on Cooper's behalf. We learn of Thomas and Hastings that they "had kindred intellectual and literary tastes and this established between them a free masonry of mind which took no account of racial differences" (220). Despite the disclaimer, Thomas finds that Hastings's "account" of racial politics in the United States demonstrates how badly he needs persuading, and he thus makes the shop owner a target of his rhetorical performance. In fact, the two meet in Hastings's "counting room," and the pun serves as a key to the political economic anatomy of the subsequent dialogue. This setting accentuates the economic imperatives of the ensuing drama of persuasion.

To be sure, Thomas's relentless rhetorical engagement of Hastings lays out an ethics of community living *as rhetorical action* for *Christian Recorder* readers. Thomas applies for a position on behalf of Cooper, telling his friend's story to Hastings, who calls Cooper's dismissal "a shame" and says that he is "sorry to see it." Yet, Hastings asks, "[W]hat can be done to help it?" Of course, Hastings might offer Cooper employment at this point, but a much longer lesson is required to secure the young man a position and to convince Hastings of the larger implications of Cooper's story. Despite the supposed "free masonry of minds" and the abeyance of racialist considerations between the two "friends," Thomas inscribes their discussion into the discourse of race and labor that animated the pages of the *Christian Recorder* more generally. Referring to the offenses Cooper has suffered, Thomas says,

> Mr. Hastings, you see them, and I feel them, and I fear that I am growing morbid over them, and not only myself, but other educated men of my race, and that, I think, is a thing to be deprecated. Between the white people and the colored people of this country there is a unanimity of interest and I know that our interests and duties all lie in one direction. Can men corrupt and intimidate voters in the South without a reflex influence being felt in the North? You may protect yourself from what you call the pauper of Europe, but you will not be equally able to defend yourself from the depressed laborer of the new South, and as an American citizen, I dread any turn of the screw which will lower the rate of wages here; and I like to feel as an American citizen that whatever concerns the nation concerns me. But I feel that this prejudice against my race compresses my soul, narrows my political horizon and makes me feel that I am an alien in the land of my birth. (222)

In Thomas's appeal to a "unanimity of interests" between races, we recognize one of Harper's core preceptive statements, but the statement is anything but "color blind." Thomas's mapping of a national color line reveals the contingent promise of this collective impulse. Employing the "accusatory 'you'" that Shirley Wilson Logan locates in Harper's addresses to white audiences, Thomas signals the existing divergence of "interests," prompting a profession of his own alienation. The sovereignty of Thomas's self-identification is shown to be contingent on a Euro-American other, the "pauper of Europe," referring to the Irish and other immigrant groups. Whatever Thomas's claim to American citizenship might be, he understands that it is deferred by racial prejudice, which, as he says, "compresses my soul, narrows my political horizon and makes me feel that I am an alien in the land of my birth." Though the race line might divide black and white America, it joins Afro- and Euro-Americans in Thomas's take on the national labor scene.[7] The "depressed labor of the new South" and the "pauper of Europe" share a dangerous "alien" quality against which, it seems some "protect[ion]" must be raised. Hastings's response acknowledges the validity of Thomas's testimony: "'I wish, Mr. Thomas, that some of the men who are writing and talking about the Negro problem would only come in contact with the thoughtful men of your race. I think it would greatly modify their views" (222).

Thomas's unwillingness to squarely accept this compliment is an important nuance of Harper's representation of persuasiveness, as the subtleties of rhetorical exchange figure pervasive ideological differences. By suggesting that Thomas's exemplary intelligence and eloquence would persuade "some of the men who are writing and talking about the Negro problem," Hastings actually detracts attention from the content of Thomas's political economic critique and from his own culpability with regard to "the Negro problem." Thomas does not allow the dialogue to reach consensus, accentuating the pervasiveness not only of racial oppression, but of the black intellectuality it elides. The divergence of their positions is signaled through the use of the second-person address. "[Y]ou know us as your servants," Thomas explains: "The law takes cognizance of our crimes. Your charitable institutions of our poverty, but what do any of you know of our best and most thoughtful men and women? When we write how many of you ever read our books and papers . . . ?" Thomas thus positions himself within a larger community of intellectuals and highlights the degree to which such a community has been disrupted through the disciplining discourses of law and charity. The invisibility of African American persuasiveness is shown to be systematic and not, as Hastings's compliment implies, a neutral lack of "contact."

Denied the option of consensus, and thus the recognition of his ostensible magnanimity, Hastings is forced to acknowledge the seriousness of Thomas's critique, remarking, "You draw a dark picture." But with his next comment, Hastings seeks again to distance himself from any complicity: "I confess that I feel pained at the condition of affairs in the South," Hastings asks, "but what can we do in the South?" Again, Thomas will not allow Hastings rhetorical escape through the assumptions of compartmentalized social relations. Given Harper's neo-abolitionist insistence on the race-national and economic connection between North and South, we should not be surprised by Thomas's answer to Hastings's question: "Set the South a better example" (222). Hastings, like Harper's readers, is thus reminded that it is the color line politics *in the North* that have initiated this dialogue in the first place. Thomas instantiates the essential connection between Southern and Northern labor, a connection the drama of the novel will bear out; the racial hierarchy of the "new South" is shown to epitomize the general racial order of the state itself.

Harper's reference to the "new South" is ironic, for what captures Thomas's attention is not the newness of the South, but a very specific oldness, the continuity of racial oppression across generations and across regional divides. The New South rhetoric, to which Harper's novel responds, is a race-nationalist legitimation of the initiation of state capitalism, which depended on the containment and control of black workers (Singh 490–494). The control of this racial caste system solidified alongside the myth-making of U.S. democratic exceptionalism, and the negotiation of such blatant contradictions marked a watershed passage in the history of racial hegemony. In his landmark address to the New England Club on December 21, 1886, Henry Grady presented his Northern audience with this vision of national economic power. In Grady's vision of the New South, black workers and white owners are happy collaborators in the building of a national economy which joins North and South inexorably and restores the brotherhood of "Puritan and Cavalier," as Grady phrases it in his construction of a white-masculinist world history.[8] Indeed, in Grady's New South rhetoric, the black worker becomes only a figure in a triangular reconfiguration of white national identity. Such racialized versions of postwar democracy constituted a pervasive popular discourse, which Nina Silber has termed "the romance of reunion."[9] Grady refers to black Southern labor as the most "prosperous laboring population" in the country (89): "Faith has been kept with [the negro], in spite of calumnious assertions to the contrary by those who assume to speak for us or by frank opponents. Faith will be kept with him in the future, if the South holds her reason and integrity" (90). The telos of Grady's "reason" is the logic of laissez-faire, which elides the racial oppression of the New South, an exploitation which Grady dismisses as a "calumnious" accusation. Yet when Grady asserts that "in the summing up the free negro counts more than he did as a slave," the mathematical metaphor quite plainly articulates the logic underwriting the commodification of black labor in the South (87).[10] Grady's insistence that "the white is the superior race"—this seemingly preternatural fear of miscegenation—impugns the social viability of black political power. And yet it is not black political power per se that Grady fears, but a black constituency co-opted by his white political foes: "If the negroes were skillfully led—and leaders would not be lacking—it would give them a balance of power—a thing not to be considered" (99).

The social assumptions that normalize the color line are the foundation of the ethical landscape that Thomas, as an agent of African American persuasion, must alter in the Northern urban space of A.P. When confronted by the suggestion that his own position resonates with the very prejudice he claims to deplore, Hastings becomes defensive and ironically mobilizes an even more explicitly color-blind line of argument:

> You bring a heavy verdict against us. I hardly think it can be sustained
> . . . [the Negro] has freedom and enfranchisement and with these two
> great rights he must work out his social redemption and political situation . . . You tell me to put myself in your place. I think if I were a

colored young man that I would develop every faculty and use every power which God had given me for the improvement and development of my race . . . No Mr. Thomas, while you blame us for our transgressions and shortcomings, do not fail to do all you can to rouse up all the latent energies of your young men to do their part worthily as American citizens and to add their quota to the strength and progress of the nation. (223)

Hastings's use of the collective pronoun "us" in reference to whites (perhaps Northern whites) suggests his ideological distance from Thomas in this moment, and indeed, it is Thomas's persuasion that has positioned him thus, denying him the disingenuous liberal ground of racial largesse. Hastings assumes "freedom and enfranchisement" as a leveling of the social field, which should allow African Americans to achieve their own "social redemption." However, political "freedom," which Hastings views as a positive force, is contingent on race division in Thomas's account of economic injustice.

Harper's post-Reconstruction preceptive script was responsive, then, to the transformed rhetoric of racial oppression, one suited for the liberal moment. Hastings is said to "take no account of racial differences," but Harper frames this not as the spirit of democracy, but as a dangerous denial of existing social conditions in the United States. Hastings, echoing many commentators of the post-Reconstruction era, argued that, within the logic of the free market, African Americans possessed all the elements of citizenship needed to succeed, and must work out their own destiny. Hastings paraphrases Henry Grady's "New South" address when he claims that "the Negro . . . has freedom and enfranchisement and with these two great rights he must work out his social redemption and political solution" (223). Or, as Grady argues regarding the limits of national jurisdiction, "To liberty and enfranchisement is as far as law can carry the negro. The rest must be left to conscience and common sense" (90).

Thomas carefully qualifies his acceptance of this precept. Acknowledging the "truth and pertinence" of Hastings's espousal of self-reliance, Thomas asks him to "bear with me just a few moments while I give an illustration of what I mean" (223). Thomas then recounts stories of segregation in the North, which suggest the limits of "freedom and enfranchisement." Thomas imagines an emerging modern state different from and in fact elided by white reunion romance, a modern vision that inspires increasing anxiety in Hastings:

Is it not fearfully unwise to keep alive in freedom the old animosities of slavery? To-day the Negro shares citizenship with you. He is not arraying himself against your social order; his hands are not dripping with dynamite, nor is he waving in your face the crimson banner of anarchy, but he is increasing in numbers and growing in intelligence, and is it not madness and folly to subject him to social and public inequalities, which are calculated to form and keep alive a hatred of race as a reaction against pride of caste? (224–225)

Here Harper mobilizes the pervasive cultural anxiety regarding an increasingly radicalized labor force.[11] Written and published at the apex of labor organization and working-class unrest and violence in white and African American communities, something of a threat is suggested in Thomas's rhetorical performance, the evocation of a revolutionary specter.[12] Clearly, such a strategy stresses the lawfulness of black citizens, but also suggests a scenario in which continued barriers to political and economic power leave those radicals without other options. In both of these passages, Harper does not threaten class violence but represents it as an avenue African Americans, as of yet, have not chosen.[13]

In *Trial and Triumph*, Harper represents the force of this argument by having Hastings come to such drastic conclusions himself. Alluding to the ongoing oppression and increasingly staunch resistance of Catholic Irish under British colonialism, Hastings worries that ignoring the struggle of black labor might be "helping create a black Ireland in our Gulf States." In Harper's "black Ireland" analogy, what British imperialism is to the Catholic Irish, Jim Crow is to African Americans. Thomas's persuasiveness is registered by Hastings's new perspective. "Mr. Thomas," he admits, "you have given me a new view of the matter . . . we have so long looked upon the colored man as a pliable and submissive being that we have never learned to look at any hatred on his part as an element of danger." Hastings is finally disabused of the notion of black passivity, which underwrites the New South ideology and its complementary Northern liberal racism. It is here that Hastings himself comes to understand the situation of race relations through the European lens that Thomas has employed. The co-composition of Hastings's new position is a model of enthymematic connection across the color line.

Hastings realizes his own "supineness" in rolling over to the prevailing racial sentiment regarding the labor market, assuming the malleability and passivity of black labor in his conception of the national political culture. He has read the implicit threat posited in Thomas's discourse on race–labor relations, but Thomas will not validate the reading or ameliorate Hastings's anxiety regarding a black rebellion. It is at this moment of high anxiety that Thomas leaves off the discussion and returns to the ostensible reason for his visit, an errand we might now see as a measure of the efficacy of the political-economic knowledge Thomas and Hastings produce through their dialogue: "But really I have been forgetting my errand. Have you any opening in your store for my young friend?" (225). Hastings says that he does indeed have an opening, and so Thomas's persuasiveness keeps Charley Cooper within the fold of the struggling black community of A.P. by establishing ethical precepts across the color line.

Thomas's own sojourn in the segregated labor market maintains the specter of labor unrest from installment to installment of the novel, throwing the
national "trial" of African American self-making into high relief. Typical
of the novel's strategy, the "crushing effect" of racialist hiring practices is
projected through a European lens onto the life of Thomas. Returning to his
grounding precepts, Thomas resolves to persevere despite the power of "popular prejudice," the blunt force of racial logic on the color line. Through his
determined efforts, Thomas eventually secures employment with a builder,
"Wm. C. Nell, an Englishman who had not been long enough in America
to be fully saturated by its Christless and inhuman prejudices." So pleased is
Nell by Thomas's skillful craftsmanship that "he did not notice the indignant
scowls on the faces of his workmen, and their murmurs of disapprobation as
they uttered." Finally, the workers stop work with a protest of sorts:

> At length they took off their aprons, laid down their tools and asked to
> be discharged from work.
> "Why, what does this mean," asked the astonished Englishman.
> "It means we will not work with a nigger."
> "Why, I don't understand? What is the matter with him?"
> "Why, there's nothing the matter, only he's a nigger, and we never
> put niggers on an equality with us, and we never will."
> "But I am a stranger in this country, and I don't understand you."
> "Well he's a nigger, and we don't want niggers for nothing."

Contrast this mode of argumentation with Thomas's eloquence or, for
that matter, the chaste rationality of Mrs. Lasette. When Nell offers to let
Thomas work alone, separated from the white workers, they put a finer
point on their ultimatum: "We won't work for a man who employs niggers." Up to this point of her career, Harper did not attempt a great deal of
dialect, *Sketches of Southern Life* being the major exception. When she did
write dialect, it was as often in formulation of white characters. Here, the
coarse English of the workers suggests an ignorance at the root of "popular
prejudice," to use Ransom's phrase. This racial closing of ranks disabuses
the Englishman of any undue optimism regarding the "land of liberty" in
which he finds "an undreamed of tyranny [has] entered his workshop."
Readers learn that the builder, fearing the reaction of his workers, "bit his
lip" in deference to the circular logic of racial hatred. The capitulation of
business owners is experienced by the Reverend Lomax as well. When he
asks the builder of a church if he will hire an African American, the man
replies that he "would willingly do so, but . . . can not" (234). Again, his
reason is fear of a "strike." These experiences lead Thomas again to compare the experience of black workers to their European counterparts. "I am
denied [the] right to sell my labor in any workshop in this city same as the
men of other nationalities and to receive with them a fair day's wages for a
fair day's work" (244).

The functional connection between rhetorical pedagogy and political economy is spelled out clearly in the conversations of the "salon" Lasette hosts. "Mrs. Lasette threw open her parlors for the gathering together of the best thinkers and workers of the race," we learn, "meeting to discuss any question of vital importance to the welfare of the colored people of the nation." The opening narration of the installment further spells out Lasette's rationale for gathering dedicated "thinkers and workers" as a project of race-national solidarity, and more specifically, as a practice of dedication to her "ill-fated sisters" in the South. Mr. Thomas also speaks the precept of solidarity within the "colored nation" in his exchange with Rev. Lomax, who despite his position in the community repeatedly comes under the didactic tutelage of Thomas. Recounting his own failure to employ African American carpenters in the building of a church, Lomax's relative lack of imagination regarding the function of the church for the race draws Thomas into a leadership role. Recalling the racially segregated labor market in which he and others have struggled, he declares the need for "better communication between us than we now possess" and for a "labor bureau [to be] established not as a charity among us, but as a business [to] find out the different industries that will employ men irrespective of color" (249). Thomas's vision for the church appeals to those *Christian Recorder* readers who might devote "their lives to our common cause." Thomas references the apostle John, who wrote late in life to reaffirm the virtues of Christian faith: "I write unto you, young men, because you are strong" (1 John 2:14). Characteristically orienting her lesson with *topoi* of biblical composition, Harper thus offers instruction on the manner in which rhetoric works as a constitutive force in the community. Pedagogy and economic mission are inseparable in Thomas's preceptive script.

Thomas's carpentry skills and his rhetorical skills are not mutually exclusive. While he built a reputation for himself on the job, he was also able to "teach [others] by his own experience not to be too easily discouraged, but to trust to pluck more than luck" (245). Like the heroes and heroines of Harper's previous fictions, Thomas demonstrates a way of being that exemplifies the ethical imperatives of uplift. His counsel to his neighbors—often summary and citation from Harper's own political speeches—is the focal point around which African American community forms.

LIFTING UP ANNETTE HARCOURT: RHETORICAL TRAINING AND AFRICAN AMERICAN WOMANHOOD

Lasette and Thomas's rhetorical skill propels *Trial and Triumph* as a teaching text as does the embattled education of Annette Harcourt. Harcourt's potential as a poet and defender of the race, which proves to be prodigious, remains perilously contingent early in the story. Her education is a perpetual matter of debate among those who approach the question as a matter of utility, framing Harcourt's position as a New Southern subject within the greater network of A.P.'s social setting. In a fictional oeuvre replete with teachers and students, *Trial and Triumph* stands out, meditating on educational policy and practice from the first to the last chapter. Just as she teaches against the racial precepts of the color line, Harper challenges the gender line maintained even among those in a nationally construed African American community. She counters the prevailing opinion that young women, of whom Harcourt is the synecdochal figure, are not worthy of a thorough education, revealing the racial self-hatred at the heart of this retrogressive pedagogy most explicitly in the exchanges between Harcourt and Mrs. Lasette. Lasette's pedagogical mothering of the entire community of A.P. is a model of discursive uplift practice. Through an elaborate dialogue between Lasette and young Annette Harcourt, Harper continues to turn the *topos* of black Ireland to didactic effect. Harcourt, a young orphan with intellectual promise but moral confusion, is the subject of Lasette's persuasive skill, the very figure of race character imperiled. Orchestrated by Lasette, this persuasive gambit enables the argument for race pride, or resistance to racial self-hatred, a cultural legacy Harper taught against. Where Thomas anatomizes the social power of such racialism in the national labor market, Lasette uses the outsider trope to demonstrate the daily consequences of class and gender distinctions within African America.

Harper staged these lessons of race-national progress in the ostensibly democratic institutional context of a de-segregated school in the North. Like Thomas, Lasette was once Harcourt's teacher, but lost his position after the integration of local schools. "Public opinion," we learn, "had advanced far enough to admit the colored children into the different schools . . . but it was not prepared . . . to admit the colored teachers" (186). As evident in her first novels, Harper's documentary fictional settings raise the cultural constraints with which uplift educators had to contend. *Trial and Triumph*'s coverage of the "mixed schools" debate suggests a significant rift within the reform community on the issue of school integration. The novel appeared in the *Christian Recorder* alongside a number of letters and editorials that bear out these conflicting visions for educational reform. Katie D. Chapman's May 24, 1888, article raises many of the same complex issues that are dealt with in Harper's novel. However, unlike Harper, Chapman resisted the integration of schools on the grounds that "[r]ace pride is not developed in a mixed school" (1). Thomas and Lasette take a historical long view of the matter in challenging this separatist position, relaying Harper's longstanding support for the racial integration of social institutions, no less in schools than in the labor market. Seeming to discount the possibility of emigration, Thomas argues that if African Americans "are to remain in this country," integration is a necessity. Lasette "feel[s] with Mr. Thomas that the mixing of the schools is a stride in the march of the nation . . . the progress of the centuries." Thomas finishes this co-articulated argument asserting that "it is through obstacles overcome, suffering endured and the tests of trial that strength is obtained, courage manifested and character developed" (204–205). Race pride, in other words, would not be learned by avoiding the challenge of integration.

Although Harper appears to have favored the integration of schools, her concern for the underdevelopment of "race pride" is pronounced. In one of the novel's central dialogues, it is this very lack that Annette Harcourt demonstrates, and it is a self-conception that threatens to undermine her potential. What Harcourt learns in school about herself and the power of racial sentiment marks the turning point in the novel. Forced to sit next to each other—to enact integration as it were—Harcourt and her classmate, Mary Joseph, come into conflict. After a verbal battle with Joseph, a distraught Harcourt seeks out Lasette and vows to quit the school. Lasette dissuades her, helping her make sense not only of Mary Joseph's barbs, but also of the racialist discourse in which they operate. "Ireland and Africa . . . were not ready for annexation?" Lasette asks jokingly, and Harcourt replies, "No, and never will be, I hope." With some encouragement, Harcourt tells her story:

> "Well, a mean old thing, she went and told her horrid old father, and just as I was coming along he took hold of my arm and said he had heard that I had called his daughter, Miss Mary Joseph, a poor white mick and that if I did it again he would give me a good thrashing, and that for two pins he would do it then. . . . Oh, but I do hate these Irish. I don't like them for anything. Grandmother says that an Irishman is only a negro turned wrong side out, and I told her so yesterday morning when she was fussing with me."
>
> "Say, rather, when we were fussing together; I don't think the fault was all on her side."
>
> "But Mrs. Lasette, she had no business calling me a nigger."
>
> "Of course not; but would you have liked it [any] better if she had called you a negro?"
>
> "No; I don't want her to call me anything of the kind, neither negro nor nigger. She shan't even call me black."
>
> "But, Annette, are you not black?"
>
> "I don't care if I am, she shan't call me so." (217)

Harcourt's retort reiterates a racialist joke that was common in the urban North where Irish and African Americans came into considerable conflict. The logic of equivalence in the joke's racial accusation is, however, ambiguous. The equivalence of "Irishman" and "negro" is a startling expression of self-hatred, a violent calling out of one's own name in which Harcourt makes her own identity the measure of social baseness. As in Thomas's dialogues, comparison to the Irish puts the race-national politicization of African American identity in perspective. Lasette, obviously still the girl's teacher in the broadest sense, makes no excuse for the classmate's use of the racialist epithet, but begins to question Harcourt's logic. If she will not accept "nigger" as a personal designation, will she accept "negro"? As in the case of the white workers who refused to work with a "nigger," Harcourt seems unwilling or unable to reason through the powerful interpolative force of the racial epithet, "nigger." Lasette continues with her questions:

> "But suppose you met her hurrying to school, and you said to her, 'how red and rosy you look this morning,' would that make her angry?"
> "I don't suppose that it would."
> "But suppose she would say to you, 'Annette, how black your face is this morning,' how would you feel?"
> "I should feel like slapping her."
> "Why so; do you think because Miss Joseph—"
> "Don't call her Miss, she is so mean and hateful . . ."
> "Well, if it were not for signs there's no mistaking I should think you had a lot of Irish blood in your veins, and had kissed the blarney stone."
> "No I haven't and if I had I would try to let—"

"[L]et" what, we might ask—taking our cue from Harper's conspicuous hyphen—the dreaded Irish blood from her own veins? Again, Lasette's persuasive tactics highlight Harcourt's inability to reason while in the thrall of what we might think of as a literalist racialism in which "white" and "black" might be equivalent or opposite. Lasette counters these essentialist notions with Harper's signature call to race pride, providing Harcourt with a sustaining precept drawn from the Song of Solomon, one she was unable to obtain in her school: "I am black but comely, the sun has looked down upon me, but I will make you who despise me feel that I am your superior" (215–220). Lasette offers Harcourt a new presentation of racial womanhood, chaste in language, strong in pride, and unwilling to be drawn reactively into the self-destructive logic of the color line.

On the "gala day" of her graduation, Harcourt's next engagement in public language raises a quite different sensation in A.P. With her address, "The Mission of the Negro," she proves herself to be the pedagogical standard bearer of Harper's rhetorical drama. Only through the persuasive force of Lasette's race pride is Harcourt herself able to take her place at the podium as a force of progressive persuasion. As both the poor and relatively comfortable members of the city's African American community gather "to hear Annette speak her piece," the young woman's public language becomes a constitutive site of race pride and of cross-class African American identity:

> Annette had passed a highly successful examination, and was to graduate from the normal school, and as a matter of course, her neighbors

wanted to hear Annette "speak her piece" as they called the commencement theme, and also to see how she was going to behave before
all "them people." They were, generally speaking, too unaspiring to
feel envious toward any one of their race who excelled them intellectually, and so there was little jealously of Annette . . . in fact some of her
neighbors felt a kind of pride in thought that Tennis Court would turn
out a girl who could stand on the same platform and graduate alongside of some of their employers' daughters. If they could not stand there
themselves they were proud that one of their race could. (239)

As a race-national orator, Harcourt is a striking success as her graduation-
day speech makes clear. She performs the constitutive, pedagogical work
espoused by Lasette and Thomas. The narrator makes assumptions about
the "unaspiring" black people of Tennis Court who might find a sense of
their own worth in Harcourt's example. One such auditor, who claims to
feel "like the boy when some one threatened to slap off his face," said,
"[Y]ou can slap off my face, but I have a big brother and you can't slap off
his face." According to the didactic narrator, such an occasion for "race
pride" stands in contrast to the lessons learned from "literature [African
Americans] read [which] was mostly from the hands of the white men who
would paint them in any colors which suited their prejudices" (238–240).
Indeed, Harcourt's case for "The Mission of the Negro" is the antithesis
to such literature. Described as a "remarkable production," the address
traces the history of Africans through the Middle Passage, slavery, and
Reconstruction, and predicts a "grandly constructive future" (241). Having affected all of her auditors through the force of her oratory, Harcourt
reproduces the integrative power of Lasette's persuasiveness.

HARPER'S PEDAGOGY AND THE
QUESTION OF VERNACULAR RHETORIC

Harcourt's rhetorical training and eventual eloquence raise questions about
the place of African American vernacular rhetorics in Harper's pedagogy.
As we focus on Harper's representation of persuasive style as pedagogical politics, we must also acknowledge in the novel a definite tendency to
castigate African American vernacular styles. Such ambivalence positions
Harper's work uneasily in relation to the most influential contemporary
theories of African American vernacular. In *Workings of the Spirit: The
Poetics of Afro-American Women's Writing*, Houston Baker constructs a
critical dichotomy that is as limited in its scope of textual evidence as it is
limiting in its *ars poetica* prescriptions. The privileged category in Baker's
theory of African American women's writing is "spirit work," seemingly
a feminized version of his well-known theorization of a "blues matrix."[14]
Counter-posing Baker's notion of spirit work is what he describes as a

poetics of compromise and desertion, a denial of Southern folk heritage on the part of black women writing in the North. This political-stylistic split is explained also as the difference between the "theoretical," a potentially spiritual mode, and the "historical," a spectacle of black bodies and experience presented for white approval that Baker traces from abolitionist sentimental narratives to the recovery work of a number of African American women scholars in this century (*Workings* 20–25).

Formulating a *topos* of "the daughter's departure," Baker stages highly selective and disparaging readings of passages from the writing of Pauline Hopkins, Anna Julia Cooper, and Harper herself, criticizing their obstensibly "willful . . . refus[al] to conceptualize a southern, vernacular ancestry as a site of both consuming violence and discrete value" (23). In his view, the works of these authors, in both content and linguistic style, make "a conservative appeal to white public opinion" (32). This capitulation is achieved through what Baker calls the "mulatto's embodied ambassadorship" of mixed-race characters in these fictions. The damning absence in the work of the departed daughters is, for Baker, the lack of any "fleshing out of both the southern, vernacular, communal expressivity of black mothers and grandmothers, and a portrayal of the relentless whitemale hegemony . . . that threatened ceaselessly to eradicate such expressivity" (36). Readers of turn-of-the-century black women writers of the North might well wonder how Baker justifies the claim of an "absent" figuration of "whitemale" violence in the South. Any review of Harper's public statements demonstrates her career-spanning commitment to chronicling and speaking out against such violence.

Among African American women who have responded to Baker's reading, Anne duCille's response is perhaps the most detailed.[15] DuCille takes issue with Baker's "condemn[ation] . . . of black women novelists, whose settings are the urban North and whose subjects are black middle-class women . . . dismissed in the name of the vernacular . . . condemned (along with the critics who study them) for historical conservatism." In duCille's view, Baker makes the blues "the metonym for authentic blackness" and thus ironically instantiates a single standard, the very rhetorical move he bemoans in the historical work of what he sees as the mainstream of Black Studies (*Coupling* 68). DuCille worries that this "occult of true black womanhood" reinscribes dangerous cultural stereotypes about black women as "magnanimous mammies who not only endure . . . but whose primary function is to teach others to do the same" (*Skin Trade* 114). DuCille's critique opens space for my own reading of Harper by raising the question of Baker's own gender essentialism and its effacement of the experience of African Americans in the North, many of whom—ironically given Baker's own Marxian ethic—struggled in and critiqued the manifest violence of Northern capitalism.

Ought we to read *Trial and Triumph* as an instantiation of Baker's *topoi* of the "daughter's departure"? Harper often delivered her public addresses in grand Ciceronian form (Peterson, *Doers* 132). To be sure, *Trial and*

Triumph, as much as any of Harper's texts, casts aspersions on vernacular rhetorics. There is clearly a warrant for the claim that Harper retained a missionary's presumptuousness regarding the Southern folk culture to which she was foreign. Lasette is upset by Annette Harcourt's ostensibly "unlady-like . . . quarreling." When Mary Joseph refuses to be seen "eating with niggers," Harcourt employs a master trope: "I asked her if her mother didn't eat with the pigs in the old country." As well, when the Irish girl "squirmed" in expression of her distaste at being forced to sit next to an African American, Harcourt "asked her if anything was biting her," implying the girl had lice (216). Whether or not we find these remarks amusing is clearly a matter of disposition, but we might agree that they get the better of Joseph's rather flat insults. Harcourt's progressively refined sensibilities are arguably the narrative's central pedagogical point of reader reference. Be that as it may, Lasette's admonishment effaces neither the wit nor the pleasure of these verbal turns, even if they do become an instructive counterpoint in Harper's preceptive narration.

In a discussion on the style of worship in African American churches, Thomas also registers Harper's disdain for rhetorical reliance on vernacular expression, calling for "Christly men, who will be more anxious to create and develop moral earnestness than to excite transient emotions." Thomas worries about a local reverend whose charge was "an honest, well meaning, but an ignorant congregation" who need "lifting . . . to more rational forms of worship." The reverend, it seems, shares his congregation's ostensibly inappropriate expressive style. "He tried to imitate [the congregation] and made a complete failure. He even tried to moan as they do in worship but it didn't come out natural." Even though Harper holds up an elite sermonic idiom as a desirable standard, she is clear on the historical function of what we might call a bluesy style of worship and of preaching. Lasette is not surprised that the reverend's affective "imitation" lacked authenticity:

> These dear old people whose moaning during service, seems even now so pitiful and weird, I think learned to mourn out in prayers, thoughts and feelings wrung from their agonizing hearts, which they did not dare express when they were forced to have their meetings under the surveillance of a white man." (187)

The reverend appropriates a style that cannot be, given his history, authentically his own. Without making any apologies for Harper's dichotomous construction of an irrational folk expression, we can interpret her didactic choices in accordance with the imperatives of her own rhetorical context within the black press. Also, while Harper did not work in dialect—"blues strategies," as Baker defines it—we should not dismiss out of hand the political importance of the rhetorical skill of which Lasette and Thomas are exemplars. Through a series of careful associations, Thomas literally brings white shop owner Hastings to the point of reversing his position.

Lasette's line of questioning brings Annette Harcourt to terms with the absurdity of her own racialist logic. What is more, Thomas, in his sojourn through the segregated labor market of the North, finds an important precedent in his slave heritage: "I am going to be like the runaway slave who, when asked, 'Where is your pass?' raised his fist and said 'Dem is my passes'" (186). Thomas claims the hard-won wisdom of his slave past as a characterological precept.

Through Harper's representation of a range of rhetorical styles within A.P., style becomes a marker of the class and generational divide within the black community. While Harper's ambivalence regarding vernacular modes certainly speaks of her own class privilege and rhetorical training, it is a hard case to make, as Baker does, that this ambivalence signals Harper's political capitulation to "white bourgeois" culture. Rather, by foregrounding the historical specificity of these different modes of black speech, Harper traces the common history of an African American nation, which has become increasingly divided by class interests and access to education. Baker's assertion that Harper staged some betrayal of poor Southern African Americans does not account for the novel's explicit arguments on the national labor scene, or, more generally, Harper's constant professions of solidarity with African-Americans in the South. There is no teleology of white style in Harper's texts; her own classically educated discourse is not the marker of citizenship within, in Baker's terms, an "American noplace—a mulatto utopia" (30). As we have seen, Harper's texts do not write poor Southern black people out of the race-national future. In fact, such a thing is categorically impossible in Harper's rhetorical oeuvre. Rather, like so many among her reform milieu, Harper argued that there could be no future without the entire race. Indeed, Thomas's critique of the New South challenges any separation of Northern and Southern fortunes. Such were the imperatives of uplift generally and, more specifically, of Harper's rhetorical pedagogy.

5 Not as a Mere Dependent

The Historic Mission of African American Women's Rhetoric at the End of the Century

The Black Women's Club Movement of the 1890s arose as a direct response to the "most difficult years for Black people since the abolition of slavery."[1] The repeal of the 1875 Civil Rights Act in 1883 and the *Plessy v. Ferguson* ruling exemplify the juridical framework of state–capitalist collusion, which resulted in Jim Crow labor relations and legal segregation nationally. Too often, on grounds of disciplinary and period focus, the work of African American reformers is bracketed from an account of the modern nation state. As Nikhil Pal Singh argues, "[T]he New South project . . . was a distinctively *modernizing* one that was forged in corporate board rooms by northern industrialists like Andrew Carnegie working in an alliance with emergent urban industrialist interests in the South."[2] According to Singh, historians to this day continue the nineteenth-century effacing of race-labor injustices, framing these forces and the work of those who resisted them "within a synthetic account of capitalist-nation formation" (492–493). In their writing and reform work, clubwomen such as Frances Harper, Ida B. Wells, Mary Ann Shadd Cary, Fannie Barrier Williams, and Anna Julia Cooper composed an ethic of race-womanly character that challenged the foundational precepts of race and gender identity within the operations of United States political economy.

In the 1890s, even as the U.S. political economy increasingly produced relations of social *dependence* through economic underdevelopment and class-caste hierarchy, "independence" became an economic and characterological virtue; as a late-century article of cultural faith, the individualist creed masked the systemic logic of institutional life in this country.[3] True to their abolitionist lineage, Harper and the club movement sought to undermine the laissez-faire ideology that replaced slavery as the pretext for racial segregation and reinforced the dependence–independence binary at the heart of U.S. national exceptionalism. Throughout these chapters, we have traced the rhetorical tactics of African American reformers challenging mainstream notions of "independence" by employing their pedagogies of character to de-center the monadic subject as construed within the prevailing market culture. As a matter of social reform, racial self-determination was conceived as a cross-class effort intended to lift impoverished African

Americans out of poverty and to cultivate the African American nation collectively beyond the constraints of racial caste.

"Lifting as we climb" served as the slogan of the National Association of Colored Women (NACW), of which Harper was a founding member and, in 1897, elected vice president (Boyd 225). This precept pledged reform audiences to racial solidarity across class divisions, as well as divisions of region and education. Codes and practices of uplift offered grassroots political responses to Jim Crow life after Reconstruction, and in the preceptive address of African American women like Harper, a potent language for the rhetorical engagements of reform work. However, there were divisions even among those practitioners of uplift politics, divisions marking a pedagogical boundary between neo-immediatist uplift and coerced conformity. As Kevin K. Gaines argues, African American uplift played out the contradictions between "blacks' communal quest for social justice and individualistic imperatives of survival." Gaines stipulates that in many of its incarnations, uplift was a "promotion of bourgeois morality [and] patriarchal authority" meant to impress upon "the white world" the progress and potential of African Americans. Unlike Harper's neo-immediatist strain of uplift reform, such appeals to white public opinion paid "scant attention to those elements of the state and civil society that combined to control black labor." These practices of uplift "like white supremacy [were] ultimately subject to the logic of market values and minstrel representations prescribing the subordinate social place of African Americans" (2–10). In much uplift rhetoric, the impoverished African American remained a figure of debasement, albeit a sentimental figure, a problem for those teaching race pride and proclaiming "the progress of the race" as a social imperative. In such historical narratives of progress, poor black Southern workers represented a past from which it was deemed necessary to escape and a characterological liability to remedy.

As demonstrated in previous chapters, Harper, along with the most radical of the African American immediatists, were constrained to address the ostensible degradation of Southern slaves as well as the haunting social influence of slavery among free people of color in the North. Neo-immediatist uplift, however, brought the anti-state ethic of radical antislavery rhetoric into the Gilded Age. As argued in the last chapter, dependence was a key construct in the characterological assault on African American morality and, not coincidentally, also in justifying the coercion and exploitation of black labor in the post-Reconstruction South. Fictionalizing the alleged social dependency of impoverished African American workers in the New South, Harper crafted her most expansive precepts of common humanity. According to Harper and other members of the club movement of the 1890s, the historical mission of black women's character was inseparable from the destiny of the nation. Indeed, millennialism offered a common language for imperialists, robber barons, Klansmen, and African American feminist reformers, all of whom, albeit to radically disparate ends, claimed the ethos of the emerging nation state's exceptionalist character. Amid the pervasive proclamations of national reunification and Southern redemption that served as justification for the post-Reconstruction political economy, African American women publicized their own sense of the changing times as a matter of character talk in an effort to humanize and reinterpret African Americans' daily economic and social struggles. Clubwomen developed complementary arguments about historical progression that gained authority from the exceptionalist narrative even while articulating the political claims and needs of those marginalized within its social order.

The complexity and contradictions in Harper's rhetoric of dependence are evident in her 1891 address, "Duty to Dependent Races," delivered in Washington, D.C., before the National Council of Women, on whose national board she served. This address exemplifies the complicated position of Harper as an activist in the nascent and changeable multiracial reform community of the late nineteenth century. In her address, Harper focused on the widespread lynching of African Americans, the most dramatic manifestation of the more general culture of terror that eclipsed official "independence" in the South. Harper's laborite novel *Trial and Triumph* forwards the address's central argument—give us these tools, the logic of the drama runs, and indeed we will achieve independence. "Duty to Dependent Races" was delivered with a number of other addresses under the general heading of "Charities and Philanthropies." As Shirley Wilson Logan notes, Harper's address faced the "immediate challenge" of countering "the essentialized characterization of a 'dependent race'" by disputing the preconceptions sounded by her fellow presenters, the prevailing racial common sense regarding "the condition of black people in America at the time—their causes, effects, and remedy" (*We are Coming* 62–63). At every turn in her text, Harper is at pains to represent African Americans "not as a mere dependent asking for Northern sympathy or Southern compassion, but as a member of the body politic who has a claim upon the nation for justice . . . which is the right of every race" (86).

This is not to say that Harper entirely vilified the dependence reform argument. In the late century, for every claim Harper made for the self-determining character of her race, she also hailed her audience as dependents within a wider existential, political, and spiritual collective. As argued in the last chapter, in her public addresses, poems, and fictions, Harper taught against the pedagogy of prevailing economic systems that impeded labor agency and thus created a dependent class systematically. As the century continued, this critique, which casts dependence as a product of political-economic brutality rather than as a characterological flaw, was articulated increasingly through the language of racial uplift, evincing the ideological contradictions noted previously. Decrying the intensification of lynching in the South, Harper notes, "Outside of America, I know of no other civilized country, Catholic, Protestant, or even Muhammadan, where men are still lynched, murdered and even burned for real or supposed crimes." She argues that any government that "has power to tax a man in peace and draft him in war" but will not exercise its power to secure for all citizens "life . . . liberty . . . [and] . . . due process of law . . . is vicious." "The strongest nation on earth," Harper asserts, "cannot afford to deal unjustly towards its weakest and feeblest members." And yet, in making this anti-lynching argument, the weakness and feebleness of African Americans is presented as necessary evidence of state crimes.

According to similar reasoning, the "ignorance" Harper attributes to Southern African Americans is crucial evidence of the necessity of a national educational system, rather than evidence of a characterological flaw (83). To be sure, Harper, like many of her Protestant compatriots, was invested in representing dependence itself as the inevitable state of human relations for good and for ill, a mutual dependence premised on a "common Christianity."

Figure 5.1 A photograph of Frances Harper from H. F. Kletzing's 1897 *Progress of a Race: or, the Remarkable Advancement of the American Negro.* Manuscripts, Archives and Rare Books Division, Schomburg Center for Research in Black Culture, The New York Public Library, Astor, Lenox and Tilden Foundation.

Harper carefully distinguishes from the "terrible perversions" of colonizing Christianity, the former constituting a "religion glowing with love and replete with life . . . which will be to all weaker races an uplifting power and not a degrading influence" (90–91). Clubwomen did not simply counter charges of dependency; from the perspective of the contemporaneous political discourse, their texts often had a more radical purpose. As Nancy Fraser and Linda Gordon conclude, reformers in the United States in the 1890s attempted to rehabilitate the idea of dependency ("A Genealogy" 132). This rehabilitation sought to raise the category not simply to the status of an understandable or acceptable weakness. Precepts of the moral strength required for productive mutual dependence came to predominate Harper's work in this era. In the rhetoric of the most radical of clubwomen, dependency between the state and its citizens and among social subjects more generally became itself a necessary model for economic as well as spiritual life.

As she had many times at national, multiracial forums, Harper followed unstinting criticisms of state immorality with a centering call to subjects not fully bound by state allegiance. Like the Paul of Galatians to whom she alludes in the following passage, Harper made her address to fellow Christians:

> Be reconciled to God for making a man black, permitting him to become part of your body politic, and sharing one roof or acre of our goodly heritage. Be reconciled to the Christ of Calvary, who said, "And I, if I be lifted up, will draw all men to me," and "it is better for a man that a millstone were hanged about his neck, and he were drowned in the depths of the sea, that he should offend one of these little ones that believe in me. . . . There is neither Greek nor Jew, circumcision nor uncircumcision, Scythian nor Barbarian, bond nor free, but Christ is all, and in all." ("Duty to Dependent Races" 91)

The all-absorbing identification with Christ echoes Harper's "We Are All Bound up Together" address, delivered in 1866 to the largely white audience of the National Women's Rights Convention in New York. This intersubjectivity dissolves religious, national, and cultural divisions. Harper's participation in the internationally focused Universal Peace Union also suggests the universalist goals always underwriting more particularist calls to character.[4] Even in these years, at the height of New Southern violence and segregation, Harper recorded her lasting hope in an ideally democratic republic. The remainder of this chapter examines the rhetorical pedagogy Harper articulated along the conceptual continuum of the dependence–independence binary as she taught the characterological means of affiliational language.

AFRICAN AMERICAN WOMANHOOD IN THE RACIAL STATE

Among the participants of the clubwomen's movement, Ida B. Wells had a strong reputation for her uncompromising opposition to the corruption and weakness of the law. Wells led an international campaign against "lynch law" in the South and was influential among a number of women's organizations.[5] She founded her own newspaper, the *Free Speech*, and published numerous pamphlets documenting the national scope of white terror in the South. Harper and Wells held common political commitments to anti-lynching and civil rights protections, for all the apparent differences in their rhetorical practices. Melba Joyce Boyd rightly characterizes the two women's "ideological and activist politics" as existing "in concert" (220–221). Angela Davis credits Wells's journalism and oratory as a central force in inaugurating the clubwomen's movement. In retribution for her campaign against lynching, the *Memphis Free Speech* was burned to the ground and her life was threatened. As Paula Giddings notes, it was fortunate that when the destruction occurred, Wells was in

Figure 5.2   Ida B. Wells is rightfully remembered as a groundbreaking journalist and uncompromising crusader for racial justice. Manuscripts, Archives and Rare Books Division, Schomburg Center for Research in Black Culture, The New York Public Library, Astor, Lenox and Tilden Foundation.

Philadelphia, having taken up a "long-standing invitation" from Harper. From Philadelphia, Wells went to New York, where she continued her work through a series of articles in the *New York Age*, which helped catalyze women's rights and anti-lynching activity among clubwomen.[6] In October of 1892, at a rally in New York's Lyric Hall, a "moving presentation" by Wells raised a good deal of money and led immediately to the formation of the Women's Loyal Union, Boston's Women's Era Club, and the NACW, which, as mentioned earlier, Harper co-founded (Giddings, *When and Where* 28–30). In her autobiography, Wells would identify this as the "real beginning of the club movement among the colored women in this country" (*Crusade for Justice* 81).

Just as surely as Wells's uncompromising example spurred the development of the club movement, her theoretical acumen impacted the rhetorical pedagogy of clubwomen in the 1890s. As the pre-eminent voice of protest against lynching, Wells exposed the sentimentalized defense of lynching as a mask for preserving old notions of white Southern women's purity. Wells was a brilliant rhetorician, deconstructing the cultural and political maintenance of white supremacism, which developed new justifications for "lynch law" as the century progressed. No one more successfully challenged the widespread allegations of the rape of white women by African American men, which became the leading rationale for lynching. Through careful research largely in white newspapers including the *Chicago Tribune*, Wells demonstrated how such charges were systematically claimed without evidence and used as justification for the lynching of black men, many of whom had achieved economic success and were thus viewed as a threat. When Wells's friend Thomas Moss and his business associates were lynched in Memphis, Wells noted that "they had committed no crime against white women"—a fact that "opened [her] eyes to what lynching really was. An excuse to get rid of Negroes who were acquiring wealth and property and thus keep the race terrorized and 'keep the nigger down'" (*Crusade for Justice* 64). Striking at core characterological precepts of white supremacism and patriarchal privilege, she openly questions the hegemonic common places of race and sexuality and the devastating political figure of the black male sexual aggressor:

> Nobody in this section of the country believes the old thread-bare lie that Negro men rape white women. If Southern white men are not careful, they will over-reach themselves and public sentiment will have a reaction; a conclusion will then be reached which will be very damaging to the moral reputation of their women. (*Southern Horrors* 52)

Wells performs a transgressive reversal in these lines, one that upsets a central topos of lynch law by rejecting the premised right of white countrymen to control a class of dependent white women.

By challenging the "thread-bare" assumptions about a de-humanizing, predatory sexuality and the race-sexual fidelity of white Southern women, Wells raises the devastating double standard regarding the relative value of African American women's "virtue." As was her usual tactic, Wells cites a "leading journal in South Carolina," which reported,

> It is not the same thing for a white man to assault a colored woman as for a colored man to assault a white woman, because the colored woman had no finer feelings nor virtue to be outraged. Yet colored women have always had far more reason to complain of white men in this respect than ever white women have had of Negroes. (*Southern Horrors* 127)

This double standard, which positioned African American women outside the cultural protection of true womanhood, had its roots in the slave economy. Even as miscegenation laws outlawed any sexual relation between African American men and white women, the routine rape of African American women by white men provided a means of increasing the slave population (Carby, *Reconstructing Womanhood* 30–31).

As Giddings argues, African American clubwomen had before them the task of inventing a new morality within the conceptual framework of "true womanhood." This was in part a matter of re-teaching womanhood across the class divide (85). As a matter of rhetorical practice for women working in the public sphere, the revaluation of ideological codes of gender performance was essential for claiming a new discursive space for African American women's virtue. This historical defense of womanhood divided clubwomen along a continuum of reform rhetoric, marking a pedagogical divergence over the extent to which white public opinion could be or ought to be mollified. Such a "defense" was often as simple as cataloguing the exemplary lives and accomplishments of African American women. Establishing proof of African American women's moral character became a crucial act for the articulation of protest rhetoric.

By exposing the economic and political factors that motivated the assault on African American women's character, clubwomen like Wells and Harper cast African American women as a potent political force, one that disrupted the privatizing discourses aligned against them, and invoked a collective African American community.[7] In "Coloured Women of America," published in the *Englishwoman's Review* in 1878, Harper argued that "women as [a] class are quite equal to the men in energy and executive capacity." As evidence, Harper's character portraits reassert a familiar ethos of her reform argument, that of the independent republican producer—farmers and merchants working, saving, and acquiring land—to model the potential for success contingent on free integration of African Americans into the economy. As exemplars of robust economic citizenship, Harper significantly held up "widows and unaided women" who joined the agricultural labor force, made inroads into the professions, owned land, and hired their own employees (*BCD* 272–73).

Harper was among a small group of African American women to speak as members of the Women's Representative Congress at the 1893 Chicago World's Columbian Exposition. Alan Trachtenberg calls the Columbian Exposition "an oasis of fantasy and fable at a time of crisis," a "pedagogy" of benevolent American world leadership (208–209).[8] Harper used her opportunity at this prestigious forum to forecast the progress of reform in her address, "Woman's Political Future." There, at an event meant to celebrate and evince the nation's progress, Harper heralded the historicity of women's character against the violence of white terror authorized by an indifferent state:

> If the fifteenth century discovered America to the Old World, the nineteenth is discovering woman to herself . . . Not discovering new worlds, but that of filling this old world with fairer and higher aims than the greed of gold and the lust for power, is hers . . . [T]o-day we stand on the threshold of woman's era, and woman's work is grandly constructive . . . As the saffron tints and crimson flushes of morn herald the coming day, so the social and political advancement which woman has already gained bears the promise of the rising of the full-orbed sun of emancipation. The result will not be to make home less happy, but society more holy; yet I do not think the mere extension of the ballot a panacea for all the ills of our national life. What we need to-day is not simply more voters, but better voters. To-day there are red-handed in our republic, who walk unwhipped of justice . . . brutal and cowardly men, who torture, burn and lynch their fellow-men . . . More than the changing of institutions we need the development of a national conscience and upbuilding of national character . . . and it is the women of a country who help mold its character, and . . . influence if not determine its destiny. (433–434)

As she had since the beginning of her career, Harper bases the notion of moral character on a foundational state of self-knowledge and a process of self-examination "discovering woman to herself." This insularity opens immediately to the project of "higher aims" than the accumulative drive of "greed and gold and the lust for power," forces that clubwomen associated with industrial capitalism and which, Harper here implies, delay the advent of "emancipation." Lynch law was the instantiation of the post-Reconstruction eclipse of civil rights and equal protections, and for Harper and Wells, it was the mark of the nation's brutality and cowardice. In Harper's argument, the exceptional social progress heralded by the Columbian Exposition depended on women's influence over "national conscience and . . . national character." Here, Harper delivers her jeremiadic call to republican motherhood, the claims of which grew increasingly expansive in the late century.

As "Woman's Political Future" continues, Harper predicts that along with the traditional role of moral persuader, "[t]o [women] is apparently coming the added responsibility of political power" (435). However, women's suffrage is posited here not as the ultimate goal, but as a simple preparation for "the coming glory of God." Her denial that suffrage would prove a social "panacea" belies the post-Reconstruction skepticism Harper reserved for institutional politics. Thus, without denying the inherently conservative impulses in her work, we can acknowledge Harper's eschewal of "changing institutions" in a neo-immediatist context. As argued in the last chapter, by the 1880s, Harper's coalitional address was markedly post-Republican. Indeed, the millennial accents of the clubwomen's rhetoric suggest the degree to which the non-state emphasis of abolitionism continued to influence their work.

Given Harper's general response to the collapse of Reconstruction, we should not, perhaps, be surprised by the sustained critique of governmental institutions that marks her late work. What is the value of a ballot, she suggests, in the hands of one who would murder? In the *African Methodist Episcopal Church Review* in 1884, along with Frederick Douglass, William Still, T. Thomas Fortune, Henry McNeal Turner, and others, Harper responded to the question, "The Democratic Return to Power—Its Effect?" (Foreman 197). As part of her response, Harper suggested that "for the next twenty years the colored people take no feverish interest in the success or failure of either party" and focus instead on developing "an intelligent and virtuous manhood, and a tender, strong and true womanhood." This should not be understood, however, as Harper's abdication of civil rights protest. Shirley Wilson Logan argues that Harper's assertion that "we can afford to wait for political strength while developing moral and spiritual power" is an appeal to racial self determination and not racial accommodation (*We Are Coming* 153).

Teaching the precepts and idioms of human duty and interconnection more fundamental than citizenship, Harper practiced a familiar race-national politics of the Afro-Protestant press. In his analysis of Harper's "Enlightened Motherhood," a lecture delivered at a gathering of the Brooklyn Literary Society on November 15, 1892, Russ Castronovo reads Harper as locating the best hope of the racial nation "snugly on domestic doorsteps." To be sure, the lecture holds the training of character to be the generative ground of a progressing racial collective. Offering strict advice on avoiding coercive or intemperate husbands, Harper returns to long-standing precepts of egalitarian marriage and republican motherhood. Harper claims that by training children for lives of moral purpose, mothers give the world "something better than the results of arrogance, aggressiveness, and indomitable power"—a collective social conscience which can "uplift the race" (*BCD* 292). Like any number of other lectures and texts written over her career, "Enlightened Motherhood" claims privileged space for women's pedagogical practice. As Castronovo argues, this rhetoric of "disconnection" from the state had great use value for African American women attempting to subvert the "masculinist state." Harper's "black republican motherhood" was perhaps less a matter of attempting a transcendence than an attempt to establish "nonnational" citizenship that would "function *below* bureaucratic levels of the state in everyday subterranean incrustations that withstand interpellation" (206–207). For a reform leader articulating a logic of affiliation, Harper invented a constitutive rhetoric intended to create just the kind of discursive space Castronovo evokes.

What, then, did Harper teach Chicago Exposition visitors about social dependence in the first "Columbian" era? What, under the auspices of the Women's Representative Congress, did she teach them about African American womanhood? As argued in the introduction, Harper's theory of women's political future takes up republican and Protestant millennialist sources of cultural authority to make a claim to a national ethos. This jeremiad, however, served a specific teaching function for African American women. For Harper, the "upbuilding of national character" rested on a new literacy, which she and the clubwomen modeled in themselves and called for in others. Thus, their pedagogy operated within a self-reflexive logic, in which reform rhetoric cultivated the private introspection necessary to rightly judge the public role of African American women's political voices. In the historical theory underwriting their rhetorical pedagogy, the self-reliance of women might bring about national transformation.

Though Harper barred racial descriptors from her NACW rhetoric, in the work of clubwomen as a whole, it is the character of African American women that bears the (rhetorical) burden of this historical mission. And if "lifting as we climb," the slogan of the NACW, posits the responsibility for "improvement" on African Americans themselves, it is the argument of this chapter that, for Harper, the "climb" always involved a lessons about economic hierarchy itself, both at a national level and within the tenuous black middle class. As was her wont from the very first of her abolitionist writings and lectures, Harper was not shy about criticizing the "isolation" of portions of her privileged audience.[9]

Also speaking at the Women's Congress in the Chicago Exposition, Anna Julia Cooper, like Harper, refused to be silent about racial oppression in her address (Logan 114). Cooper's *A Voice from the South* offers perhaps the most extensive pedagogical argument regarding the importance of women's social influence. Cooper, one of the first African American women to earn a doctorate in the United States, was Harper's compatriot in the NACW and a staunch advocate of higher education for African American women. She introduces her collection of essays with the metaphor of a national trial in which "[o]ne important witness has not yet been heard from. The summing up of the evidence deposed, and the charge to the jury have been made—but no word from the Black Woman" (ii). Like Harper, Cooper called for the rhetorical resources of African American women, arguing that the state's ethical viability cannot be settled without their judgment.

A logic of historical "progression" structures Cooper's argument, as does the claim that "the foundation stones of our future as a race" are anchored by "a regenerating womanhood" (25). Positing this regenerative power as the antithesis of a long world history of Anglo-Saxon barbarism, Cooper suggests a periodization for American history. In this scheme, the initial pioneer period is followed by a "wealth producing period," followed by an "era of thought and reform," which Cooper heralded as emergent. Cooper located her argument for the importance of education for African American women in this critical moment of race-national destiny. "Because [women's] sentiments must strike the keynote and give the dominant tone to . . . the era about to dawn," their intellectual preparation was crucial. As the following passage suggests, Cooper held women's influence to be the impetus of historical progression itself, the transition from "a wealth producing period" to a world imagined through the moral lens of the Black Women's Club Movement:

> You will not find political economists declaring that the only possible adjustment between laborers and capitalists is that of selfishness and rapacity—that each must get all he can and keep all that he gets, while the world cries laissez faire and the lawyers explain, "it is the beautiful working of law of supply and demand;" in fine, you will not find the law of love shut out from the affairs of men after the feminine half of the world's truth is completed. (58)

The idea that a feminine force had yet to express itself historically, and that that expression would be a regenerative force, informs Cooper's vision of an African American future. In an essay entitled "Has America a Race Problem; If So, How Can It Best Be Solved?" Cooper offers a theory of social adjustment as a means of arguing against "race prejudice," as well as immigration restrictions. Cooper asserts that *"equilibrium, not repression, among conflicting forces is the condition of natural harmony, of permanent progress, and of universal freedom"* (160). According to Cooper's theory of history, any law limiting the education or political freedom of African Americans is a historical aberration, retrogressive and ultimately destined to give way to a proper balance of social power. In this line of reasoning, social conflict is not simply competition, but another, world-historical form of mutual dependence.

Published in 1892, the same year as Cooper's collection, Harper's last novel, *Iola Leroy, or Shadows Uplifted*, is the text on which her current critical reputation is largely based and a central text in the discourse of club-women. Like *Minnie's Sacrifice* in 1869, the novel champions the historic mission of African American women's moral character before and after the Civil War. Late in the novel, in a chapter that recounts a club-like salon of educated African Americans, the Reverend Charmicle asserts the historical progressionist argument: "[T]he evils of society . . . are no solvents as potent as love and justice, and our greatest need is not more wealth and learning, but a religion replete with life and glowing with love. Let this be the impelling force in the race and it cannot fail to rise in the scale of character and condition" (260). Such claims can be found in Harper's oeuvre from her earliest abolitionist writing and oratory. However, despite the faith in providential agency claimed in this passage, the novel works as a historical catalogue of the barriers to such progress. Referencing the culture of white supremacist terrorism in the South, Harper was at pains to publicize the "savage elements in our civilization, which hear the advancing tread of the Negro and would retard his coming" (259).

In the radically contingent personhood of Iola, who survives the dehumanizing effects of slavery on African American women, Harper wrought her most powerful pedagogical heroine. The pedagogy of *Iola Leroy*, like that of Harper's other fictions, reconfigures the precepts by which African American social progress was assessed.[10] Here again, the assertion of progress resulting from exceptional character serves as a political heuristic. Like its predecessor, *Minnie's Sacrifice*, *Iola Leroy* follows the story of a mulatta from before the Civil War to Reconstruction, recounting her transformations in legal status and race-national consciousness. Iola, raised as a wealthy planter's daughter, is reduced to slave status as her mother Marie's slave status is revealed. With the end of the war, Iola devotes herself to service to "the race," and, like Minnie before her, she chooses African American affiliation despite a number of opportunities to pass as white. Iola's ambiguous racial identity allows Harper to encode her theories on race relations in her heroine's social experience.

Giving voice to Harper's precepts of African American uplift and modeling a discursive politics for women reformers, Iola's determined sojourn across eras in the racial state teaches lessons of character fit for the post-Reconstruction moment. As the rest of this chapter argues, Harper situated the rhetorical pedagogy of the novel around powerful commonplaces of social dependence and independence, which structure the sweeping historical trajectory of *Iola Leroy* and the quotidian actions and words of its character's daily lives. Lauren Berlant explains this journey as one "about an arduous pilgrimage to full citizenship in American law and the public sphere . . . from sexual domination in domestic and laboring spaces . . . to public renunciation of the nation for the pseudo-democratic promises it makes" (24). With this apt description of *Iola Leroy* as a protest novel, we must consider as well how the polemicized practice of self-making, what Berlant conceives as a "pilgrimage," operates pedagogically within the progressive logic of African American character talk. As a survivor of the slave system and an exemplar of clubwoman politics in the "woman's era," Iola embodies the brightest hopes for racial self-determination. Iola's improbable control over her own body figures not only her feminine purity according to the code of true womanhood, but also the ethic of self-determination found throughout the discourse of racial uplift.

The writing and oratory of Fannie Barrier Williams offers another version of moral character and the ethic of self-determination. Williams's short history, "The Club Movement among Colored Women of America," was included in the 1900 collection *A New Negro for a New Century*, edited by Booker T. Washington, N. B. Wood, and Williams herself.[11] A founding member and eventually the leader of the NACW, Williams's representation of a "new negro" differs from Harper, Wells, and Cooper's re-evaluation of black women's character as a site of political protest. Like many middle-class reformers, Williams explains the work of uplift as the "force of a new intelligence against the old ignorance. The struggle of an enlightened conscience against the whole brood of social miseries born out of the stress and pain of a hated past" (428). Williams's deep investment in countering claims of dependence sets her apart from her compatriots' more radical view of social dependence as a political pedagogy. Williams's ethic of self-determination puts the burden of change on poor African Americans much more so than on the violent political-economic system in which they were trapped. Her sense of black women's historicity is that "[s]he is needed to change the old idea of things implanted in the minds of the white race and there sustained and hardened into a national habit by the debasing influence of slavery estimates. The woman is needed as an educator of public opinion" (426).

Williams's address at the Chicago Exhibition, "The Intellectual Progress of the Colored Women," teaches racial imitation at the expense of immediatist invention. As Shirley Wilson Logan argues,

[Williams] created a picture of women struggling to "catch up" with their white sisters in all things and to develop morally and intellectually in order to achieve the "blessedness of intelligent womanhood." She pictured black women not as claiming a rightful equality as Harper had . . . but as striving to earn the equality . . . She dwelled upon what she called a "lack of morals" among the formerly enslaved and emphasized the need, after emancipation, for learning family values . . . Williams and other black women felt that racial advancement would follow on the heels of social respectability. (105)

As we have seen, Harper was also apt to bemoan the intellectual and moral habits of the so-called dependent poor, but in nearly every case, such complaints implicated the political-economic power responsible for creating the conditions of dependence. As Paula Giddings asserts, Williams was not primarily interested in "defending" the history of the race or redefining codes of "true womanhood." Williams instead lauds the clubwomen as a historic class of elite black women charged with teaching struggling black women how to adapt themselves to bourgeois social norms, writing that the "terms good and bad, bright and dull, plain and beautiful are now as applicable to colored women as to women of other races" (402). Clearly, the Victorian virtues of the clubwomen whose photographs adorn Williams's essay are the crucial figures in her evidentiary argument. However, the oppressive codes of characterological morality themselves are left unchallenged.

Harper herself was not completely free of this class and generational bias. Her maternal condescension at times suggests a de-valuation of the black worker's intellect and character. One example of such condescension is found late in *Iola Leroy* in a discussion among the educated elite of the novel's African American community. One character says, "I am sorry to see a number of our young men growing away from the influence of the church and drifting into prisons" (259). To represent such imprisonment as a "drifting" is problematic, the word, of course, signifying a lack of resolve and character in Harper's lexicon. Harper acknowledges that the rise in black imprisonment, in one character's words, "is owing to a partial administration of law in meting out punishment to colored offenders," and yet the characterological charge against African Americans remains. The same conversation yields the wisdom that race leaders should "pass it along the lines, that to be willfully ignorant is to be shamefully criminal" (260). Even as she devoted her life to advocacy of impoverished African Americans, Harper shared in part in Williams's assumptions of a regrettable "spirit of dependency" among those she considered to be her charge (Williams 427). However, there remains a key distinction between Williams's elitist version of reform and Harper's more radical critique of dependence in that, for Williams, individual transformation was the primary goal of reform, while Harper's pedagogy of self-determination within mutual dependence was a means for enacting broad transformation in the political-economic system writ large.

THE POLITICAL ECONOMICS OF DEPENDENCE

Harper's re-coding of the dependence–independence binary—teaching the lesson of independence within dependence—arose from a long history of pedagogical rhetoric. In their essay "A Genealogy of 'Dependency': Tracing a Keyword of the U.S. Welfare State," Nancy Fraser and Linda Gordon follow the development and political use of notions of social dependency from sixteenth-century England to the late twentieth-century United States. In feudal England, Fraser and Gordon argue, dependency was a non-valued descriptor of laborers in a strictly stratified society. Dependency, in a sense, was seen as a very natural state and carried no "individual stigma." In the eighteenth and nineteenth centuries, however, it was the notion of independence that became "radically democratized," and within the discourse of independence, "we see the shadow of a powerful anxiety about dependency." Dependence, which "had been a normal and unstigmatized condition became deviant and stigmatized" (123–126). The authors argue that in colonial America, rejecting dependence on an earthly authority became "akin to rejecting blasphemy and false gods," and thus, only dependence on God retained a positive moral register. When this radical notion of independence emerged as the dominant characterological precept in the industrial age, the question of wage labor brought about the ideology of what Fraser and Gordon call "industrial dependency." In this new dispensation, "the pauper" became an icon, introducing a "moral/psychological register" to the notion of dependency. Because it lacked a strong feudal tradition, "the United States was especially hospitable to elaborating dependency as a defect of individual character," rather than as an inherent byproduct of wealth-based economic systems (131).

Fraser and Gordon conclude in the United States, racialized and gendered subjects of dependence were the politicized identities that accompanied the rise of late capitalism and the "welfare state." Like the historians of racial oppression referred to throughout these chapters, Fraser and Gordon note that it was through arguments about intrinsic character that systematic oppression was legitimated. Certainly, George Fitzhugh's treatise, *Cannibals All, or Slaves without Masters*, examined in Chapter 2, is a vivid example of such identity politics. It was the figure of "the slave" that became the "characterological distillation" of political as well as "economic dependency." Such interpolations were, as we have seen, juxtaposed purposefully with that of the white wage earner. The slave and "housewife" were crucial categories of dependence that allowed the white male worker to be constructed as a position of independence at a time when there was widespread anxiety regarding the contingent freedom of wage labor. Thus while "all relations of subordination had previously counted as dependency relations, now capital-labor relations were exempted" (Fraser and Gordon 129–131). In many of her speeches, Harper spoke out directly against how the notion of economic dependency was being hegemonically subverted to justify the formation of a new underclass in service of the nation's unprecedented capitalist expansion. Harper's re-teaching of fundamental social relations inverts the dependence–independence binary, arguing that it is in fact the state that is dependent on those it most manifestly disenfranchises.

Though documenting the coercive labor conditions of black workers in the South, *Iola Leroy* also trains a critical lens on the segregated Northern labor market. Iola reiterates her claim that "every woman should have some skill or art which would insure her at least a comfortable support," and that "there would be less unhappy marriages if labor were more honored among women." True to her longstanding commitment to the precepts of free labor culture, Harper understood the need to reform public opinion concerning not only race and gender, but also the culture of work itself. For Harper, labor was as surely a path to self-determination for women as for men. Iola's stated belief that "every woman ought to know how to earn her own living" is a clear enough challenge to gendered notions of domestic dependency. Securing employment, however, is only one component of Iola's mission if we pay attention to the rhetorical pedagogy of the novel. After several attempts, demonstrating a necessary resilience and determination in the face of racial prejudice, Iola finds a position as a private nurse. Harper gives Iola's white employer, Mrs. Cloten, the final say on the matter of labor segregation and racial prejudice:

> In dealing with Southern prejudice against the Negro, we Northerners could do it with better grace if we divested ourselves of our own. We irritate the South by our criticisms, and while I confess that there is much that is reprehensible in their treatment of colored people, yet if our Northern civilization is higher than theirs we should "criticize by creation." We should stamp ourselves on the South, and not let the South stamp itself on us. (205–212)

In Mrs. Cloten, Iola finds a white woman who shares her reform sensibilities. The notion that the force of example might bring about cultural change is fully in keeping with Harper's precept regarding the persuasive force of moral character. Since her earliest poems, Harper held to this pedagogy of material demonstration, of principled and powerfully symbolic action within the labor market.

However, beyond her specific claims regarding the contingency of economic independence for African American women and men, Harper problematizes the notion of social dependence through an appeal to a common humanity that is itself conceived as radically contingent. It is, in fact, a necessity that all Christians understand their own dependence on the power of the God that had

> heaved up your mountains with grandeur, flooded your rivers with majesty, crowned your vales with fertility and enriched your mines with wealth . . . Excluding Alaska, you have, I think, nearly three hundred millions of square miles. Be reconciled to God for making a man black, permitting him to become part of your body politic, and sharing one roof or acre of our goodly heritage. ("Duty to Dependent Races" 91)

In the logic of this passage, it is only through an obedience to God's will that the vast resources of the United States shift from the sequestered holdings of a "you" to "our goodly heritage." In the convergence of this address, a mutual dependence on God's abundance mandates a sharing of the enormous national resources, which are posited as themselves a gift for common use and not property to be withheld.

In the late century, Harper had occasion to consider the coercion of African American labor and rhetorical power. In her 1891 *A.M.E. Church Review* essay entitled "Temperance," discussed in Chapter 3, Harper repeatedly strays from the ostensible subject implied in her title to a discussion of "the crimes of the reconstruction period" and the appalling increase in "men fallen basely and brutally murdered since the war in Southern lands." This jeremiad against lynching is framed historically in a manner that should now be familiar, that is, as a criticism of the immorality of the state:

> After his emancipation, his enslavers had the need of his labor, and his deliverers a use for his ballot, and as he was freed partly as a military necessity, it may have been equally pertinent to have given him his vote as a political necessity. I shall not attempt to dwell on the failures of reconstruction . . . A government that can protect its citizens and will not, is a vicious government; a government that would protect its citizens and cannot is a weak government. Let the intellectuality in our race, which has been used in advocating the claims of the Republican party, grapple with the inherent weakness or viciousness in our government, which has power to tax men in peace and draft them in war, and yet fails to make their lives sacred under the shadow of its Constitution. (qtd. in Boyd 199).

In the utilitarian schema Harper charts, North and South no longer exist as such, but rather are united in their common exploitation of African American resources. The paragraph break marks a disjunction in the political-economic narrative she has initiated. Harper begins by noting the successful efforts of planters to substitute a system of peonage for the slave system and keep black laborers politically neutralized by means of the lynching she decries. Harper notes that Republicans ultimately pushed black suffrage only to swell the ranks of their own constituency. Her self-impeachment is a striking acknowledgment that her own political and intellectual efforts during Reconstruction were used to legitimate a fundamentally corrupt state politics. The Constitution is rendered ominously in shadow, suggesting its juridical failure and the ultimately baseless liberatory "claims of the Republican party," which Harper herself had once legitimated at the podium and in the presses.

It is against the backdrop of this economic critique that Harper makes a seemingly more conservative argument for racial self-help, criticizing many of the allegedly inept or corrupt black politicians of Reconstruction for not being "self-sacrificing lovers of the race." Amid the rhetorical space of the "hush harbor" provided by the forum of the *A.M.E. Church Review*, Harper did not avoid some disparaging comments about the first generation of African American legislators.[12] She says of those African Americans serving as "legislators and officeholders," "I scarcely remember having seen one colored man holding any important position, whom I had known, either by person or reputation, as having been either a leader, or very prominent in the anti-slavery agitation" (qtd. in Boyd 199). These comments are consistent with Harper's general skepticism about the progressive potential of government. Countering *Atlanta Constitution* editor Henry Grady's claims about the general dependency of African American character—a circular argument in which the enforced poverty and disenfranchisement of black Southerners serves as evidence of character—Harper reasons,

> Power will naturally gravitate into the strongest hands, be they white or black; and to strengthen our hands, and base our race-life on those divine certitudes, which are the only safe foundations of either individuals or nations, is of more vital importance to us than being the appendage of any political party. Let the race that expends so much for pleasure, learn to expend more for strength. Let the young people all over the country form themselves into reading clubs, and gather information from ancient lore and modern learning to throw light on the unresolved problems of our modern civilization. Let them learn to unite with the great moral and philanthropic movements of the day, and add their quota to the progress and development of the country. (qtd. in Boyd 201)

As a means of marshalling of the intellectual resources of the race, Harper prescribes the kinds of voluntary organizations of which she herself was an active member and which were beginning to flourish in the late century. In Harper's rhetorical culture, intellectual self-determination figures crucially not only in cultivating the African American nation but also in the "progress and development" of the state itself.

Like Harper, Ida B. Wells also reverses the prevailing racialist logic of economic dependence, arguing that it is "[t]o Northern capital and Afro-American labor the South owes its rehabilitation. If labor is withdrawn capital will not remain. The Afro-American is thus the backbone of the South" (*Southern Horrors* 68). Indeed, in a chapter entitled "Self Help," Wells constructs a radical version of self-help as political resistance:

> Nothing is more definitely settled than [the African American] must act for himself. I have shown how he may employ the boycott, emigration and the press, and I feel that by a combination of all these agencies can be effectually stamped out lynch laws . . . "the gods help those who help themselves." (72)

Such a version of self-help is far removed from Williams's capitulation to white public opinion. Rather than a conservative characterological charge, self-help is presented as a difficult necessity in the post–civil rights era. Similarly, Anna Julia Cooper's 1899 editorial in *The Southern Workman and Hampton School Record*, "The Colored Woman as Wage-Earner," also turns to economics to directly confront the privatized notion of women's dependence within the African American community. In making her claim for the powerful economic agency of African American women, Cooper places them at the center of the livelihood of the community without resorting to the sentimental claims of true womanhood. Cooper notes that unlike white women, African American women in the workforce are many, and she asks that in assessing the meaning of this phenomenon, her readers set "[s]entiment aside." Of domestic duties, Cooper notes, "[T]he highest services can not be measured by dollars and cents." Acknowledging the traditionalist perspective on women's work in the home, Cooper writes, "It is sordid to talk about paying mothers to be mothers, and giving a wage to wife to be wife!" Understanding her transgression, Cooper asks that her readers stay focused on the "dry but fundamental principles of economics," noting that the "fact remains that a large percentage of the productive labor of the world is done by women," and citing an Atlanta University study that found African American women to be the primary earners in more than half of African American families. She goes on to speak of marriage, much as Harper does in her domestic fictions, as a most honorable and socially regenerative, contractual arrangement (200–201).

In an attempt to shed the ideological constraints of sentiment, Cooper argues for the fundamental dependence of society upon maternity in a manner worthy of republican motherhood but based more squarely on the physiological labor of those assumed domestic roles. Cooper goes so far as to suggest metaphorically a notion that even now remains well within the political margin, that the bearing of children is itself a form of "labor" which should be considered in economic terms. She argues that "by her foresight and wisdom, her calm insight and tact, her thrift and frugality, her fertility of resource and largeness of hope and faith, the colored woman can prove that a prudent marriage is the very best investment that a working man can make" (205). To be sure, Cooper's estimation of the economic agency of African American women, like Harper's as expressed in "Woman's Political Future," counters not only the charges of a black dependent character in society as a whole, but also the assumption of women's dependence on men within the African American community itself. Their insistence on women's economic and rhetorical agency telegraphs how the clubwomen positioned their mission at a contentious intersection of racial and gender politics.

The precept of interdependence within a society of collective duty underwrote Harper's pedagogy of uplift and her practice of pedagogical fiction. As do her previous novels, *Iola Leroy* argues for uplift fealty across class and regional lines. The literary romance genre provided Harper with the means of countering cultural assumptions regarding essentially dependent feminine character. As Hazel Carby argues in the case of *Iola Leroy*, the romance plot is refigured as a political union, a coalition of like-minded and mutually committed ethical life practices (79–80). To achieve this refiguration, Harper conflates rhetorical skill with romantic affections: as Iola discourses on the future of the race, Iola's suitor Dr. Latimer is "spellbound" along with the rest of Iola's auditors. "She is strangely beautiful!" Latimer remarks: "As Iola finished, there was a ring of triumph in her voice, as if she were reviewing a path she had trodden with bleeding feet, and seen it change to lines of living light. Her soul seemed to be flashing through the rare loveliness of her face and etherealizing its beauty" (257).

Thus, from the outset, the impetus for romance is underwritten by needful participation in the "select company" of race leaders. The description of Iola's speaking self as "strange" and "ethereal" suggests the degree to which she models the millennial language of racial progress. Through a parallel romance plot, Harper offers her readers a lesson about the internalization of racism that often accompanied class divisions within the African American community. Like that of Iola and Latimer, the marriage of Iola's brother Harry Leroy and Miss Delany is a pedagogy of both race-loyalty and integration. After Miss Delany and Harry court and eventually marry, Harry warns his sister before the two women have met that Miss Delany is dark complected: "Neither hair nor complexion show the least hint of blood admixture." Iola responds,

> "I am glad of it. . . . Every person of unmixed blood who succeeds in any department of literature, art, or science is a living argument for the capacity of the race."
>
> "Yes," responded Harry, "for it is not the white blood which is on trial before the world." (199)

Even more than the marriage of Iola and Latimer, the marriage of Harry and Miss Delany offers a pedagogical example of race solidarity. Their union across ostensible racial difference figures Harper's life-long call for cross-class coalition within the African American community and thus reiterates Harper's conviction that marriage represents a potent political act of racial self-determination.

OF PROGRESS AND SELF-RELIANCE: CLUBWOMEN AS SPONSORS OF LITERACY

Without question, the quest for education and literacy has always been of central importance to African American political agendas, with education held to be the means of improving oneself and the racial state. The arbiters of characterological pedagogy mediated the public debate over the means and ends of education. The dispute between Booker T. Washington and W. E. B. Du Bois is the most well-known example of a more pervasive split among reformers regarding the politics of pedagogy and curriculum. By the time of the emergence of national African American clubwomen's groups, Washington had gained great power and influence across successive presidential administrations, serving as an unofficial advisor for Theodore Roosevelt, William McKinley, and William Taft. Washington's pedagogy offers an instructive contrast to the neo-immediatist impulse within African American uplift reform. As a pedagogue, Washington has been widely understood as an accommodationist for the white racial state. In her autobiography, Wells summarizes the pedagogy of "the Tuskegee machine" this way:

> Mr. Washington's theory had been that we ought not to spend our time agitating for our rights; that we had better give attention to trying to be first-class people in a jim crow car than insisting that the jim crow car should be abolished; that we should spend more time practicing industrial pursuits and getting education to fit us for this work than in going to college and striving for a college education. And of course, fighting for political rights had no place whatsoever in his plans. (265)

Washington's accommodation of New Southern business interests and his access to capital allowed his organization to dominate "[b]lack higher education, business, the press, and political patronage" (Giddings 101–108). As Giddings notes, though they were almost universally supportive of "industrial education," the pedagogical orientations of clubwomen did split recognizably along the Washingtonian–Du Boisian line.[13]

Du Bois's argument in support of university education for African Americans has become an exemplar of pedagogical orientation; like his abolitionist predecessors, he understood education as the necessary ground of character-making and thus social progress. Du Bois's pedagogical writing at the turn of the century resonated strongly with the clubwomen who proceeded him in the race-national public sphere. Like them, Du Bois looked hopefully to the future of the race, calling for an expansion of the school system developing in the South (*Souls* 131–136). *Souls of Black Folks* includes repeated representations of souls transformed by education, and like Harper, Du Bois uses fiction to articulate a pedagogy of character for uplift.[14] As a founder and leader of the National Association for the Advancement of Colored People, Du Bois refused the Washingtonian line by trenchantly addressing national civil rights abuses.

The pedagogical poetics of clubwomen, however, were too variable and nuanced to be subsumed under any binary (Knupfer 160). Deborah Brandt's notion of literacy "sponsorship" provides a more supple critical construct for understanding the constitutive self-understanding of the clubwomen as literacy workers. Brandt argues that sponsors of literacy "are any agents, local or distant, concrete or abstract, who enable, support, teach, model, as well as recruit, regulate, suppress, or withhold literacy." Brandt's work endeavors to "connect literacy as an individual development to literacy as an economic development" (166). Brandt's theory acknowledges that literacy, its standards and the selective deployment of its technologies, is in every case an act of politics. Clearly African American activists understood the violent, as well as the liberatory, potential of literacy "sponsorship." Hazel Carby argues that in *Iola Leroy,*

Harper intended to "demystify . . . the power of language to liberate as well as subordinate" (*Reconstructing* 83).

Harper and her compatriots engaged the theoretical questions of African American literacy and schooling at the discursive interstices of dependence and independence. The clubwomen represented the function of education, like that of motherhood, as a means of uplift; for example, Harper's 1892 address to the Brooklyn Literary Society, "Enlightened Motherhood," links the work of mothering and teaching inextricably as work for "the race." At the national and local levels, clubwomen engaged in a diversity of teaching practices and reforms. These efforts included the defense of higher education for women, as well as industrial training, the fostering of race pride, and the importance of moral education. In her brief history of the club movement, Fannie Barrier Williams documents the commitment of clubs to issues of moral education:

> The mothers' meetings established in connection with almost every club have probably had a more direct and beneficial influence on the everyday problems of motherhood and home-making than any other activity. Meetings of this sort have been the chief feature of the women's clubs organized by the Tuskegee teachers among the women of the hard plantation life, within reach of the Tuskegee Institute. Thousands of these women in the rural life of the South continue to live under the shadow of bondage conditions. There has come to them scarcely a ray of light as to a better way of how to live for themselves and their offspring . . . It is to the credit of the high usefulness of the colored club woman that she has taken the initiative in doing something to reach and help a class of women who have lived isolated from all the regenerating and uplifting influences of freedom and education. It is the first touch of sympathy that has connected the progressive colored woman with her neglected and unprogressive sister. (418)

Williams ties the work of clubwomen to the pedagogical program of Booker T. Washington, her *New Negro for a New Century* co-editor. Coupled with her privileging of white public opinion, we might question the clubwomen's "high usefulness," premised so conspicuously with the "unprogressive sisters" of the South.[15] This example of Williams's rhetoric serves not to vilify her politics, and certainly not to reinforce a binary assessment of clubwomen, but to suggest that the rhetorical practice of literacy sponsorship operated along a continuum in which the belief in education was shared, but not necessarily the underlying goals. In "Duty to Dependent Races," Harper also expresses her concerns about the legacy of illiteracy stemming from a history of enslavement, but unlike Williams, she uses the fact of black print illiteracy as impetus for a larger political-economic solution, one which the work of clubwomen was originally meant to supplement:

Let the nation, which once consented to his abasement under a system which made it a crime to teach him to read his Bible, feel it a privilege as well as a duty to reverse the old processes of the past by supplanting his darkness with light, not simply by providing the Negro, but the whole region in which he lives, with national education. No child can be blamed because he was born in the midst of squalor, poverty, and ignorance, but society is criminal if it permits him to grow up without proper efforts for ameliorating his condition. (89)

As sponsors of literacy, then, Harper and other radical clubwomen articulated a relentlessly historicizing pedagogy, which highlighted the violence of withholding education as well as its liberatory uses. In their argument, social dependence through illiteracy is a historical means of social control.

Anna Julia Cooper rearticulated the prevailing pedagogy of dependence–independence in much the same rhetorical manner as Harper. In her essay "The Higher Education of Women," Cooper argued that education, and the education of women specifically, was a necessary element for social progress. Just as Cooper argues that a racial balance must be struck, so gender must be balanced as well. "I claim," Cooper writes, "that it is the prevalence of the Higher Education among women . . . [which will] enable and encourage women to administer to the world." This education is crucial, according to Cooper, in "transmitting the potential forces of her soul into dynamic factors that [have] given symmetry and completeness to the world's agency" (57). Such an assertion is, of course, in full keeping with the clubwomen's sense of their own historical mission. "[P]ut your ear close to the pulse of the time," Cooper suggests, "What is the banner cry of all the activities of the last half decade? . . . Is it not compassion for the poor and unfortunate" (58–59). Into this dawning age of reform, Cooper weaves the rise of African American literature. Praising white writers including Harriet Beecher Stowe and Albion Tourgee, who had taken up the cause of African American civil rights, in "One Phase of American Literature," Cooper asserts the need for African American writers to come onto the public stage. In keeping with her general theory of historical progression, Cooper imagines how the emergence of an African American literature would counter the political obfuscations of white literary hegemony and represent "honestly and appreciatively . . . both the Negro as he is, and the white man . . . as seen from the Negro's standpoint" (224).

Harper, whom Cooper acknowledges as one of the century's most notable African American poets, echoes Cooper's assessment of literary politics in *Iola Leroy*. Self-sacrificing as all of Harper's pedagogical characters, Iola wishes she "could do something more for our people than I am doing . . . I would like to do something of lasting service" (262). In response, Dr. Latimer, Iola's future husband, advises her to "write a good, strong book." This self-reflexive moment in the novel is part of a larger strategy to historicize the centrality of literacy acquisition to the social constitution of African American community. Such historical conjecture serves an explicitly pedagogical rhetorical function. For Harper's primary audience, African American clubwomen, this tactic gives them a frame of reference for the political importance of their own work as sponsors of literacy, connecting it to a revolutionary impulse among enslaved African Americans of the early century and the Reconstruction-era politics of "freedmen's education." For white readers, as at least an imagined audience for Harper's work, the representation of a self-sufficient African American community would counter notions of social dependency.[16]

In contrast to *Trial and Triumph*, the pedagogical vision of *Iola Leroy* looks back to the era of slavery, positing the accumulated knowledge of enslaved generations as a source of character lessons and practical political wisdom. A theory of dependence underwrites Harper's lessons about the generational relations within the community of African American uplift. The novel opens with a history of the rhetorical practices of the enslaved, claiming them as part of a lineage of African American rhetorical skill. Harper shows how despite the enforced print-illiteracy of its members, the political community of the enslaved was sustained and radicalized through alternative literate practices. In the opening chapter, "The Mystery of Market Speech," with the Confederacy on the brink of collapse and the Union army approaching, the enslaved had crucial need of both information and the skills to interpret it:

> During the dark days of the Rebellion, when the bondman was turning his eyes to the American flag, and learning to hail it as an ensign of deliverance, some of the shrewder slaves, coming in contact with their masters and overhearing their conversations, invented a phraseology to convey in the most unsuspected manner news to each other from the battle-field . . . [U]nder [an] apparently careless exterior there was an undercurrent of thought which escaped the cognizance of their masters. In conveying tidings of the war, if they wished to announce a victory of the Union army, they said the butter was fresh, or that the fish and eggs were in good condition. If defeat befell them, then the butter and other produce were rancid or stale. (9)

The drama of this novel of the New South bears out the shifting meaning of the "American flag," moving forward from the initial hope of Emancipation. In this era of segregation and racial terror, Harper was apt to figure the symbols of nationalism with greater menace and ambiguity, as we saw in her imagery of the shadowed Constitution. Whatever her ambivalence regarding the institutions of government, Harper's faith in rhetoric was as strong as ever, grounded in the long tradition of resistant rhetorical politics that she documents in the novel. The secret system of this "market speech" allows the enslaved to keep current with war news under the nose of their "masters." At the secret "prayer meeting," however, they can speak more plainly of the war and their options:

> "Oh, sho, chile" said Linda, "I can't read de newspapers, but ole Missus' face is newspaper nuff for me. I looks at her ebery mornin' wen she comes inter dis kitchen. Ef her face is long an' she walks kine o' droopy den I thinks things is gwine wrong for dem. But ef she comes out yere looking mighty pleased, an' larffin all ober her face, an' steppin' so frisky, den I knows de Sesech is gittin' de bes' ob de Yankees. (10)

To be sure, such a portrait of political intelligence and organization countered pervasive assumptions regarding the essential ignorance and dependence of slaves. It served as well as a renunciation of the "happy slave" myth; by representing the politics of resistance behind the performance of mannered deference and unthinking contentedness, Harper put the lie to the minstrel image of the slave figure.

The acquisition of print literacy by the character of Robert, whose representation reiterates the recollections of any number of slave narrators, makes him an important figure within the community of slaves. The drama of Robert's literacy acquisition echoes the work of slave narrators who emphasized the inventiveness necessary to gain such skills. Robert's mistress, his owner's wife Mrs. Johnson, is said to have "taught him to read on the same principle she would have taught a pet animal amusing tricks." That Robert was able to "use the machinery she had put in his hands to help overthrow the institution" of slavery speaks to his inventiveness, intelligence, and determination, which is to say, the quality of his character (16). If we apply Brandt's notion of literacy sponsorship, Mrs. Johnson becomes an unwitting conduit of emancipation, as she aids the slave community in circumventing the political liability of enforced print illiteracy. Robert, who, we are told, "enjoyed the distinction of being a good reader," serves a crucial political function in the slave community. Having read a newspaper, he is able to explain the Union army's policy of accepting escaped slaves as "contraband" and thus assure his compatriots that "the Yankees" would not, as had been rumored, send "runaways back to their masters" (15–16). Based on this information, a majority of the people present at the meeting make the decision to flee slavery for the Union line.

As the historical progression of the novel continues, the uses of literacy for racial integrity and progress are taken up by Iola herself as an agent of the Radical Republicanism that characterized Harper's own Reconstruction politics. The chapter titled "Flames in the School-Room" recounts Iola's participation in the Freedmen's education effort after the Civil War. Her work is cut short by the arson of neo-Confederate vigilantism, what Iola understands as the "unreasoning malice" of the students' "former owners" (146–147). However, in one brief chapter, we learn enough about

Iola as a pedagogue and perhaps about Harper's understanding of her own
work in context of the freedmen's education movement during the 1870s:

> One day a gentleman came to the school and wished to address the
> children. Iola suspended the regular order of the school, and the gentle-
> man essayed to talk to them on the achievements of the white race, such
> as building steamboats and carrying on business. Finally, he asked how
> they did it?
>   "They've got money," chorused the children.
>   "But how did they get it?"
>   "They took it from us," chimed the youngsters. Iola smiled, and the
> gentleman was nonplussed; but he could not deny that one of the pow-
> ers of knowledge is the power of the strong to oppress the weak. (147)

Iola's smile suggests her pleasure at the manner in which the students
responded. In the children's sense of a communal "us" and their astute joke
regarding the economics of white supremacism, perhaps Houston Baker
could find a blues note to appreciate as the white supremacist orator is
made the dupe of the children's rhetorical skill. The children's economic
critique recalls an assessment of the economics of slavery posited in the
prayer meeting scene, where one character's complaint about the exploitation of slave labor finds expression in verse: "They eat the meat and give us
the bones, / Eat the cherries and give us the stones" (17). Only vigilantism
and arson, the material destruction of the school, can halt the progress of
such intelligence.

The culminating representation of African American literacy as the agency
of social independence comes near the end of the novel in a "conversazione"
attended by "a select company of earnest men and women deeply interested
in the welfare of the race" (246). The activities and political-economic concerns of the conversazione recall the conventions, meetings, and literary
groups of the club movement, and Harper is careful to frame this chapter,
titled "Friends in Council," as a model for how both formal and informal
opportunities for socio-political discourse demand interpretive skills relevant to the political-economic moment. As well, Harper shows how these
types of "councils" have their roots in the radical activities of slave meetings. Robert, the only one present who had taken part in the novel's slave
meeting, remarks at the conclusion of the conversazione:

> "I . . . was thinking of the wonderful changes that have come to us since
> the war. When I sat in those well-lighted, beautifully-furnished rooms,
> I was thinking of the meetings we used to have in bygone days. How we
> used to go by stealth into lonely woods and gloomy swamps."

Marie, Iola's mother, responds to Robert that she "would gladly welcome
such a conference at any time," opining that "such meetings would be so

helpful to our young people" (261). Thus, Harper cues her readership to the historical and political legacy of their own literate acts. The slave meeting serves at once as a model of political communication and as a marker of the socio-political distance the race has come. Iola's own contribution to the meeting, her "Education of Mothers" address, merges with the narrative voice and gains the omniscient authority of the voice of history itself. The address recalls Harper's "Enlightened Motherhood" address, charging mothers with the moral-pedagogical duty, in Iola's words, to "instill into our young people that the true strength of a race means purity in women and uprightness in men . . . [a]nd where there this is wanting neither wealth nor culture can make up the deficiency" (254).

The characterological charges of racial progress give over to the jeremiad against lynching. The Reverend Charmicle gives his view of the situation in the South:

> From the unfortunate conditions which slavery has entailed upon [the South] . . . I dread the results of that racial feeling which ever and anon breaks out into restlessness and crime . . . I also fear that in some sections, as colored men increase in wealth and intelligence, there will be an increase of race rivalry and jealousy. It is said that savages, by putting their ears to the ground, can hear a far-off tread. So, to-day, I fear that there are savage elements in our civilization which hear the advancing tread of the Negro and would retard his coming. It is the incarnation of these elements that I dread. (259)

As in a number of Harper's public orations, the fact of lynching is the primary and tragic evidence in the case against national exceptionalist assumptions. The following comments arise in response to the one white orator, Rev. Cantor, and his address entitled "Patriotism," in which he posits Anglo-Saxons as the finest moral example of a "master race" proving itself as the "most Christian, and humane of that branch of the human family." The African American Professor Gradnor asserts:

> I think . . . that what our country needs is truth more than flattery. I do not think that our moral life keeps pace with our mental development and material progress. I know of no civilized country on the globe, Catholic, Protestant, or Mohammedan, where life is less secure than it is in the South . . . Does not true patriotism demand that citizenship should be as much protected in Christian America as it was in heathen Rome? (250)

This self-citation from "Duty to Dependent Races" recalls Harper's longstanding critique of the moral pretension of the state. In response, Miss Delany, an African American teacher, articulates a pedagogical approach to such problems. "I want my pupils," she says, "to do all in their power to make this country worthy of their deepest devotion and loftiest patriotism" (251). As always, the characterological burden remains the key to Harper's pedagogy. The burden of duty lies with the state in the logic of this precept.

Iola Leroy re-circulates many of Harper's previous texts, as Hazel Carby notes, making the novel strictly consistent with the political-philosophical position of Harper's earliest reform work. As Castronovo notes, this is due as much to the persistence of the material conditions that most concerned Harper, as to the rhetorical resources and precedents available to her (207). One striking example of this consistency is her return to the Moses figure. Harper would reprint the long poem *Moses: A Story of the Nile* in 1893 (originally published in 1869), and with the revisions, there was "no mistaking the identification of African-Americans as a new Israel" (*BCD* 326). Yet the genre of the historical romance, for which there was a market, allowed the extended analysis of character development that gave Harper an opportunity to refocus her pedagogical address. A year before the reprint, *Iola Leroy* referenced Harper's own 1857 *National Anti-Slavery Standard* editorial, "Could We Trace the Record of Every Human Heart," this time allowing her heroine to articulate the biblical character's political significance. Iola tells her uncle Robert, "The characters of the Old Testament I most admire are Moses and Nehemiah. They were willing to put aside their own advantages for their race and country" (265). These lines are spoken as a praiseful comparison to Dr. Latimer, the mulatto who like Iola herself had made the coalitional choice to live life as an African American—to make, that is, the Mosaic choice of race affiliation and life service to the building of a national African American community.

Iola's choices, the sort made by all of Harper's pedagogical literary characters, evince a moral character that engages the dependence–independence binary as a matter of racial duty. Racial ambiguity—the bizarre option to *choose* race affiliation—is a condition unique to the educated Northern mulatta; therefore, the "tragic mulatta" plot allowed Harper to instruct her Northern, educated, African American audience regarding the ethics of their relation to Southern African Americans. Iola and Latimer's renunciation of white privilege is an ethical choice of race-national interdependence over independence from that collective, an isolationist independence. To "be born white in this country," Robert reminds Iola, "is to be born to an inheritance of privileges, to hold in your hands the keys that open you the doors of every occupation, advantage, opportunity and achievement." Iola counters that "the gain would not have been worth the cost" of living life as a "moral cripple" (266).

In avoiding the moral disability of conformism, Iola figures the variety of individual independence that paradoxically underwrites Harper's defense of social dependence. To be free of accumulative desire constitutes characterological independence, recalling Foucault's self that is "too much real" and needs to be resisted, as well as the Protestant notions of self-control that always inspired Harper's rhetoric. This adversarial relationship—the self-sacrificing practice of inter-subjectivity—is central to Harper's reform argument. As we saw in Chapter One in the penultimate lines of her first known fiction, "true happiness consists not so much in the fruition of our wishes as in the regulation of desires and the full development and right culture of our whole natures" ("The Two Offers" 114–115). As a stark contrast to this ethical code, consider Harper's representation of the Confederates of the planter class, and Iola's father in particular: "Young, vivacious, impulsive, and undisciplined, without the restraining influence of a mother's love or the guidance of a father's hand, Leroy found himself with vast possessions, abundant leisure, unsettled principles, and uncontrolled desire" (61). As always in Harper's canon of didactic narratives, undisciplined wealth destroys the self-control on which civilization depends.

It is the independence from desire for economic privilege and social distinction that characterizes Iola and Latimer as Mosaic heroine and hero. Their marriage, as Nancy Cott and Anne duCille argue, subsumes physical passion under political commitment to African American community; independence from secular desire, then, amounts to independence for the larger community (duCille, *Coupling* 32–33). The literate communities Harper represents in *Iola Leroy* exemplify the need for African American judgment and perspective, modes of literacy around which community could cohere. The Mosaic character is the intersection of race-national integrity and the political-economic pressure that makes such independence not only a characterological virtue, but also a daily necessity. For all of Moses's heroism, he was, of course, a figure of dispossession, a wanderer. *Iola Leroy* is a novel of wandering, but also of homecoming. The novel is structured as a search for mothers and the reintegration of families scattered by the slave system. The neo-Confederate burning of her freedmen's school sets Iola wandering again, and the segregated labor market of the North keeps her wandering. Her activist union with Latimer figures a resting place and a self-sufficiency that, once reproduced throughout a multitude of families and communities, will form the foundation for the African American nation.

Afterword

Reviewing generations of commentary on the life and work of Frances Harper reveals paradigmatic shifts in the institutions of African American writing. The rhetorical skills that had most recommended Harper to her contemporaries became evidence of anachronism in subsequent generations. Whether praiseful or disparaging, commentators have continued to assess Harper in terms of pedagogical character and race-national fidelity. Writing for an audience long since established through the organizing force of the African American press, Harper's fellow reformers, those who knew Harper or shared her vision of racial progress, made judgments about her writing itself, as well as the exemplary lived ethic of uplift politics that she embodied. William Still's portrait of Harper in *The Underground Railroad: A Record of Facts, Authentic Narratives, Letters*, with its reproductions of Harper's own writing and speeches, is the most ambitious reframing of Harper's example.[1] Twentieth-century editors and scholars, who subsequently took as their mission the formation of an African American literary canon, tended to judge Harper by her poetry alone, applying criteria that largely overlooked or rejected the nation-building function of her rhetorical pedagogy. The praiseful biographical sketches of her abolitionist compatriots, by comparison, written when she was still in the midst of her career, make a race-national endorsement of Harper's literary efforts. I conclude this writing picking up these earlier threads of reception to suggest the trajectory of Harper's legacy and of African American reform rhetoric more generally.

Still's 1870 retrospective makes a strong appeal to the pedagogical character of Harper's work with the hope

> that the rising generation at least will take encouragement by her example and find an argument of rare force in favor of mental and moral equality, and above all be awakened to see how prejudices and difficulties may be surmounted by continual struggles, intelligence and a virtuous character. (779)

Here, of course, Still restates Harper's own tenacious ethical code, that common characterological precept of uplift. Still uses his perspective as a correspondent to uncover the connection between her writing and the living truth behind it, portraying Harper's private womanly character as consistent with her public ethos. "It may be well to add," Still writes, "that Mrs. Harper's letters from which we have copied were simply private, never intended for publication; and while they bear obvious marks of truthfulness, discrimination and impartiality, it becomes us to say that a more strictly conscientious woman we have never known" (778). This privatizing tendency aside, Still recommends the example of Harper's persuasiveness, noting that "[t]he earnest advice which she gives on the subject of temperance and moral reform generally causes some to reflect, even among adults, and induces a number of poor children to attend day and Sabbath schools." Still's account also circulates Harper's challenging address to the reformer class. "The condition of this class, she feels, appeals loudly for a remedy to respectable colored citizens," Still notes, "and whilst not discouraged, she is often quite saddened at the supineness of the better class" (778). Repeatedly, the social effect of such elite moral lethargy, this "supineness," drew Harper's attention as a writer and orator facing the problem of class divisions within the African American reform community.

Other leaders of the abolitionist generation praised Harper in her lifetime with a similar pedagogical emphasis. William Wells Brown, literary innovator and important early chronicler of African American history, included Harper in his exemplary gallery of contemporary figures in *The Rising Son; or, The Antecedents and Advancement of the Colored Race*, published in 1874. Ranking Harper as one of the "persons who have contributed, of their ability, towards the Freedom of the Race," Brown places Harper approvingly among the intellectual and political leadership of the abolitionist generation, praising her effectiveness as a reform writer and speaker (418). "As a speaker," Brown asserts,

> she ranks deservedly high; her arguments are forcible, her appeals pathetic, her logic fervent, her imagination fervid, her delivery original and easy. Mrs. Harper is dignified both in public and in private yet witty and sociable. She is the ablest colored lady who has ever appeared in public in our country, and is an honor to the race she represents. (525)

Brown's lavish praise of Harper's work recognizes her rhetorical prowess, by which she advocated "most effectually by both pen and speech for the overthrow of slavery, and for ten years before the commencement of the Rebellion, the press throughout the free states reordered her efforts as amongst the ablest made in the country" (524). He thus credits Harper with flawless representative status as an exemplar of race character and right rhetorical action, just the kind of rhetorical and ethical personhood modeled in Harper's fictions. He attributes to Harper not "a single instance" of "discredit" in "seventeen years of public labor," an achievement that "accomplished a great deal in the way of removing prejudice" (524).

Critical fortunes change, however. In the interim between Still and Brown's pedagogic reception of Harper and the reclamation of her work by feminist and rhetorical-studies scholars a century later, the emerging institution of African American literary study cast Harper in something like an aesthetic pre-history, an era of utilitarian sentimentality thankfully left behind. W. E. B. Du Bois passed literary judgments on Harper that reverberated through a post-reform aesthetic strain of early twentieth-century literature, one which defined itself in opposition to the didactic tradition of Harper's rhetoric. Du Bois's notice at Harper's death in 1911 seems lost somewhere between dismissal and acknowledgment. "She was not a great singer," as Du Bois has it, "but she had some sense of song; she was not a great writer, but she wrote much worth reading" ("Writers" 20–21).

This backhanded praise resonates through the canon building of the early twentieth century, especially in the preface of the *Book of American Negro Poetry*, edited by James Weldon Johnson and published in 1922. Johnson all but classes Harper and many of her contemporaries "between Phillis Wheatley and [Paul Lawrence] Dunbar" as admirable mediocrities, claiming they ought to be "considered more in light of what they attempted than of what they accomplished" (26). Johnson allows that "it may be said that none of these poets strike a deep native strain or sound a distinctively original note either in matter or in form" (34). This privileging of originality is quite telling; as a rhetorician, Harper was more concerned with deeply communal language and knowledge—the familiar, rather than the "original." Harper practiced her craft within a complex rhetorical culture that cannot be reduced to any dualistic limit between derivation and originality, as Frances Smith Foster suggests. Rhetoric demands continuously original derivation "in matter" and "in form." Bound to criteria such as originality and verisimilitude, literary studies has "confused the original with the imitation or improvisation with the inability to replicate" ("Gender, Genre" 51). These confusions are of an arhetorical quality, and Foster's assertion captures insightfully the literary bracketing of rhetorical inventiveness. She argues that both gender and the scholarly reification of genre account for the general overlooking of the Afro-Protestant press as an archive of unknown writers, an archive that as Foster's research has demonstrated, demands greater attention (50–52). Harper's work, of course, demonstrates that these biases have a long history in African American reform movements. As I have argued, the genres most readily available to Harper, of which she was a skillful innovator, served her pedagogical purposes very well. What some literary scholars may identify as a lack of artistic resonance, nineteenth-century reformers easily attribute to Harper's disciplined adherence to rhetorical tactics that, more importantly, carried the historical and discursive force of commonplace virtue.

Held strictly to aesthetic codes of African American literary modernism, Harper's work continued to receive condescending treatment as the century wore on. *To Make a Poet Black*, Saunders J. Redding's influential

1939 anthology of African American poetry, echoes Du Bois again; Redding pays Harper a glancing compliment, writing that "as a writer of prose Miss Watkins is to be remembered rather for what she attempted than for what she accomplished" (43). Harper's great flaw, by Redding's account, is her failure to take poetic craft beyond what he calls the "doctrinal treatment" of the abolitionist era. Redding cites Harper's 1861 letter to *Anglo African Magazine* editor Thomas Hamilton, in which she argues for African American writing focused "less [on] issues that are particular and more of feelings that are general . . . We are blessed with hearts and brains that compass more than ourselves in our present plight," Harper reasoned with Hamilton, concluding that African American writers "must look to the future which, God willing, will be better than the present or the past, and delve into the heart of the world" (qtd. in Redding 39). In a final damning judgment on Harper as "a full-fledged member of the propagandist group," Redding faults Harper for failing, like her reform contemporaries including William Wells Brown, to follow her own advice to Thomas Hamilton. Redding passes broad judgment on the literature that followed the era of "slave biographies," works that in his estimation, "were still infected by the deadly virus" of reformist sentimentality. Redding's posture as cultural physician assessing the resilience of a "deadly virus" carried on from the tradition of the slave narrative, raises questions about the criteria by which he styled himself an arbiter of a "truer artistic outlook" (39).

I cite Redding's multifaceted criticism at length because in its willful misreading of Harper's work, it serves well to highlight what it omits, namely, Harper's rhetorical craft and the social situation of her writing and oratory. Consider for instance the following:

> But she was seriously limited by the nature and method of her appeal. Immensely popular as a reader ("elocutionist"), the demands of her audience for the sentimental treatment of the old subjects sometimes overwhelmed her. On the occasions when she was free "to delve into the heart of the world" she was apt to gush with pathetic sentimentality over such subjects as wronged innocence, the evils of strong drink, and the blessed state of childhood. (40)

Since the eighteenth century, abolitionists understood the rhetorical possibilities and political expedience of railing against "wronged innocence" as an ethical key to the depth of corruption that engendered slavery. As for Harper's commitment to temperance, which Redding seems here to regret, scholarship has irrefutably established its critical importance to what we now call first-wave feminism. After reading the preceding chapters, the broader political and theoretical value of Harper's ostensibly overly sentimental treatments should be apparent.

Redding was not satisfied to castigate Harper's literary efforts in just one genre. "Miss Watkins's prose is less commendable than her poetry," he judged: "Her prose is frankly propagandistic" (43). Of *Iola Leroy; or Shadows Uplifted*, published in 1893, Redding writes,

> It is a poor thing as a novel, or even as a piece of prose, too obviously forced and overwritten, and too sensational to lift it from the plane of possible to probable. . . . Her knowledge of slave life and of slave character was obviously secondhand, and the judgments she utters on life and character conventional and trite. (43)

Readers of *Iola Leroy* should question the literary criteria by which this claim of improbability is lodged against Harper's narrative.[2] Were the political failures of Reconstruction and their social fallout not "probable" exigencies for readers of the novel? Were the struggles of African American women within the reform community represented in the novel any less "probable"? As I have suggested, Redding's criticism of Harper's ostensible "simplicity of thought and expression," which he finds to be the "keynote" of her writing, seems to wholly discount the intended social function underwriting the rhetorical theory of Harper's canon. Still's praiseful biography, in its attention to Harper's rhetorical intention, makes a telling contrast:

> Mrs. Harper reads the best magazines and ablest weeklies, as well as more elaborate works, not excepting such authors as De Tocqueville, Mill, Ruskin, Buckle, Guizot, &c. In espousing the cause of the oppressed as a poet and lecturer, had she neglected to fortify her mind in the manner she did, she would have been weighed and found wanting long since. Before friends and foes, the learned and the unlearned, North and South, Mrs. Harper has pleaded the cause of her race in a manner that has commanded the greatest respect. (778)

Rather than reduce Harper to a set of literary criteria, Still's assessment judges Harper holistically and puts the emphasis on the social function of her prodigious, and we should add largely self-attained, education. By Still's account, Harper is a formidable intellectual upon whose work much depended. In Still's portrait of Harper working persuasively with a diversity of audiences and commanding their respect, we receive a record of the fortitude of her rhetorical practice.

Harper's National Association of Colored Women compatriot, Hallie Q. Brown, author of the 1926 *Homespun Heroines and Other Women of Distinction*, offered a posthumous biographical sketch of Harper written in the same preceptive idiom that Harper pioneered. As a public-school teacher, a "women's dean" at Tuskegee Institute, and a professor of elocution at Wilberforce University, Brown was herself a significant pedagogical figure who carried the theory of moral suasion forward into the twentieth century.[3] In both the foreword and introduction to *Homespun Heroines*, Brown offers advice for reading about the "history making women of our race," a variety of instruction very much in the spirit of Harper's rhetorical pedagogy (vii). "These sketches," Brown professes of her biographical portraits, "breathe aspirations, hope, courage, patience, fortitude, faith" (v). Clearly, Harper and Brown oriented their pedagogical stances according to a common set of uplift virtues. Brown continues on in a Harperian vein, asserting the subject-forming force of the text in question, a force that in her words "not only furnishes useful information, but—what is even more—inspires to finer character growth and racial development" (v). Brown's hope for the didactic force of her "women of distinction" resonates strongly with the comments Harper made about her own fiction. *Homespun Heroines*, Brown claims, "has been prepared with the hope that they will read it and derive fresh strength and courage from its records to stimulate and cause them to cleave more tenaciously to the truth and battle more heroically for the right" (vii). In her praise of Harper's rhetorical invention of a constitutive craft engendering self-perpetuating pedagogical bonds, a cleaving to virtue and struggle, Brown proves herself to be Harper's ideal student.

I have chosen to give Hallie Q. Brown the last word, so to speak, because her assessment, studiously attending to the didactic function of Harper's work, resonates so strongly with the analysis of the preceding chapters. In my own account of Harper's life and work, I have attempted to read, in the manner of Brown, William Still, and William Wells Brown, with a careful attention to Harper's writing and oratory as rhetorical action taken within the flux of social contingency. As a generative craft of social invention, Harper's work was a "gift," as Brown puts it, a "valuable acquisition to the cause" of abolitionism and the other reform projects it inspired (99). The rhetorical pedagogy forwarded in the work of Frances Ellen Watkins Harper challenges us still to reflect critically on our own rhetorical practices as a matter of social as well as compositional craft, a set of habits that either close or open possibilities for useful knowledge and social change.

Appendix
A Selected Chronology of Writing and Oratory by Frances Ellen Watkins Harper

The following references, re-gathered, are meant to provide a useful guide to allow readers some holistic sense of Harper's long and productive career. More than any other scholar, Frances Smith Foster, through her assiduous archival research, has established the scope and depth of Harper's career. The interpretive work of this study relies at every turn on her landmark collections, *A Brighter Coming Day: A Frances Ellen Watkins Harper Reader* and *Minnie's Sacrifice, Sowing and Reaping, Trial and Triumph: Three Rediscovered Novels. Brighter Coming Day* is the best single source of bibliographic information on Harper's work. As Smith Foster and others have established, the publication history of Harper's work is complicated, and a fuller account is made difficult by the current lack of extant manuscripts. The publication of individual poems is not listed here, and I have included only a selection of her extant speeches. Also included here are pseudonymously authored fictions published in the *Anglo African Magazine*, which were identified by Carla Peterson. Harper published often in the *Christian Recorder*, and I have retrieved additional references from Accessible Archive (http://www.accessible. com/accessible/), which holds its entire run. This chronology is also based on *The Complete Poems of Frances Ellen Watkins*, edited by Maryemma Graham, and Melba Joyce Boyd's *Discarded Legacy: Politics and Poetics in the Life of Frances E.W. Harper, 1825–1911*. Additional sources for this chronology include Carla Peterson's *Doers of the Word: African-American Speakers and Writers in the North (1830–1880)* and *The Pen Is Ours: A Listing of Writings by and about African-American Women before 1910 with Secondary Bibliography to the Present*, edited by Jean Fagan Yellin and Cynthia D. Bond.

SELECTED CHRONOLOGY

Forest Leaves (poems), publisher and exact date unknown.
Poems on Miscellaneous Subjects, Boston: J. B. Yerrinton and Son, 1854, and published in the same year in Philadelphia by Merrihew and Thompson Printers.

Both editions were republished in 1855, and Merrihew and Thompson reprinted the volume in 1857 and again in 1871, which was listed as the twentieth edition of the volume.

"Our Greatest Want" (essay), *Anglo African Magazine*, May 1859: 160.

"The Two Offers" (short fiction), *Anglo African Magazine*, September 1859: 288–291; October 1859: 311–313.

"Chit Chat, or Fancy Sketches" (short fiction published under the name Jane Rustic), *Anglo African Magazine*, November 1859: 340–343.

"Town and Country, or Fancy Sketches" (short fiction published under the name Jane Rustic), *Anglo African Magazine*, December 1859: 383–385.

"Home Influence and Negro Courage" (short fiction published under the name Jane Rustic), *Anglo African Magazine*, January 1860: 8–11.

"Zombi, or Fancy Sketches" (short fiction published under the name Jane Rustic), *Anglo African Magazine*, February 1860: 33–37.

"The Triumph of Freedom—a Dream" (short fiction), *Weekly Anglo African*, 1860: 21–23.

"An Appeal for the Philadelphia Rescuers" (letter to the editor), *Weekly Anglo-African*, 23 June 1860.

"Ethiopia," "Bury Me in a Free Land," "The Dying Christian," "Thank God for Little Children," "The Air of Freedom," and "President Lincoln's Proclamation of Emancipation" (reprinted poems), *The Freedman's Book*, ed. Lydia Maria Child, Cambridge: Cambridge University Press, 1865.

"We Are All Bound Up Together" (oration), *The Proceedings of the Eleventh National Woman's Rights Convention*, New York: Robert J. Johnson, May 10, 1866.

Letters from the South from 1867 to 1871, published in abolitionist journals or reprinted in William Still's 1872 *The Underground Railroad*, are reprinted in Smith Foster's *Brighter Coming Day: A Frances Ellen Watkins Harper Reader*, 122–134.

Moses: A Story of the Nile (poetry), Philadelphia: Merrihew and Son, 1869–1870. This volume was reprinted in 1889 and 1893 and again in 1901 as *Idylls of the Bible*.

Minnie's Sacrifice (serial novel), *Christian Recorder*, 20 March 1869–25 September 1869.

Poems, Philadelphia: Merrihew and Son, 1871.

Sketches of Southern Life, Philadelphia: Merrihew and Son, 1872, 1873, 1887, Editions of this text were also published by Ferguson Bros (Philadelphia) in 1888, 1891, 1893, and 1896.

"The Great Problem to Be Solved," an address at the Centennial Anniversary of the Pennsylvania Society for Promoting the Abolition of Slavery. Philadelphia, 14 April 1875.

"Fancy Etchings" (short fiction), *Christian Recorder*, 20 February 1873: 1.

"Fancy Etchings" (short fiction), *Christian Recorder*, 10 April 1873: 1.

"Fancy Etchings" (short fiction), *Christian Recorder*, 24 April 1873: 1

"Fancy Etchings" (short fiction), *Christian Recorder*, 1 May 1873: 1

"Fancy Etchings" (short fiction), *Christian Recorder*, 22 May 1873: 1

"Fancy Etchings" (short fiction), *Christian Recorder*, 3 July 1873: 1.

"Fancy Sketches" (short fiction), *Christian Recorder*, 15 January 1874: 1.

Sowing and Reaping (serial novel), *Christian Recorder*, 10 August 1876–February 8, 1877.

"Colored Women of America" (essay), *Englishwoman's Review*, 15 January 1878: 10–15.

"A Factor in Human Progress," *African Methodist Episcopal Review* 2 (1885): 14–18.

Trial and Triumph (serial novel), *Christian Recorder*, 4 October 1888–14 February 1889.

"The Woman's Christian Temperance Union and the Colored Woman," *African Methodist Episcopal Church Review* 4 (1888): 313–316.

Iola Leroy, or, Shadows Uplift, Philadelphia: Garrigues Bros, 1892.

"Enlightened Motherhood" (oration), an address by Mrs. Frances E. W. Harper to the Brooklyn Literary Society, 15 November 1892.

"Woman's Political Future" (oration), *World Congress of Representative Women 1893 Proceedings*, May Wright Sewall, ed. Chicago: Rand McNally, 1894, 433–437.

"Duty to Dependent Races" (oration), National Council of Women of the United States, Transactions, 86–91, Philadelphia: National Council of Women of the United States, 1891.

The Sparrow's Fall and Other Poems, publisher and exact date unknown, circa 1894.

Atlanta Offering: Poems, Philadelphia: George S. Ferguson Company, 1895.

Martyr of Alabama and Other Poems, publisher and exact date unknown, circa 1895.

Poems, Philadelphia: self-published, 1895.

"True and False Politeness" (essay), *African Methodist Episcopal Church Review* 14 (1898): 399–445.

Notes

NOTES TO THE INTRODUCTION

1. For a discussion of black abolitionist response to the Fugitive Slave Law of 1850 and the mass meetings held to organize against it, see Quarles (197–205).
2. *Poems on Miscellaneous Subjects* sold at least a thousand copies within four years and was reprinted yearly for the next twenty years. As Frances Smith Foster points out, the success of this book alone merits further rethinking about Harper's prominence in nineteenth-century U.S. literature ("Gender, Genre" 47–48).
3. Shirley Wilson Logan identifies three modes of rhetorical instruction in the African American press: the hands-on experience provided by the publication of newspaper, broadsides, and other texts; direct rhetorical instruction appearing in the periodicals; and commentary on oratory (*Liberating Language* 8). While in many instances, Harper's work clearly belongs in the third category, Harper's fiction perhaps constitutes a fourth category. As I argue in what follows, the fictional delivery of instruction provided a collective space for reflecting on and theorizing all manner of rhetorical action.
4. As Alan Trachtenberg has argued, the cultural role of the Columbian Exposition was largely to establish the unity of the nation amid the contentious, turbulent social relations of the state fractured by race and class (216–217).
5. "Clearly," Cott notes, "Rush argued neither for justice with regard to women's opportunities for learning nor for women's participation in the advancement of knowledge. His reasoning was utilitarian; his plan for female education was functional . . . [female education] would preserve the family as an agency of moral instruction, facilitate male entrepreneurship, and generalize frugality and economic discipline. Without threatening male dominance, it would make women more capable adjuncts of their husbands and families" (105).
6. British and American Quakers were among the first programmatic abolitionists, organizing a powerful practice of immediatism. Harper worked across church lines throughout her career, and certainly, Quaker-led reform initiates and Quaker theology informed her thinking about abolitionist action in the marketplace.
7. As in her transformational free labor poetics up through the war, Harper's post-Reconstruction theorization of black labor stages rhetorical situations in which inhere, as Susan Willis explains it, "the social contradictions and crisis of a given mode of production" (21). In dramas of rhetorical struggle, persuasion, or the lack thereof, is represented as the movement of history itself.
8. Warren Susman argues that with the twentieth-century transition from *character* to *personality*, the governing notion of self-in-society shifted from self-mastery and self-development to individual expressiveness. For Susman, personality emerged in the United States as a new mode of modern

self-consciousness and a "vocabulary" and as the successor to characterological self-understanding of the early modern age of nation states (274–276).

9. The turn to constitutive rhetoric, according to Maurice Charland, works
around the modern social theory informing in traditional rhetorical valua-
tions of persuasion. Foregrounding the prior rhetorical assumption of subjects
embodying some predictable and stable set of motives prevents rhetoricians
from making a fetish of the ontological ground from which rhetors speak or
write and on which audiences receive language. Charland brackets the persuasive intention of individual rhetors, finding a more telling locus of rhetorical force within the vicissitudes of "identification," the narrative interactions
that provide the occasions for the self-understanding of historically specific
"coherent subjects" as the "locus for action and experience" (221).

10. "Pedagogic rhetoric," then, is for Miller the *sine qua non* of rhetorical action
as cultural practice. Miller claims that "persuasion is always a matter of trust
that precedes any form of its expression and that its worthiness for that trust
will be verified against multiple discursive conventions obviously revises the
possibility of one rhetorical tradition" (8).

11. The "domestic literacy narrative" of *Minnie's Sacrifice*, according to Sarah
Robbins, expands the pedagogical domain of "a new American motherhood,
expanded to include the freedwomen of the South and the heritage of their
slavery experience" (183).

12. As Boyd notes, Harper's lecture tour for the African Methodist Episcopal
Church followed the theme of "Literacy, Land, and Liberation," a title which
is itself a crystalline expression of uplift and civil rights principle (119–120).

13. Throughout this book, I rely on two landmark collections of Harper's work,
both edited by Frances Smith Foster, *A Brighter Coming Day: A Frances
Ellen Watkins Harper Reader* and *Minnie's Sacrifice, Sowing and Reaping,
Trial and Triumph: Three Rediscovered Novels*. Unless clearly indicated otherwise, subsequent references to *Minnie's Sacrifice* will be made parentheti-
cally to *MS*. Parenthetical references to *Sowing and Reaping* and *Trial and
Triumph* will be made to *SW* and *TT*, respectively.

14. Despite the elitist assumptions of Blair's pedagogy, Shirley Wilson Logan
suggests that African American reformers like William J. Watkins and Frances Harper worked within the broad parameters of Blair's principles (*Liberating Language* 97–98).

15. William Still's biographical sketch of Harper in *The Underground Railroad*
is the best single record of the reception of her oratory. To be sure, Still's
painstaking effort to establish Harper's eloquence suggests the pedagogical
significance of rhetorical skill as a marker of character.

16. To be fair, I must mention Williams's gesture of including blank pages for
reader contributions to the genealogical project of *Keywords*. As Williams
notes, in "the use of our common language, in so important an area, this is
the only spirit in which this work can be properly done" (26).

17. As the work of historians of character like Rael and Susman suggests, to
understand race and gender in the nineteenth century as a matter of discursive politics, we need to test our own theoretical presuppositions, our post-
modern theories of subject formation, for example, within a broader field
of characterological imperatives. The interdependence of race, gender, class,
and nationalism was negotiated from all political perspectives at the site of
character, the inevitable rhetorical frame of social identity.

18. The ideological emergence of racial egalitarianism and, across the diaspora,
African appeals to natural rights in the revolutionary era in the West constituted an opening of possibility in the long reign of what David Brion Davis
calls simply "anti-black racism." Centuries of global, historically accreted

white supremacist ideology continuous with technological and political economic modernity in the Western hemisphere imposed profound constraints
on the politics of African American character.

19. The ban on slave literacy was enforced with increasing strictness as the
century moved toward the Civil War, and "free Negroes" in the North
struggled with expense and access. And yet, in the circular logic of the
vicious assault on African character, illiteracy was damning evidence of
inherent inhumanity. The argument about slave illiteracy was a circular
argument in which reading and writing were outlawed and the enslaved
were nonetheless argued to be incapable of reason, which, by the standards
of the Enlightenment, was tantamount to an accusation of being incapable
of self-control in society.

20. Consider, for example, Jefferson's claims about the character traits of slaves,
each of which is a patent justification of tyranny, the groundwork, in other
words, of "happy slave" mythology.

21. Subsequent references to Harper's work collected in Frances Smith Foster's
Brighter Coming Day: A Frances Ellen Watkins Reader will be made paren-
thetically to *BCD*.

22. Despite a number of historical correctives, the role of African Americans
themselves in the abolitionist movement is still underrepresented. A few of
the most notable exceptions are Benjamin Quarles's *Black Abolitionists*, *Witness for Freedom: African American Voices on Race, Slavery, and Emancipation*, edited by C. Peter Ripley; and John Goodman's *Of One Blood:
Abolitionism and the Origins of Racial Equality*.

23. Though the so-called racial dictatorship may in real senses have crumbled
in 1865, scholars of native and immigration history could well dispute that
such a tectonic shift came so early. Omi and Winant assert the era of reform
ushered in by Emancipation advanced social justice and human rights at the
level of policy, but also through a more diffuse sociality which, though never
named as such, can be understood as rhetorical. Omi and Winant identify the
social power and symbolic force of racial liberation politics in the 1960s and
the "rearticulation of racial meaning" (96–101). Surely the argument can be
extended to African American abolitionists, whose oppositional arguments
about racial equality and race-national pride forged the discursive ground for
the next generation of civil-rights activists.

24. At this moment in 1866, like many other supporters of the Radical agenda,
Harper was most likely reacting specifically to Andrew Johnson's vetoes of
Reconstruction legislation such as the Freedmen's Bureau extension bill in
1865 and the 1866 Civil Rights Bill.

25. As Louis S. Gerteis argues, utilitarianism was ultimately the most persuasive
mode of abolitionism among white Northerners, insofar as it made market-
based arguments about the superiority of "free" versus slave labor. Utilitarian
and egalitarian creeds merged into what we might call with some trepida-
tion popular abolitionist sentiment (36–37). African American abolitionists
themselves, Harper included, appealed to the values of social freedom as the
greatest civic utility.

26. Nikhil Pal Singh argues that nation-state formation is still obscured in
the field of U.S. cultural studies due to the endurance of the American
exceptionalist perspective on the post–Civil War era. In this critical narrative, according to Singh, the continued subjugation of black workers
during Reconstruction is explained as a product of socioeconomic stag-
nation in the South, and thus a romantic and ahistorical agrarian myth
of slavocracy lore is ironically reproduced. Such regional distinctions, so
ingrained in the field of American studies, fail "to locate the history and

development of the South within a synthetic account of capitalist nation-formation" (493). The irony of this critical failure is intensified when we consider the polemic of radical reformers themselves who refused to acknowledge regional distinctions in their own critique of national power. Indeed, as early as the 1840s, well before the Civil War presented itself as an inevitability, African American abolitionists denounced the Northern political logic of the Jacksonian era as irretrievably Southern in its policy dictates. By the time Harper joined the abolitionist lecture circuit in 1854, implicating the Northern power structure in the moral quagmire of slavery was a quintessential gesture.

27. Nancy Fraser's public-sphere theory, as discussed in Chapter 3, offers a more nuanced model for analysis of the rhetorical means of publicity as a political practice. Fraser advances the claim that Jurgen Habermas's account of the changing "structure" of the public sphere confuses rhetorical with social structures, arguing that the history of the public sphere alone cannot be written because it was through the very exclusion of such counter-publics that the more powerful publics gain definition. Such exclusions rely on the assumption of equality among citizens and the importance of barring "special interests" from the discourse of the public good.

NOTES TO CHAPTER 1

1. In his invaluable 1891 historical, *The Afro-American Press and Its Editors,* Garland Penn grants great importance to the *Anglo African Magazine.* The criteria of his praise tell us much about the rhetorical mission of the African American press during the antebellum period. "[The *Anglo African Magazine*] lived to see the Afro-American on the march to an intellectual position and to civil citizenship; and with this consciousness it died peacefully in the arms of its promoters." Of Thomas and Robert Hamilton, who owned, edited, and led the paper through its successful run, Penn writes, "Their names will be treasured in the archives of history in connection with that of Phillips, Garrison, and a phalanx of others, whose arms are stacked by the Jordan of eternal rest" (88).

2. That constitutive subjectivity, the subjects of persuasion to whom Harper's *Anglo African* texts are so often addressed, were readers of a rightfully proud African heritage whose generation was destined to demonstrate its exceptional character as productive citizens and moral reformers in the United States. A considerable variety of genre and topic appeared in the paper, but the majority of the authors appealed to many of the same precept—the call on the collective will of a racial nation, Anglo-Africans duty-bound to the enslaved of the race and to self-improvement on their behalf. This is not to suggest that any one race-national agenda dominated the *Anglo African Magazine* or African American reform generally. As would be the case increasingly, Harper made her preceptive calls to character at these very fault lines.

3. Eddie S. Glaude's history of race and religion offers insights into the rhetorical use of the book of Exodus in crafting African American "nation language." His focus on the centrality of Exodus to the collective practice of "racial solidarity" has informed my own analysis of Harper's work. Glaude's critical survey of many sources identifies obligation as an intersubjective mechanism of collective identification. The rhetorical pedagogy I trace in Harper's writing builds these bonds of solidarity and obligation didactically, teaching the language with which those constitutive bonds can be created (Glaude 16–18).

4. Abolitionists viewed the rhetorical culture of the antebellum period as a casualty of a corrupt market culture and the weak moral will of the state. Gag laws in Congress forbidding antislavery petitions, violence against abolitionist speakers and publishers, and general stigmatizing of abolitionists as fanatical all contributed to the constraints in which abolitionist rhetors worked. For a defense of abolitionists' rhetorical practices, see Wendell Phillips's "The Philosophy of the Abolition Movement" (*Speeches, Lectures, Letters* 98–153).

5. During the Lincoln–Douglas debates, Stephen Douglas used the term repeatedly to predict a disagreeably egalitarian future of "negro citizenship." Douglas queried his audience, "[I]f you desire to allow [African Americans] to come into the State and settle with the white man, if you desire them to vote on an equality with yourselves, and to make them eligible to office, to serve on juries, and to adjudge your rights, then support Mr. Lincoln and the Black Republican party, who are in favor of the citizenship of the negro" (Sparks 95).

6. While Cmiel offers a rich account of the political history of eloquence, he offers no analysis of the changes wrought on United States rhetorical cultures by the emergence of African American eloquence. However, as an overview of major shifts in nineteenth-century rhetorical culture and as a model of scholarship on the politics of style and pedagogy, Cmiel's study *Democratic Eloquence: The Fight Over Popular Speech in Nineteenth Century America* is indispensable.

7. As I outlined in the Introduction, I read the discursive circulation of Harper's work in a manner consistent with Steven Mailloux's theorization of "rhetorical hermeneutics," in which writing, speaking, and reading are "simultaneously productive and interpretive" (31–32).

8. Phillips's address given before the Massachusetts Anti-Slavery Society in Boston on January 27, 1853, "Philosophy of Abolitionism," is itself a theory of rhetorical action. Responding to the gradualist logic of moderate abolitionists critical of aggressive immediatism, Phillips defends immediatist rhetoric at length, arguing that "our course, more than all other efforts, has caused that agitation which has awakened these new converts" (99).

9. Shirley Wilson Logan argues that Harper's primary rhetorical tactics were those of "convergence" and "divergence." Through careful reading across Harper's oratorical career, Logan demonstrates her tactical interpolative address and her skill at manipulating the exigencies of given rhetorical situations. I follow Logan's attention to Harper's shifting collective ethos, though I attend more closely to the ideological imperatives and public-sphere debates that formed the exigency to which Harper responded.

10. Jacqueline Bacon's sense of the rhetorical flexibility of jeremiad rhetoric offers an important qualification for any too-general theory of jeremiad rhetoric by Sojourner Truth, Maria Stewart, and Harper, among others. In particular, Bacon notes the use of jeremiad rhetoric to speak to gender divisions within the African American abolitionist community (207–208).

11. Foucault considered the Christian techniques of the self as an ethical departure from Hellenistic modes. Foucault's most concise explanation of Hellenistic practices of the self (and his most explicit defense of their residual political potential) can be found in *Ethics, Subjectivity and Truth* (207–280).

12. For a discussion of Harper's likely political and theological paths to Unitarianism, see Rosencrans in its entirety. Although she does not follow this line of inquiry, Rosencrans makes the point that the social activist theology of the A.M.E. and Unitarian churches was similar in stipulating service and connection to a humanity much broader than any denominational limit (2). In

practice, this clearly would have provided discursive continuity for a reform writer and orator like Harper, who published and spoke across church–institutional lines.

13. Lani Guinier and Gerald Torres assert the diagnostic function of race in *The Miner's Canary: Enlisting Race, Resisting Power, Transforming Democracy*, arguing that race relations in the United States reveal the more general workings of power within our societies.

14. Hazel Carby's work on nineteenth-century novels by African American women strongly informs my historical understanding of Harper's domestic topoi, and more specifically, their crucial importance for didactic rhetorics of African American womanhood. Carby writes, "The dominating ideology to define the boundaries of acceptable female behavior from the 1820s until the Civil War was the 'cult of true womanhood,'" arguing that enslaved African American women, because of their position within the social and political economy of slavery, were ideologically excluded from the category of true womanhood (23–24).

15. Michael Bennett notes that as an abolitionist, Harper had a "consuming interest in the intersection between the private bodies of the nation's inhabitants and the public democratic body of which they were a part." Focusing on poems including "The Slave Mother," "Eliza Harris," and "To the Cleveland Union Savers," all poems that confront readers with the domination of slave women's bodies, Bennett attributes to Harper a poetics of "bodily democracy," which was founded on the notion of extending "democracy to the realm of the body politics and control over one's own sexuality" (45).

16. Peterson claims that the "idiosyncratic style" of the "Sketches" leaves no doubt as to the authorship ("Literary Transnationalism" 192).

17. Harper sounds core didactic principles as she explains to the other wedding guests the benefits of imitation: "To despise imitation entirely, is to throw away a cardinal source of improvement; we had never learned to talk had we, from our cradles, despised to imitate sound" (341).

18. Melba Joyce Boyd characterizes this polemical fiction as one employed "in an integrative capacity with the women's movement through the Woman's Christian Temperance Union" (202). This important observation frames my analysis of Harper's work as a discursive practice in both its textual craft and its social circulation.

NOTES TO CHAPTER 2

1. Obama provided a map of the discursive structures productive of "a cycle of violence, blight and neglect that continues to haunt us." He noted the lasting impact of "[s]egregated schools [that] were and are inferior schools; we still haven't fixed them, 50 years after *Brown v. Board of Education*. And the inferior education they provided, then and now, helps explain the pervasive achievement gap between today's black and white students. Legalized discrimination—where blacks were prevented, often through violence, from owning property, or loans were not granted to African-American business owners, or black homeowners could not access FHA mortgages, or blacks were excluded from unions or the police force or the fire department—meant that black families could not amass any meaningful wealth to bequeath to future generations" (*New York Times*, 18 March 2008).

2. Crenshaw's notion of "intersectionality" is the essential to her critical race methodology, a central intention of which is to "disrupt the tendencies to see race and gender as exclusive or separable." For Crenshaw, this critical

operation is necessary to address the specific kinds of social oppression victim-izing women of color, subjects "at the bottom of multiple hierarchies" (114). I follow Crenshaw in addressing the historically difficult politics of African American women's intersectional discursive position. However, as a critical term for rhetorical studies, I attend to invention within discursive constraint.

3. In the Senate on December 5, 1866, in his resolution declaring "The True Principles of Reconstruction," Sen. Charles Sumner asserted the illegality of the provisional Southern state governments, which, with the encourage-ment of President Andrew Johnson, were quickly working to re-establish themselves in the national apparatus. Rep. Thaddeus Stevens's speech in the House following the ratification of Thirteenth Amendment identified the crushing irony of the possible effect of this legislation so loudly celebrated as the culminating moment of the abolition movement. Because the ratification of the amendment bolstered the official population of former slave states, the Congressional representation of the late Confederacy would gain a majority in Congress. Of this possible Democratic advantage, Stevens would only say, "I need not depict the ruin that would follow" (17). Sumner was more expan-sive in his doom-saying, arguing that the twenty-nine added representatives for the South, if unchecked, would result in the most far-reaching gains for the Southern oligarchy, potentially, the re-institution of slavery (Du Bois, *Black Reconstruction* 265).

4. Gillian Brown makes this argument specifically in the case of Stowe's *Uncle Tom's Cabin*. Brown's reading of Stowe's redeployment of domestic ideol-ogy and its attendant subjectivities has influenced my argument about moral character as a central political category, elaborated extensively in a literary public sphere. Harper, as Brown argues in the case of Stowe, uses the ideal of the domestic sphere to demonstrate "the contagion of the market" within private life (13–16). Harper's poetry and fiction circulate the well-used per-suasive gambits of this domestic rhetoric.

5. On April 9, 1866, just a month before Harper spoke in New York at the Elev-enth Annual Women's Rights Convention, Johnson vetoed the first national Civil Rights Act, the first veto in U.S. history to be overridden. This action signaled the degree to which Johnson intended to claim executive privilege in opposing the Radical 39th Congress. Harper was one of many advocates for Radical Reconstruction to denounce Johnson in uncompromising terms (Foner, *Reconstruction* 249–251).

6. In letters from the Southern lecture circuit, Harper explained this sanction against black public speech as part of the larger culture of silence in the South, one analogous to the South's political circumscription. "Freedom of speech," she noted in a July 26, 1867, letter published in the *National Anti-Slavery Standard*, "has been an outlaw in the South" (*BCD* 124). Harper posited the resulting ignorance, like the poverty of the majority of the South-ern population, as "the two materials" which provided a viable social field for the Democratic Party (*BCD* 130).

7. The consolidation of capital into the hands of powerful industrialists is certainly a hallmark of Reconstruction. As Theodore Allen argues, racial oppression is the system of social control in which racialist narratives of identity are used to justify the exploitation of workers. Racial slavery, thus, is only one form of racial oppression. Allen finds this racialism to be ancillary to the actual material conditions of servitude (134–135). The legitimating narratives of racial oppression are thus used to obscure primitive accumula-tion, in Marx's definition, and a range of class-exploitative practices. While Allen finds this system to be analogous to gender oppression, it is far from his emphasis (28).

8. Smith Foster suggests "Words for the Hour" was written during the Civil War, a warranted suggestion (*Brighter* 185). The "battle-field" to be held in this poem could well refer to a federally occupied South.

9. I want not to idealize Child's text as pedagogically exemplary, nor for that matter, any of the ostensibly progressive projects of "Freedmen's education." As Butchart notes, despite the very real differences of pedagogy and political intention, the general orientation of the movement as a whole demanded that recently emancipated slaves meet the socio-economic standards of white Northern middle-class culture. Overall, Southern schools were far from an adequate response to the social situation of emancipated African Americans, who had none of the material requirements to found the kind of new subjectivity demanded in the didactic texts of the Southern schools (167–168).

10. Unfortunately, the penultimate chapter of the novel in which the murder occurs is not extant. With Frances Smith Foster, who recovered Harper's *Christian Recorder* novels, we must hope that future archival research will bring all the missing chapters to light.

11. The language of the experiment was long used to forward conjecture about the state of the labor of emancipated slaves. Seymour Drescher's history of British Emancipation in the West Indies captures the combination of economic theory and racial expectations structuring the political discourse after Emancipation (8). In the disparaging assessments of white elites, the capacity of African-descended laborers confined black personhood to labor's terms.

12. Boyd notes that Harper took as her theme for these tours "Land, Literacy and Liberty" (120). Certainly this is suggestive of what we know of her Southern lecture work based on letters sent to William Still and from contemporaneous notices of her appearances, most of which are exceptionally laudatory. It is evident in her letters from the South that even while she travelled and worked in the South, she was gathering material that would structure the rhetorical pedagogy of *Minnie's Sacrifice*.

13. There is excellent scholarship on the literary and rhetorical function of mulatto and mulatta characters. Carby reads such characters as both cultural expression and critical "exploration" of race relations (89). Dismissed by some critics as race-national traitory or "racial ambivalence," Harper's deployment of mixed-race characters, heroines in particular, seems clearly to intend just the opposite (Tate 144–145). *Minnie's Sacrifice*, like *Iola Leroy, or, Shadows Uplifted* at the end of the century, pledged readers with racial solidarity.

14. Nearing the end of his life, Stevens made the redistribution of Southern lands his final radical stand as a Radical leader. "Explaining it to the House on March 19, he proposed that all public lands belonging to the ten states in question be forfeited, and that the president seize the property specified by the second Confiscation Act. He also wanted commissioners appointed in each state to take over the confiscated land, which was to be distributed among the freedmen, each head of a family receiving forty acres to be held in trust for ten years prior to being turned over to the recipients." The initiative would never succeed before or after Stevens's death (Trefousse 210–211).

15. Logan undertakes a broader analysis of Harper's appeal to a complicated multiracial "community of interests," identifying a rhetoric of "convergence and divergence" that served as a means for negotiating her coalitional politics across racial lines (*We are Coming* 44–45). This insight informs my analysis of Harper's rhetorical pedagogy, which often took the form of a racial pledge to rhetorical action, and as such, parsing of loyalties.

16. Reid's example of the potential black voter comes in the form of an idiot minstrel character, one which he offered enigmatically as important information for those meditating on the prospects of negro suffrage. See, for example, his

characterization of what he calls in one chapter title "The Plantation Negro Character" (546–573).

17. Historians of the Ku Klux Klan have stressed that the politically and financially enfranchised black man and Southern Unionists were the primary targets of Klan lynching and harassment (Tourgee, *Invisible* 60–71). In letters written during her lecture tours, Harper acknowledged the potential danger of speaking publicly as a black Republican, citing examples of black women who were beaten or murdered for ostensibly "incendiary speech." Harper reported, "I am drawn into conversation. 'What are you lecturing about?' the question comes up, and if I say, among other topics politics, then I may look for onset. There is a sensitiveness on this subject, a dread, it may be, that some one will 'put the devil in the nigger's head,' or exert some influence inimical to them" (qtd. in *BCD* 123).

NOTES TO CHAPTER 3

1. In her *Homespun Heroines*, Hallie Q. Brown praises Harper's rhetorical prowess, or "forensic ability," and marks her achievements, among them, the WCTU's posthumous honoring of Harper's "life-long services" by placing her on the organization's "Red Letter Calendar" (102–103).

2. For Harper, the disillusioned Republican and temperance activist, there could be no more poignant demonstration of an immoral political economy than the "Whiskey Ring" scandal of 1875–1876, which was the result of distillers and federal tax collectors conspiring to misrepresent the taxable amount of alcohol produced. This scandal reached all the way into the Grant administration (Blocker 98–99).

3. As Jack S. Blocker demonstrates, the temperance activities of 1873–1874 occurred at the local, state, and national levels. Women were inspired to challenge the liquor interests for a variety of reasons and understood their work according to different values and political goals. Likewise, the reaction of different communities and the press to the pervasive reform activity of these years diverged according to complex social factors. Amid the complexity, the historical significance of the crusade as a national political event as well as its subsequent impact on reform movements is considerable (3–6).

4. Rosenthal's speculation about Harper's "deracialized discourse" seems to ignore, in its emphasis on *literary* artifact, that the majority of Harper's comments on temperance circulated within a carefully racialized discourse. When Rosenthal does venture outside the bounds of the literary text, I am suspicious of her readings. The suggestion that Harper meant simply to "level . . . the differences between races" is misguided in the context of the rest of Harper's writing. The economic conditions that Harper's temperance rhetoric foregrounds were the same that oppressed African Americans, not a field Harper identified as "level" in any sense. Certainly, as Rosenthal suggests, Harper understood economic subjectivity as primary over and above racial subjectivity. I would argue, however, that Harper's gestures toward the "communality between the races" (162) must be read as situational rhetoric within a larger critique of a profoundly stratified economy.

5. In particular, William Wells Brown, Harriet Jacobs, Harriet Beecher Stowe, and Lydia Maria Child provided Harper with models for race-critical, tragic mulatta narrative. For a lengthier discussion of the various political uses of the figure of the mulatta, see Carby's *Reconstructing Womanhood* (88–94).

6. Douglass names specific newspapers guilty of such mischaracterizations. He told his sizeable audience, "No one has a right to speak to another without

that other's permission. Social equality and civil equality rest upon an entirely different basis, and well enough the American people know it; yet to inflame a popular prejudice, respectable papers like the *New York Times* and the *Chicago Tribune*, persist in describing the Civil Rights Bill as a Social Rights Bill" (Douglass 5: 122).

7. In Harper's fiction, didactic attention is regularly paid to people's practices of buying clothes, an activity providing an index of characterological assessment and of course a matter of specific didactic prescription. Insistence on treating crafts people fairly in trade is but another variation on Harper's central message of just economic relations governed by the virtues of character.

8. It would be hard to over-emphasize the pervasive abuse of alcohol across social lines and the resulting social costs for women in the nineteenth century. With relatively scarce opportunities for the types of employment that might provide economic independence, women were of course dangerously dependent on husbands and fathers for family livelihoods. The expansion of the liquor trade and the rise of alcoholism put great numbers of women at risk for economic disaster in the instance of inebriate patriarchs squandering family monies as a result of their addiction. Both inside and outside the home, women were inevitably targets of drunken men's violence. Jack S. Blocker Jr. notes that national newspaper readers in the 1870s would most certainly have been aware of this violence against women because it was so widely publicized, often in sensationalistic detail (100–110).

9. In *The Feminization of American Culture*, Ann Douglas traces the feminine "doctrine of influence" in the late eighteenth and nineteenth centuries, making an excellent case for its prevalence in burgeoning, mass-mediated public consciousness and arguing that, ultimately, the notion of "influence" constituted a "pattern of defeat within victory." As a cultural practice, notably in the explosion of women's writing in the mid-nineteenth century, "influence" in Douglas's estimation was articulated as an *alternative to* and not a *means of* access to political power for women. While Douglas is not as dismissive of sentimental culture overall as these comments suggest, I use her criticism as a point of departure because it raises a contentious point not only in twentieth-century cultural history, but also one which existed as an active dialectic within nineteenth-century women's politics. We must place the factionalism of the WCTU platform in this context and in so doing, read Willard as a careful negotiator of a powerful ideological construction.

10. Clifford's mother, an archetypal character in Harper's oeuvre as well as in the slave narrative and sentimental literature of reform activism, makes him "take the pledge," and it is her Christian reform sensibilities that make Clifford both an eligible bachelor and also eligible as the novel's hero. Clifford is a member of the temperance movement and Harper's model of an ethical capitalist, for whom the bottom line is the civic good and not sheer profit.

11. Reading Walt Whitman's poetics of the 1840s in the context of the temperance movement, the auspices under which Whitman wrote the majority of his fiction, Michael Warner asserts that the "temperance movement *invented* addiction . . . In temperance rhetoric, the concept [of addiction] loses the sense of an active self-abnegation on the part of the will. Desire and will become distinct" (32). This "picture of the body's own heteronomy" places Whitman's serial novel *Franklin Evans; or, The Inebriate* (1842) "on the cutting edge of addiction theory," in which the temperance pledge figures "a much more radical valuing of the will . . . the receding horizon of [a] relatively absolute voluntarity" (32–33). Although the differences between the politics and poetics of Whitman and Harper are dramatic, Warner's reading provides insights into the addiction theory of the temperance movement as well as its implicit concern

(made explicit in Whitman's and Harper's texts) with the relationship between individual and civic identity, which is to say the ethical proving ground of moral character. It is, in fact, such acts of self-control that were repeatedly modeled by temperance writers and orators, narratives of self-mastery, and by turns, of the ruinous failure of self-mastery.

12. For a discussion of the sensationalism of temperance fiction, see Reynolds's *Beneath the American Renaissance* (65–73).

13. Fraser suggests a pattern, which such interpublicity tends to follow. First, "'oppositional' forms of needs talk . . . arise" contributing to the crystallization of new social identities. These counter-discourses draw the response of "reprivatization" (*Unruly Practices* 171). Harper's dialogue represents such a pattern quite clearly.

14. John Gough was likely the most well-known temperance orator of the century. His own story of escape "from the thralldom of a common drunkard" was a very well-known narrative (Warden 219).

15. The influential Washingtonian temperance movement of the 1840s and 1850s was known for its religious fervor as well as its sensationalistic narratives detailing the depravity of inebriates. See Reynolds's introduction to *The Serpent in the Cup*.

16. Hazel Carby, among others, has noted that in the activist literature of nineteenth-century African American women, marriage plots were used to figure the consummation not of romantic love, but of a community of resistance. Carby focuses her reading on Harper's later novel, *Iola Leroy*, and in my last chapter, I examine this rhetorical use of the marriage plot in a discussion of *Minnie's Sacrifice*. Minnie and Louis's marriage forms a political coalition "in which they could clasp hands . . . and find their duty and their pleasure in living for the welfare and happiness of *our* race, as Minnie would often say" (67). Minnie and Louis headed South to work in the "Freedmen's movement," while Gordon and Clifford find their mission among the abject subjects of the drunken economy. Critic Anne duCille adds an important qualification to Carby's notion of the sublimation of sexual pleasure in African American women's writing: She notes that such "literary passionlessness . . . metaphorically extends to black women . . . autonomy and moral authority" while in popular fiction and tragic fact, black women's sexuality was subject to "white supremacist masculinity" (43–45). Certainly, this argument could be extended to cover the practice of temperance rhetoric I have discussed in this chapter.

NOTES TO CHAPTER 4

1. One of the most tragic of these events were the so-called New York City "Draft Riots" of 1863. For the most detailed historical analysis of the riots, see Bernstein.

2. Harper's title signifies on Frederick Douglass's well-known address, "The Trials and Triumphs of the Self-Made Man." In this address, Douglass praises the attributes of self-made men and declares that "America," because of its general respect for labor, is the pre-eminent ground of self-making. Douglass offers one qualification to his extreme faith in America's opportunities, that being the racial prejudice that threatens the viability of free-labor culture. Harper's novel addresses the same dynamics of self-making, all the while studiously revising the masculinist frame of Douglass's address.

3. While their social struggles by no means disappeared in the second half of the century, Irish Americans gained social status along with political power

and lost much of the racial stigma they had previously suffered. This process of gaining white-skin privilege, or "becoming white," as Noel Ignatiev has phrased it, was taken by African American commentators as an object lesson in the instrumental power of racial rhetoric. Easton is studiously blithe in his suggestion that "there is nothing malignant in the nature and exercise of that prejudice" exercised against Irish immigrants, and yet his sense of white privilege in the United States is acute.

4. Matthew Frye Jacobsen's analysis of the Irish as racially ambiguous suggests the diversity of rhetorical use to which reference to the Irish was put among nineteenth-century commentators (48–53).

5. Irish Catholic patriot Daniel O'Connell is a point of identification through-out Douglass's voluminous oratorical oeuvre. Influential in securing Catho-lic Emancipation in British-ruled Ireland, O'Connell wielded considerable power from the podium, where crowds thronged to hear "the Liberator," and eventually from his seat in Parliament as well.

6. Fortune's construction of a revolutionary African lineage exceeds in aggres-siveness either Douglass's or Harper's black Ireland tropes, but was mild in comparison to Henry McNeal Turner's reaction. A.M.E. Bishop and then editor of the *Christian Recorder*, Turner saw the reversal of the bill as an irreconcilable act of oppression, one that justified his own separatist agenda. In an 1883 *Christian Recorder* editorial, Turner predicts "bloodshed enough over that decision to drown every member of the Supreme Court in less than two years." He argues furthermore that the reversal "absolves the allegiance of the negro to the United States." The implicit threat to the white power structure of the post-Reconstruction era pales in comparison to Turner's barb to black Republicans, reprinted in the *Christian Recorder* just after the 1883 repeal: "[T]he negro hereafter who will enlist in the armies of the government, or swear to defend the United States Constitution ought to be hung by the neck" (1). Clearly, this assertion of black self-determination is quite different from Harper's.

7. Harper's sense that the community of racially disenfranchised people exceeds the African American community is suggested later in the novel when Thomas equates "lynch law with its burnings and hangings [and] our national policy in regard to the Indians and Chinese" (236).

8. Grady's self-congratulatory explanation of race relations in the South oddly echoes the Protestant narratives of historical "progress" so common in the abolitionist and neo-abolitionist presses: "But what of the negro? Let the record speak to the point. No section shows a more prosperous laboring population than the negroes of the South, none in fuller sympathy with the employing and land-owning class . . . We understand that when Lincoln signed the emancipation proclamation, your victory was assured, for he then committed you to the cause of human liberty, against which the arms of man cannot prevail—while those of our statesmen who trusted to make slavery the corner-stone of the Confederacy doomed us to defeat as far as they could, committing us to a cause that reason could not defend or the sword maintain in sight of advancing civilization" (89). Thus Lincoln, who had been a sym-bol of abolitionist martyrs, is reconfigured as an embodiment of white union, "the sum of Puritan and Cavalier" (85).

9. Silber finds the celebration of national reconciliation to be pervasive enough late in the nineteenth century to call it a "mind-numbing mantra in American society" (1). Dominated by representations of cross-regional romance, Silber argues that this "culture of conciliation," was increasingly underwritten by an abandonment of Reconstruction and the popularization of Southern-style white supremacism. She also makes the economic connection, claiming

rightly that the culture of conciliation "was less an emotional bonding of northern and southern people and more a financial bonding between investors and business leaders in both regions" (2).

10. In claiming for the South, that it has "put business above politics," Grady makes the predictable move of placing the labor market outside the realm of political concern. Grady eschews any complaints about "carpetbaggers," claiming the South has "wiped out the place where Mason and Dixon's line used to be" (88). Thus the joining of Northern and Southern business interests parallels the metaphysical reconciliation of national white identity, the ontology underwriting New South economics. Grady obscures the offenses of race-class antagonisms by mobilizing another privatizing narrative, this one familial. That narrative is, of course, the myth of the happy slave, of "Mammy." Demonstrating his imaginative solidarity with "Plantation Romance" authors such as Thomas Dixon and Thomas Nelson Page, Grady writes, "I want no sweeter music than the crooning of my old 'mammy,' now dead and gone to rest, as I heard it when she held me in her loving arms" (97). Grady's assumptions about the passivity of black sociality are marked, and for all its language of unity, among white "brothers" and white capital, there remains in Grady's New South at least one major regional distinction, one that follows from the paternalism of the neo-planter class. In an 1887 address in Dallas, entitled "The South and Her Problems," Grady surmises that the most pressing of all Southern problems "is to carry within her body politic two separate races, and nearly equal in numbers. She must carry these races in peace—for discord means ruin. She must carry them separately—for assimilation means debasement" (96).

11. Carla Peterson argues that the dialogue between Thomas and Hastings also poses the threat of oppressed black labor in the South migrating North, expanding the labor pool and thus lowering wages ("Further Liftings" 109).

12. Both the black and white presses in the second half of the century repeatedly drew the connection between class violence in Europe and in the United States, and projected the possibility of a labor revolution. Depending on the editorial slant, of course, such projections were accordingly paranoid or welcoming. Harper, Douglass, and Stowe all inveighed the spectre of communism and anarchism as a warning against Jim Crow. For a discussion of such comparisons in abolitionist discourse, see Ernest (64–70).

13. It is difficult not to read such rhetoric as an act of scapegoating labor radicals and immigrants. Kenneth W. Warren argues that Harper was invested in representing black workers "as a non-subversive, non-revolutionary force," and a survey of Harper's oeuvre bears out such a claim (69).

14. In *Blues, Ideology and Afro-American Literature: A Vernacular Theory*, Baker lays out the poetics and politics of the "blues matrix." Drawing on African American literature and deconstructive and Marxist theory, Baker finds in the blues matrix the "'always already' of Afro-American culture" (4). The improvisational power of the blues is in its ever-changing rhetorical creation in the face of oppressive power and its inventive intertextuality. Baker's definition of spirit work is multiple and shifting, thus performing the improvisatory rhetorical power of spirit work itself. Baker calls spirit work the "classic work of verbal expressiveness" in African American culture " . . . a kaleidoscopic . . . [and] limitless cultural repertoire" in which form and content merge to form "habitable poetic territory" (*Workings* 76). His primary example of such spirit work is Zora Neale Hurston, whose poetics "take back or secure a pre-European return upon African expressive energies silenced by an enslaving trade in [African American] bodies" (50).

15. See also Hazel Carby's "Ideologies of the Black Folk: The Historical Novel of Slavery" in *Cultures of Babylon: Black Britain and African America* (146–147), and Melba Joyce Boyd's *Discarded Legacy* (18–20).

NOTES TO CHAPTER 5

1. Angela Davis contrasts the black clubwomen's organizations to those of white women, which catered primarily to the needs of middle-class women for leisure activities. Davis sets the date of the beginning of the proliferation of white women's clubs in 1868 when, excluded from the New York Press Club, women in that city and in Boston established the New England Women's Club (*Women* 128–129). This is an important detail, as it suggests the clubwomen's early conception of the club movement as a means of building what I have followed Fraser in calling a subaltern counterpublic.
2. Singh criticizes liberal historians who have practiced their own brand of rhetorical segregation by keeping this Southern history separate from more standard critiques of late-century Northern capitalism, recapitulating, in a sense, a romanticizing of the Southern ethos by positing Jim Crow, for instance, as a postponement of "southern modernity" (492).
3. As I argued in Chapter 4, the collapse of Reconstruction as an effort for black political-economic self-determination was, ironically, widely justified through the ideology of self-reliance itself, in which the dependence–independence binary was a crucial operation. The elision of capital–labor relations as a system of coercion and the continuation of racial oppression allowed apologists of the "New South" to place the blame for the underdevelopment of African American communities on African Americans themselves, as a failure of a independent individual and collective character.
4. Founded in 1866, the Universal Peace Union (UPU) was dedicated to "immediate disarmament" and called for arbitration between all the world's warring nations. The long-standing UPU president, Alfred Love, led the organization in dissent against the late-century imperialist policies of the United States (Gottfried 47–48). It is easy to see how Harper would have been attracted to the uncompromising stance of the UPU.
5. Wells did not simply denounce the legitimacy of national law in her pamphlets. She was the first to challenge the 1883 nullification of the 1875 Civil Rights Act when she refused to give up her seat in the first-class ladies coach on the train carrying her home from her teaching position in Shelby County, Tennessee. In her autobiography, she notes that the decision proved that "Negroes were not wards of the nation but citizens of the individual states" (20).
6. When the First National Conference of Colored Women convened in Boston in 1895, the black clubwomen were not simply emulating their white counterparts. They had come together to decide upon a strategy of resistance to the current propagandistic assaults on black women and the continued reign of lynch law. Responding to an attack on Ida B. Wells by the pro-lynching president of the Missouri Press Association, the conference delegates protested that "insult to Negro womanhood" and sent out " . . . to the country a unanimous endorsement of the course [Wells] had pursued in [her] agitation against lynching" (*Women* 133).
7. Among feminist readers of African American literature and culture, there is consensus that as a project of cultural politics, the black feminists' refashioned ideology of womanhood was the primary rhetorical gambit to be undertaken. Giddings argues that the sense of an urgent need to build such a "defense"

was a direct response to a pervasive assault on the moral character of African American women. Carby argues that black women of the nineteenth century contested the hegemonic assumptions of "true womanhood" as an essentially white, leisure-class identification. Carby's seminal *Reconstructing Womanhood: The Emergence of the Afro-American Woman Novelist* posits such contestation as constitutive of a polemical strain of nineteenth-century African American women's fiction. Carby traces the redeployment of true womanhood as a language of protest; in the new idiom, reform work and literary modes provided a rhetorical surplus for this protest.

8. Trachtenberg concludes that the Chicago Exposition overall was "a pedagogy, a model and a lesson not only of what the future might look like, but just as important, how it might be brought about." This future-oriented pedagogy, according to Trachtenberg, was as notable for what it failed to teach. These untaught lessons cleared symbolic space for a pedantic celebration of corporate and industrial culture as an engine of modernist social perfectionism (209–214).

9. "Do you wish to know anything of the moral and spiritual status of a people," Harper asks in the *A.M.E. Church Review* significantly, "[F]ind out, not simply how they use their working hours, but how they spend their leisure moments" (*BCD* 279).

10. As I noted in the introduction to this chapter, the clubwomen's rhetoric of the historicity of African American character was a counter-narrative to more pervasive progressivist narratives that legitimated race relations at their nadir. In particular, they countered notions of the inexorable progress of Anglo-Saxon culture that were beginning to be articulated in the "Plantation Romance," a variety of regional fiction that romanticized the slave system and Southern gentility, and relied on minstrelized representations of African American character including that of the "happy slave." This historical narrative would soon be institutionalized in the so-called "Dunning-Burgess" school of Reconstruction historiography, which cast Radical Republicanism as a travesty and "the darkest page in the saga of American history" (Foner, *Reconstruction* xix–xx).

11. By the time of the book's publication, Washington's "Tuskegee machine" was the dominant power among African American cultural politics. Giddings documents the uneasy relationship between Washington and clubwomen, noting his efforts to undermine the authority and efforts of the women who, like Ida B. Wells, defied the limitations of his "industrial" pedagogy (*When and Where* 104–106).

12. Vorris Nunley characterizes an African American "hush harbor" being "composed of the rhetorics and the commonplaces emerging from those rhetorics, articulating distinctive social epistemologies and subjectivities of African American experience and directed toward predominantly Black audiences . . . Hush harbor places become Black spaces because African American *nomos* (social convention, worldview knowledge), rhetoric, *phronesis* (practical wisdom and intelligence), tropes, and commonplaces are normative in the encounters that occur in those locations" (224). Nunley's theorization description of the discursive space of the hush harbor resonates strongly with the constitutive function I have posited for the rhetorical pedagogies of the African American press. Within the collective identification of the hush harbor of the Afro-Protestant press, Harper regularly made didactic distinctions such as those in the 1891 "Temperance."

13. Giddings's discussion of Washington's influence within the clubwomen's movement is among the best. I would underscore her demonstration that while believing in Washington's "philosophy of Black self-help, mutual aid,

and racial pride," many would not brook his abandonment of civil rights advocacy and protest over racial injustice (101–107).

14. See, for example, Chapter 13 of *Souls of Black Folks*, "The Coming of John." After receiving a college education, John returns to his rural Southern home to start a school, which he understands as a duty to the race. Du Bois's account of John's character development puts the text in the pedagogical tradition exemplified in Harper's novels.

15. Mary Jo Deegan is certainly right in criticizing dismissive critiques of Williams as "accommodationist" given the volume and complexity of her canon (xv). My point is simply to contrast Harper's heuristic deployment of character with that of Williams, which at least here is more clearly hierarchical.

16. There is no material evidence that Harper intended the novel for white readers, or that it enjoyed any substantial white readership. However, I refer back to Chapter 3 and Deborah Rosenthal's assertion that African American polemical texts always assume a white audience. Because *Iola Leroy* is composed of so many excerpts from addresses given before racially mixed audiences, this seems, in this case, to be a safe assumption.

NOTES TO THE AFTERWORD

1. In his preface, Still makes clear that his intention in publishing *The Underground Railroad* was archival and instructional. As his epigraph, Still uses a resolution from the last meeting of the Pennsylvania Anti-Slavery Society, which frames his composition as a production of a collective reform will (1). With his series of movement biographies, which culminates with Harper's, Still worked early in a genre that would continue apace with the emerging literary marketplace of African American literature in which Harper's work could be referenced as a counter-example of worthy craft.

2. In his introduction to *Iola Leroy*, in contrast to Redding's account, Still notes Harper's extensive contact with Southern African Americans after the Civil War, a depth of knowledge reflected in the novel itself (1–2). To be sure, Redding's accusation of detachment discounts years of service to enslaved African Americans and their descendants in the New South.

3. Brown's career intersected significantly with Harper's. Like Harper, Brown was a member of the Woman's Christian Temperance Union and a founding member of the National Association of Women, and her family had been active in Underground Railroad work. Brown also lectured and taught in African American schools in the Reconstruction South (Boyd 215).

Bibliography

Ahlstrom, Sidney E. *A Religious History of the American People*. New Haven, CT: Yale University Press, 1972.

Allen, Theodore W. *The Invention of the White Race: Racial Oppression and Social Control*. New York: Verso, 1994.

Asante, Molefi Kete. *The Afrocentric Idea*. Philadelphia: Temple University Press, 1998.

Bacon, Jacqueline. *The Humblest May Stand Forth: Rhetoric, Empowerment, and Abolition*. Columbia: University of South Carolina Press, 2002.

Bacon, Margaret Hope. "'One Great Bundle of Humanity': Frances Ellen Watkins Harper (1825–1911)." *Pennsylvania Magazine of History and Biography* 113.1 (1989): 21–43.

Baker, Houston. *Blues, Ideology, and Afro-American Literature: A Vernacular Theory*. Chicago: University of Chicago Press, 1984.

———. *Workings of the Spirit: The Poetics of Afro-American Women's Writing*. Chicago: University of Chicago Press, 1991.

Balibar, Etienne, and Immanuel Walerstein. *Race, Nation, Class: Ambiguous Identities*. London: Verso, 1991.

Barrier, Fannie Williams. *The New Woman of Color: The Collected Writings of Fannie Barrier Williams*. Ed. Mary Jo Deegan. DeKalb, Illinois: Northern Illinois University Press, 2002.

Benjamin, Walter. *Illuminations*. Trans. Harry Zohn. Ed. Hannah Arendt. New York: Schocken Books, 1968

Bennett, Lerone, Jr. *Before the Mayflower*. 5th ed. New York: Penguin Books, 1982.

Bennett, Michael. *Democratic Discourse: The Radical Abolition Movement and Antebellum American Literature*. New Brunswick, NJ: Rutgers University Press, 2005.

Bergman, Jill, and Debra Bernardi. *Our Sisters' Keepers: Nineteenth-Century Benevolence Literature By American Women*. Tuscaloosa: University of Alabama Press, 2005.

Berlant, Lauren. *The Queen of America Goes to Washington City*. Durham, NC: Duke University Press, 1997.

Birnbaum, Michele. "Racial Hysteria: Female Pathology and Race Politics in Frances Harper's *Iola Leroy* and W.D. Howells's and *Imperative Duty*." *African American Review* 33 (1999): 7–23.

Blocker, Jack S., Jr. *"Give To The Winds Thy Fears": The Women's Temperance Crusade, 1873–1874*. Westport, CT: Greenwood Press, 1985.

Boeckmann, Cathy. *A Question of Character: Scientific Racism and the Genres of American Fiction, 1892–1912*. Tuscaloosa: University of Alabama Press, 2000.

Bordin, Ruth. *Woman and Temperance: The Quest for Power and Liberty, 1873–1900.* Philadelphia: Temple University Press, 1981.

Boyd, Melba Joyce. *Discarded Legacy: Politics and Poetics in the Life of Frances E.W. Harper, 1825–1911.* Detroit, MI: Wayne State University Press, 1994.

Brandt, Deborah. *Literacy in American Lives.* New York: Cambridge University Press, 2001.

Brent, Linda. *Incidents in the Life of a Slave Girl.* Ed. L. Maria Child. New York: Harcourt Brace Jovanovich Publishers, 1973.

Bruce, Dickson D. *Black American Writing from the Nadir: The Evolution of Literary Tradition 1877–1915.* Baton Rouge: Louisiana State University Press, 1989.

Brown, Gillian. *Domestic Individualism: Imagining Self in Nineteenth-Century America.* Berkley: University of California Press, 1990.

Brown, Hallie Q. *Homespun Heroines and Other Women of Distinction.* New York: Oxford University Press, 1988.

Burgess, John W. *Reconstruction and the Constitution 1866–1876.* New York: Charles Scribner's Sons, 1902.

Butler, Judith. *Excitable Speech: A Politics of the Performative.* London: Routledge, 1997.

Campbell, James T. *The African Methodist Episcopal Church in the United States and South Africa.* New York: Oxford University Press, 1995.

Carby, Hazel. *Cultures in Babylon: Black Britain and African America.* London: Verso, 1999.

———. *Race Men.* Cambridge, MA: Harvard University Press, 1998.

———. *Reconstructing Womanhood: The Emergence of the Afro-American Woman Novelist.* London: Oxford, 1987.

Castronovo, Russ. *Necro Citizenship: Death, Eroticism, and the Public Sphere in the Nineteenth-Century United States.* Durham, NC: Duke University Press, 2001.

Chapman, Katie. D. "Mixed Schools." *Christian Recorder* 24 May 1888: 1.

Cherniavsky, Eva. *That Pale Mother Rising: Sentimental Discourses and the Imitation of Motherhood in 19th-Century America.* Bloomington: University of Indiana Press, 1995.

Christian, Barbara. *Black Women Novelists: The Development of a Tradition, 1892–1976.* Westport, CT: Greenwood Press, 1980.

Christmann, James. "Raising Voices, Lifting Shadows: Competing Voice-Paradigms in Frances E. W. Harper's *Iola Leroy*." *African American Review* 34 (2000): 5–18.

Clark, Gregory, and S. Michael Halloran, eds. *Oratorical Culture in Nineteenth-Century America: Transformations in the Theory and Practice of Rhetoric.* Carbondale: Southern Illinois University Press, 1993.

Clark, Norman. *Deliver Us from Evil: An Interpretation of American Prohibition* New York: Norton, 1976.

Claude, Eddie S. *Exodus! Religion, Race and Nation in Early Nineteenth-Century Black America.* Chicago: University of Chicago Press, 2000.

Cmeil, Kenneth. *Democratic Eloquence: The Fight over Popular Speech in Nineteenth-Century America.* Berkeley: University of California Press, 1990.

Collins, Patricia Hill. *Black Feminist Thought: Knowledge, Consciousness, and the Politics of Empowerment.* New York: Routledge, 2000.

Condit, Celeste Michelle. "Crafting Virtue: The Rhetorical Construction of Public Morality." *Contemporary Rhetorical Theory: A Reader.* Ed. John Louis Lucaites et al. New York: Guilford, 1999: 306–325.

Cooper, Anna Julia. *A Voice from the South.* New York: Oxford, 1988.

Crowley, John W. "Slaves to the Bottle: Gough's Autobiography and Douglass's Narrative." *In The Serpent and the Cup: Temperance in American Literature.*

Ed. David S. Reynolds and Debra J. Rosenthal. Amherst: University of Massachusetts Press, 1997: 115–135.

Crowley, Sharon and Debra Hawhee. *Ancient Rhetorics for Contemporary Students*. Needham Heights, MA: Allyn and Bacon, 1999.

Davis, Angela. *Women, Race and Class*. New York: Vintage Books, 1983.

Davis, David Brion. *Inhuman Bondage: The Rise and Fall or Slavery in the New World*. Oxford: Oxford University Press, 2006.

Douglas, Ann. *The Feminization of American Culture*. New York: Anchor Books, 1977.

Douglass, Frederick. *Frederick Douglass on Women's Rights*. Ed. Philip S. Foner. New York: De Capo Press, 1992.

———. *The Frederick Douglass Papers: Speeches, Debates, and Interviews*. Ed. John W. Blassingame. 5 vols. New Haven: Yale University Press, 1979

Drescher, Seymour. *The Mighty Experiment: Free Labor versus Slavery in British Emancipation*. New York: Oxford University Press, 2002.

Du Bois, W.E.B. *Souls of Black Folk*. New York: W.W. Norton and Co., 1999.

———. "Writers." *The Crisis* 1 (April 1911): 20–21.

duCille, Ann. *The Coupling Convention: Sex, Text, and Tradition in Black Women's Fiction*. New York: Oxford University Press, 1993.

———. *Skin Trade*. Cambridge: Oxford University Press, 1996.

Dunnning, William A. *Reconstruction, Political and Economic 1865–1877*. New York: Harper Torchbooks, 1962.

Erkkila, Betsy, and Jay Grossman, eds. *Breaking Bounds: Whitman and American Cultural Studies*. Oxford: Oxford University Press, 1996.

Ernst, John. *Liberation Historiography: African American Writers and the Challenge of History, 1794–1861*. Chapel Hill: University of North Carolina Press, 2004.

———. *Resistance and Reformation in Nineteenth-Century African-American Literature: Brown, Wilson, Jacobs, Delany, Douglass, and Harper*. Jackson: University Press of Mississippi, 1995.

Fitzhugh, George. *Cannibals All! or Slaves Without Masters*. Ed. C. Vann Woodward. Cambridge, MA: Harvard University Press, 1988.

Flax, Jane. *Disputed Subjects: Essays on Psychoanalysis, Politics and Philosophy*. New York: Routledge, 1993.

Flexner, Eleanor. *Century of Struggle: The Woman's Rights Movement in the United States*. 1959. Revised and enlarged by Ellen Fitzpatrick. Cambridge, MA: Belknap Press, 1996.

Foner, Eric. *Free Soil, Free Labor, Free Men: The Ideology of the Republican Party Before the Civil War*. New York: Oxford, 1970.

———. *Politics and Ideology in the Age of the Civil War*. New York: Oxford University Press, 1980.

———. *Reconstruction: Americas Unfinished Revolution, 1863–1877*. New York: Harper and Row, 1988.

Foreman, P. Gabrielle. *Activist Sentiments: Reading Black Women in the Nineteenth Century*. Chicago: University of Illinois Press, 2009.

Fortune, T. Thomas. *Black and White: Land, Labor and the Politics of the South*. New York: Arno Press, 1968.

Foucault, Michel. *Ethics, Subjectivity and Truth*. New York: The New Press, 1994.

Fraser, Nancy. *Justice Interruptus: Critical Reflections on the "Post-Socialist" Condition*. London: Routledge, 1997.

———. *Unruly Practices: Power, Discourse and Gender in Contemporary Social Theory*. Minneapolis: University of Minnesota Press, 1989.

Furness, William Henry. *The Blessings of Abolition: A Discourse Delivered in the First Congregational Unitarian Church, Sunday July 1, 1860*. Philadelphia: C. Sherman & Son, Printers, 1860.

Gates, Henry Louis. *The Signifying Monkey: A Theory of African-American Literary Criticism*. New York: Oxford University Press, 1988.

Gerteis, Louis. *Mortality and Utility in American Antislavery Reform*. Chapel Hill: University of North Carolina Press, 1987.

Gibian, Peter. *Oliver Wendell Holmes and the Culture of Conversation*. Cambridge: Cambridge University Press, 2001.

Giddings, Paula. *"When and Where I Enter": The Impact of Black Women on Race and Sex in America*. New York: William Morrow, 1984.

Gillette, William. *Retreat from Reconstruction 1869–1879*. Baton Rouge: Louisiana State University Press, 1979.

Gilroy, Paul. *The Black Atlantic: Modernity and Double Consciousness*. London: Verso, 1993.

Goodman, Paul. *Of One Blood: Abolitionism and the Origins of Racial Equality*. Berkeley: University of California Press, 1998.

Gordon, Ann, ed. *African American Women and the Vote, 1837–1965*. Amherst: University of Massachusetts Press, 1997.

Gordon, Dexter B. *Black Identity: Rhetoric, Ideology, and Nineteenth-Century Black Nationalism*. Carbondale: Southern Illinois University Press, 2003.

Gossett, Thomas F. *Race: The History of an Idea in America*. New York: Oxford University Press, 1997.

Gottfried, Ted. *The Fight for Peace: A History of Antiwar Movements in America*. Minneapolis: Twenty-First Century Books, 2006.

Grady, Henry. *The New South: Writings and Speeches of Henry Grady*. Savannah, GA: Beehive Press, 1971.

Grohsmeyer, Janeen. "Frances Harper." *Dictionary of Unitarian and Universalist Biography*. Unitarian Universalist Historical Society. 18 Sept. 2009 <http://www25.uua.org/uuhs/duub/articles/francesharper.html>.

Guinier, Lani, and Gerald Torres. *The Miner's Canary: Enlisting Race, Resisting Power, Transforming Democracy*. Cambridge, MA: Harvard University Press, 2002.

Gutierrez-Jones, Carl. *Critical Race Narratives: A Study of Race, Rhetoric, and Injury*. New York: New York University Press, 2001.

Harper, Frances Ellen Watkins. *A Brighter Coming Day: A Frances Ellen Watkins Harper Reader*. Ed. Frances Smith Foster. New York: The Feminist Press, 1990.

———. "A Plea Against Mere Money-Making." *The Anglo-African Magazine*. May 1859: 160.

———. *Complete Poems of Frances E. W. Harper*. Ed. Maryemma Graham. New York: Oxford, 1988.

———. "Duty to Dependent Races." *National Council of Women of the United States, Transactions*. Philadelphia: National Council of Women of the United States, 1891. 86–91.

———. "Fancy Etchings." *Christian Recorder* 1 May 1873: 1.

———. *Iola Leroy; or Shadows Uplifted*. Boston: Beacon, 1987.

———. *Minnie's Sacrifice, Sowing and Reaping, Trial and Triumph: Three Rediscovered Novels by Frances E. W. Harper*. Ed. Frances Smith Foster. Boston: Beacon, 1994.

———. "Our Greatest Want." *Anglo African Magazine* May 1859: 160.

———. *Poems on Miscellaneous Subjects*. 2nd ed. Boston: J. B. Yerrinton & Son Printers, 1857.

———. "The Two Offers." *Anglo African Magazine* (September 1859): 288–291; (October 1859): 311–313.

———. "Woman's Political Future." *World Congress of Representative Women 1893 Proceedings*. Ed. May Wright Sewall. Chicago: Rand McNally, 1894. 433–437.

Hartman, Saidiya H. *Scenes of Subjection: Terror, Slavery, and Self-Making in Nineteenth-Century America*. New York: Oxford University Press, 1997.

Higginbotham, Evelyn Brooks. "African American Women's History and the Metalanguage of Race." *Signs* 17.2 (1992): 251–274.

———. *Righteous Discontent: The Women's Movement in the Black Baptist Church, 1880–1920.* Cambridge, MA: Harvard University Press, 1993.

hooks, bell. *Yearning: Race, Gender and Cultural Politics.* Boston: South End Press, 1990.

Howe, Daniel Walker. *The Unitarian Conscience: Harvard Moral Philosophy 1805–1861.* Middletown, CT: Wesleyan University Press, 1988.

Ignatiev, Noel. *How the Irish Became White.* London: Routledge, 1995.

Johnson, James H. A., D.D. "Rev. William H. Watkins." *African Methodist Episcopal Church Review* 3 (1886): 11–12.

Johnson, James Weldon, ed. *The Book of American Negro Poetry.* New York: Harcourt, Brace, and Company, 1931.

Johnson, Nan. *Nineteenth-Century Rhetoric in North America.* Carbondale: Southern Illinois University Press, 1991.

Jones, Jacqueline. *Labor of Love, Labor of Sorrow: Black Women, Work and the Family, from Slavery to the Present.* New York: Vintage Books Random House, 1985.

———. *Soldiers of Light and Love: Northern Teachers and Georgia Blacks, 1865–1873.* Athens: University of Georgia Press, 1992.

Jordan, June. *Affirmative Acts: Political Essays.* New York: Anchor Books, 1998.

Karcher, Carolyn L. *The First Woman in the Republic: A Cultural Biography of Lydia Maria Child.* Durham, NC: Duke University Press, 1994.

Kinney, James. *Amalgamation! Race, Sex and Rhetoric in the Nineteenth-Century Novel.* Westport, CT: Greenwood Press, 1985.

Knupfer, Anne Meis. *Toward a Tenderer Humanity and a Nobler Womanhood: African American Women's Clubs in Turn-of-the-Century Chicago.* New York: New York University Press, 1996.

"Lecture on the Mission of the War." *Christian Recorder* 21 May 1864: 2.

Logan, Shirley Wilson. *Sites of Rhetorical Education in Nineteenth-Century Black America.* Carbondale: Southern Illinois University Press, 2008.

———. *"We Are Coming": The Persuasive Discourse of Nineteenth-Century Black Women.* Carbondale: Southern Illinois University Press, 1999.

Lukacs, Georg. *History and Consciousness: Studies in Marxist Dialectics.* Trans. Rodney Livingstone. Cambridge: MIT Press, 1968.

Lynch, Deidre Shauna. *The Economy of Character: Novels, Market Culture, and the Business of Inner Meaning.* Chicago: University of Chicago Press, 1998.

Mabee, Carleton. *Black Freedom: The Nonviolent Abolitionists from 1830 through the Civil War.* London: The Macmillan Company, 1970.

Mailloux, Steven. *Disciplinary Identities: Rhetorical Paths of English, Speech, and Composition.* New York: The Modern Language Association of America, 2006.

Manning, Marable. *How Capitalism Underdeveloped Black America: Problems in Race, Political Economy and Society.* Boston: South End Press, 1983.

Martin, Scott C., ed. *Cultural Change and the Market Revolution in American, 1789–1860.* New York: Rowman and Littlefield Publishers, 2005.

Mattingly, Carol. *Well-Tempered Women: Nineteenth-Century Temperance Rhetoric.* Carbondale: Southern Illinois University Press, 1998.

Mayer, Henry. *All on Fire: William Lloyd Garrison and the Abolition of Slavery.* New York: St. Martin's Press, 1998.

McInerney, Daniel J. *The Fortunate Heirs of Freedom: Abolition and Republican Thought.* Lincoln: University of Nebraska Press, 1994

McPherson, James M. *The Struggle for Equality.* Princeton, NJ: Princeton University Press, 1964.

Merish, Lori Ann. *Sentimental Materialism: Gender, Commodity Culture, and Nineteenth-Century American Literature.* Durham, NC: Duke University Press, 2000.

Miller, Kelly. *Race Adjustment and The Everlasting Stain.* New York: Arno Press, 1968.

Mills, Charles W. *The Racial Contract.* Ithaca, NY: Cornell University Press, 1997.

Moses, Wilson Jeremiah. *The Golden Age of Black Nationalism, 1850–1825.* New York. Oxford University Press, 1978.

Moody, J. Carroll, and Alice Kessler-Harris, eds. *Perspectives on American Labor History: The Problems of Synthesis.* DeKalb: Northern Illinois University Press, 1990.

Morrison, Toni. *Playing in the Dark: Whiteness and the Literary Imagination.* New York: Random House, 1993.

"Mrs. Harper on Reconstruction." *Liberator* 3 March 1865. University of Detroit Mercy Black Abolitionist Archive. Web.

Nerone, John. *Violence Against the Press: Policing the Public Sphere in U.S. History.* New York: Oxford University Press, 1994.

Nuermberger, Ruth Ketring. *The Free Produce Movement: A Quaker Protest Against Slavery.* Durham, NC: Duke University Press, 1942.

O'Connor, Lillian. *Pioneer Women Orators: Rhetoric in the Ante-Bellum Reform Movement.* New York: Columbia University Press, 1954.

Omi, Michael and Howard Winant. *Racial Formation in the United States From the 1960s to the 1990s,* Second Edition New York: Routledge Press, 1994.

Page, Thomas Nelson. *Red Rock: A Chronicle of Reconstruction.* New York: Charles Scribner's Sons, 1912.

Painter, Nell Irvin. *Sojourner Truth: A Life, A Symbol.* New York: W.W. Norton and Company, 1996.

Peterson, Carla. *Doers of the Word: African American Women Speakers and Writers in the North (1830–1880).* New Brunswick, NJ: Rutgers University Press, 1995.

———. "Further Liftings of the Veil: Gender, Class, and Labor in Frances E.W. Harper's *Iola Leroy.*" In *Listening to Silences: New Essays in Feminist Criticism.* Ed. Elaine Hedges and Shelley Fisher Fishkin. New York: Oxford Press, 1994: 97–112.

———. "Literary Transnationalism and Diasporic History: Frances Watkins Harper's 'Fancy Sketches,' 1859–1860." In *Women's Rights and Transatlantic Antislavery in the Era of Emancipation.* Ed. Kathryn Kish Sklar and James Brewer Stewart. New Haven CT: Yale University Press, 2007: 189–208.

Phillips, Wendell. *Speeches, Lectures, and Letters.* Boston: Walker, Wise, and Company, 1864.

Porter, Dorothy, ed. *Early Negro Writing 1760–1837.* Boston: Beacon Press, 1971.

Quarles, Benjamin. *Black Abolitionism.* New York: Oxford University Press, 1969.

Rael, Patrick. *Black Identity and Black Protest in the Antebellum North.* Chapel Hill: University of North Carolina Press, 2002.

Ransom, Rev. R.C. "A National Shame: Closing the Doors of Various Trades Against Colored People." *Christian Recorder* 28 June 1888: 5–6.

Redding, Saunders. *To Make a Poet Black.* Ithaca, NY: Cornell University Press, 1988.

Reid, Whitelaw. *After the War: A Southern Tour, May 1, 1865 to May 1, 1866.* Reprint. New York: Harper Torchbooks, 1965.

Reynolds, David S. *Beneath the American Renaissance: The Subversive Imagination in the Age of Emerson and Melville.* Cambridge, MA: Harvard University Press, 1988.

Richardson, Elaine B., and Ronald L. Jackson II, eds. *African American Rhetoric(s): Interdisciplinary Perspectives.* Carbondale: Southern Illinois University Press, 2004.

Ripley, C. Peter. *The Black Abolitionist Papers: The United States, 1859–1865.* Vol. 5. Chapel Hill: University of North Carolina Press, 1985.

Robbins, Sarah. "Gendering the Debate over African Americans' Education in the 1880s: Frances Harper's Reconfiguration of Atticus Haygood's Philanthropic Model." *Legacy* 2002: 81–89.

Roediger, David R. *The Wages of Whiteness: Race and the Making of the American Working Class.* London: Verso, 1991.

Rosecrans, Jane E. "Between Black and White: Frances Ellen Watkins Harper and Philadelphia Unitarianism." <http://www.uucollegium.org/07paper_Rosecrans. doc>.

Rosenthal, Debra J. "Deracialized Discourse: Temperance and Racial Ambiguity in Harper's 'The Two Offers' and *Sowing and Reaping*." In *The Serpent and the Cup: Temperance in American Literature*. Ed. David S. Reynolds and Debra J. Rosenthal. Amherst: University of Massachusetts Press, 1997: 153–164.

Royster, Jacqueline Jones. *Traces of a Stream: Literacy and Social Change Among African American Women*. Pittsburgh, PA: University of Pittsburgh Press, 2000.

Ryan, Mary. "Gender and Public Access: Women's Politics in Nineteenth Century America." In *Habermas and the Public Sphere*. Ed. Craig Calhoun. Cambridge: MIT Press, 1992: 259–288.

———. *Women in Public: Between Banners and Ballots, 1825–1880*. Baltimore, MD: Johns Hopkins University Press, 1990.

Sanchez-Eppler, Karen. *Touching Liberty: Abolition, Feminism, and the Politics of the Body*. Berkeley: University of California Press, 1993.

Saxton, Alexander. *The Rise and Fall of the White Republic: Class Politics and Mass Culture in Nineteenth-Century America*. London: Verso, 1990.

Schechter, Patricia A. "'All the Intensity of My Nature': Ida B. Wells, Anger and Politics." *Radical History Review* 70 (1998): 48–77.

Schurz, Carl. *Report on Conditions of the South*. Reprint: New York: Arno Press, 1869.

Sklar, Kathryn Kish, and James Brewer Stewart. *Women's Rights and Transatlantic Antislavery in the Era of Emancipation*. New Haven, CT: Yale University Press, 2007.

Sorisio, Carolyn. "The Spectacle of the Body: Torture in the Antislavery Writing of Lydia Maria Child and Frances E. W. Harper." *Modern Language Studies* 30.1 (Spring 2000): 45–66.

Stange, Douglas. *Patterns of Antislavery among American Unitarians, 1831–1860*. London: Associated University Presses, 1977.

Steele, Shelby. *The Content of Our Character: A New Vision of Race in America*. New York: Harper Collins Publishing, 1991.

Sterling, Dorothy, ed. *We Are Your Sister: Black Women in the Nineteenth Century*. New York: W.W. Norton and Company, 1984.

Stewart, James Brewer. "The Emergence of Racial Modernity and the Rise of the White North, 1790–1840." *Journal of the Early Republic* 18.2 (Spring 1998): 181–217.

———. *Wendell Phillips: Liberty's Hero*. Baton Rouge: Louisiana State University Press, 1986.

Still, William. *The Underground Railroad: A Record of Facts, Authentic Narratives, Letters, etc, Narrating the Hardships Hair-breadth Escapes and Death Struggles of the Slaves in their Efforts for Freedom, by Themselves and Other, or Witnessed by the Author; Together with Sketches of Some of the Largest Stockholders, and Most Liberal Aiders and Advisers, of the Road*. Philadelphia: Porter and Coates, 1872.

Stowe, Harriet Beecher. *Uncle Tom's Cabin, Or, Life Among the Lowly*. Cambridge, MA: Harvard University Press, 2009.

Strong, Douglas M. *Perfectionist Politics: Abolitionism and the Religious Tensions of American Democracy*. Syracuse, NY: Syracuse University Press, 1999.

Sundquist, Eric J. *To Wake Nations: Race in the Making of American Literature*. Cambridge, MA: Harvard University Press, 1993.

Susman, Warren. *Culture as History: The Transformation of American Society in the Twentieth Century*. New York: Pantheon Book, 1973.

Tate, Claudia. "Allegories of Black Female Desire, or, Rereading Nineteenth-Century Sentimental Narratives of Black Female Authority." In *Changing Our Own*

Words: Essays on Criticism, Theory and Writing by Black Women. Ed. Cheryl A. Wall. New Brunswick, NJ: Rutgers University Press, 1989: 98–126.

———. *Domestic Allegories of Political Desire: The Black Heroine's Text at the Turn of the Century.* New York: Oxford University Press, 1992.

Tourgee, Albion Winegar. *The Invisible Empire.* Baton Rouge: Louisiana State University Press, 1989.

Trefousse, Hans L. *Thaddeus Stevens Nineteenth-Century Egalitarian.* Chapel Hill: University of North Carolina Press, 1997.

Wald, Priscilla. *Constituting Americans: Cultural Anxiety and Narrative Form.* Durham, NC: Duke University Press, 1995.

Walden, Daniel. "Frances Ellen Watkins Harper." *Dictionary of American Negro Biography.* Ed. Rayford Whittingham Logan. New York: W.W. Norton, 1982.

Washington, Mary Helen. "Disturbing the Peace: What Happens to American Studies If You Put African American Studies at the Center?" Presidential Address to the American Studies Association, October 29, 1997.

Warner, Michael. *The Letters of the Republic: Publication and the Public Sphere in Eighteenth-Century America.* Cambridge, MA: Harvard University Press, 1990.

Warren, James Perrin. *Culture of Eloquence: Oratory and Reform in Antebellum America.* University Park: Pennsylvania State University Press, 1999.

Warren, Joyce W., and Margaret Dickie. *Challenging Boundaries: Gender and Periodization.* Athens: University of Georgia Press, 2000.

Warren, Kenneth W. *Black and White Strangers: Race and American Literary Realism.* Chicago: University of Chicago Press, 1993.

Washington, Booker T., N. B. Wood, and Fannie Barrier Williams. *A New Negro for a New Century.* New York: Arno Press, 1969

Watkins, William. "Address Delivered Before the Moral Reform Society, in Philadelphia, August 6, 1836." In *Early Negro Writing 1760–1837.* Ed. Dorothy Porter. Boston: Beacon Press, 1971: 155–166.

Wells, Ida Barnett. *Crusade For Justice: The Autobiography of Ida B. Wells.* Ed. Alfreda Duster. Chicago: University of Chicago Press, 1970.

———. *Southern Horrors and Other Writings: The Anti-Lynching Campaign of Ida B. Wells, 1892–1900.* Ed. Jacqueline Jones Royster. New York: Bedford Books, 1997.

Welter, Barbara. *The Woman Question in American History.* Hinsdale, IL: Dryden Press, 1973.

West, Cornell. *The Cornell West Reader.* New York: Basic Civitas Books, Perseus Books Group, 1999.

Wilentz, Sean. "The Rise of the American Working Class, 1776–1877, A Survey." In *Perspectives on American Labor History: The Problems of Synthesis.* Dekalb: Northern Illinois University Press, 1990.

Williams, Gilbert Anthony. *The Christian Recorder, A.M.E. Church, 1854–1902.* Jefferson, NC: McFarland and Co. Inc., 1996.

Willis, Susan. *Specifying: Black Women Writing the American Experience.* Madison: University of Wisconsin Press, 1987.

Woodward, C. Vann. *The Burden of Southern History.* 3rd ed. Baton Rouge: Louisiana State University Press, 1993.

Xi, Wang. *The Trial of Democracy: Black Suffrage and Northern Republicans, 1860–1910.* Athens: University of Georgia Press, 1997.

Yellin, Jean Fagan, and John C. Van Horne, eds. *The Abolitionist Sisterhood: Women's Political Culture in Antebellum America.* Ithaca, NY: Cornell University Press, 1994.

Yellin, Jean Fagan, and Cynthia D. Bond, eds. *The Pen is Ours: A Listing of Writings By and About African American-Women Before 1910 with Secondary Bibliography to the Present.* New York: Oxford University Press, 1991.

Index